DAILY LIFE IN

NAZI-OCCUPIED EUROPE

**Recent Titles in
The Greenwood Press Daily Life Through History Series**

Trade: Buying and Selling in World History
James M. Anderson

The Colonial South
John Schlotterbeck

A Medieval Monastery
Sherri Olson

Arthurian Britain
Deborah J. Shepherd

Victorian Women
Lydia Murdoch

The California Gold Rush
Thomas Maxwell-Long

18th-Century England, Second Edition
Kirstin Olsen

Colonial New England, Second Edition
Claudia Durst Johnson

Life in 1950s America
Nancy Hendricks

Jazz Age America
Steven L. Piott

Women in the Progressive Era
Kirstin Olsen

The Industrial United States, 1870–1900, Second Edition
Julie Husband and Jim O'Loughlin

The 1960s Counterculture
Jim Willis

Renaissance Italy, Second Edition
Elizabeth S. Cohen and Thomas V. Cohen

DAILY LIFE IN
NAZI-OCCUPIED EUROPE

HAROLD J. GOLDBERG

The Greenwood Press Daily Life Through History Series

BLOOMSBURY ACADEMIC
NEW YORK · LONDON · OXFORD · NEW DELHI · SYDNEY

BLOOMSBURY ACADEMIC
Bloomsbury Publishing Inc
1385 Broadway, New York, NY 10018, USA
50 Bedford Square, London, WC1B 3DP, UK
29 Earlsfort Terrace, Dublin 2, Ireland

BLOOMSBURY, BLOOMSBURY ACADEMIC and the Diana logo
are trademarks of Bloomsbury Publishing Plc

First published in the United States of America by ABC-CLIO 2019
Paperback edition published by Bloomsbury Academic 2024

Copyright © Bloomsbury Publishing Inc, 2024

Cover photo: Nazi swastika flag on the Arc de Triomphe after the
German occupation of Paris, June 1940. (Everett Collection Historical/Alamy)

All rights reserved. No part of this publication may be reproduced or
transmitted in any form or by any means, electronic or mechanical,
including photocopying, recording, or any information storage or retrieval
system, without prior permission in writing from the publishers.

Bloomsbury Publishing Inc does not have any control over, or responsibility for,
any third-party websites referred to or in this book. All internet addresses given
in this book were correct at the time of going to press. The author and publisher
regret any inconvenience caused if addresses have changed or sites have
ceased to exist, but can accept no responsibility for any such changes.

Library of Congress Cataloging-in-Publication Data
Names: Goldberg, Harold J., author.
Title: Daily Life in Nazi-Occupied Europe / Harold J. Goldberg.
Description: First edition. | Santa Barbara, California: Greenwood,
an imprint of ABC-CLIO, LLC, [2019] | Series: The Greenwood
Press Daily Life Through History Series |
Includes bibliographical references and index.
Identifiers: LCCN 2019025967 (print) | LCCN 2019025968 (ebook) |
ISBN 9781440859113 (paperback) | ISBN 9781440859120 (ebook)
Subjects: LCSH: World War, 1939–1945—Occupied territories. | World
War, 1939–1945—Europe. | Europe—History—1918–1945.
Classification: LCC D802.E9 G65 2019 (print) |
LCC D802.E9 (ebook) | DDC 940.53/4—dc23
LC record available at https://lccn.loc.gov/2019025967
LC ebook record available at https://lccn.loc.gov/2019025968

ISBN: HB: 978-1-4408-5911-3
PB: 979-8-7651-1601-2
ePDF: 978-1-4408-5912-0
eBook: 979-8-2160-7104-4

Series: The Greenwood Press Daily Life Through History Series

To find out more about our authors and books visit www.bloomsbury.com
and sign up for our newsletters.

For the future:
Jake, Simon, Ilja, Evelina

CONTENTS

Preface	xiii
Introduction	xvii
Timeline	xxiii
Glossary	xxix
1. POLITICAL LIFE	1
Introduction	1
Weimar Republic	2
Treaty of Versailles	3
Adolf Hitler	3
Mein Kampf	4
Elections in 1932	5
End of Democracy in Germany	7
Book Burning	7
Rearmament	8
Appeasement	9

	Austria	9
	Czechoslovakia and the Munich Pact	10
	Danzig, Poland	12
	Stalin	12
	Nazi-Soviet Pact	13
	Political Life of Poland	14
	Occupation of Poland	16
	Political Life of France	16
	Vichy	17
	The Netherlands	18
	Occupation of The Netherlands	19
	Political Life of USSR	19
	Political Life of Belgium, Greece, Yugoslavia	21
	Conclusion	22
2.	MILITARY LIFE	25
	Introduction	25
	1938	26
	Hitler Demands Danzig	26
	Nazi-Soviet Nonaggression Pact	27
	War: Poland	27
	Phony War	28
	Spring Offensive	29
	Battle of France	29
	France Surrenders	30
	Battle of Britain	30
	Trouble in the Balkans	31
	Soviet Union	31
	Invasion	32

	Reaction	33
	Leningrad	35
	Moscow	36
	Stalingrad	37
	North Africa and Italy	37
	From Stalingrad to D-Day	38
	D-Day	39
	Occupied Countries	41
	Weapons	42
	Conclusion	49
3.	ECONOMIC LIFE	51
	Introduction	51
	Irrational Economics	53
	German Economics, Racism, War Planning	53
	Blitzkrieg and Economics	54
	Germany Moves West	55
	War with the Soviet Union	55
	Defeat in Russia and Occupation Policies in Europe	56
	Occupation: Forced Labor	56
	Fritz Sauckel	57
	Economic Life: Soviet Union	59
	Crime: Soviet Union	59
	Agriculture: Soviet Union	60
	Food: Soviet Union	62
	Trade and Supply: Soviet Union	62
	Industry and Labor: Soviet Union	63
	Urban Life: Leningrad	64
	Leningrad Diaries	66

	Why Did Germany Lose, and Why Did the Allies Win?	71
	Inevitable?	71
4.	DOMESTIC AND MATERIAL LIFE	75
	Introduction	75
	Germany	76
	Poland	77
	France	84
	Various Countries	90
	The Soviet Union	100
	Testimonies	101
	Conclusion	104
5.	INTELLECTUAL LIFE	107
	Introduction	107
	Germany	108
	France	111
	The Netherlands	113
	Greece	113
	Poland	114
	Soviet Union	115
	Monuments Men	115
	Atomic Bomb	117
	France	121
	Poland	128
	Conclusion	131
6.	RECREATIONAL LIFE	133
	Introduction	133
	The Politics of Sports	134
	Entertainment in Germany	140

Contents xi

	France	142
	Poland	146
	Soviet Union	149
	Conclusion	160
7.	RELIGIOUS LIFE	163
	Introduction	163
	Germany	164
	Poland	171
	France	174
	Norway	176
	Soviet Union	177
	Belgium	179
	The Netherlands	179
	Croatia and Slovakia	180
	Conclusion	182
8.	RESISTANCE LIFE	185
	Introduction	185
	Germany	186
	France	187
	Belgium	198
	Czechoslovakia	199
	The Netherlands	200
	Poland	204
	Soviet Union	211
	Conclusion	212
9.	THE HOLOCAUST	215
	Introduction	215
	Germany	216

Poland	226
The Netherlands	232
Anne Frank	234
France	237
Denmark	240
Bulgaria	242
Soviet Union	242
Croatia and Serbia	243
Greece	244
Hungary	244
Conclusion	245
Appendix A: Films about World War II	249
Appendix B: Museums Visited	255
Bibliography	257
Index	263

PREFACE

World War II is the greatest drama in human history, the biggest war ever and a true battle of good and evil.

Ken Follett

I hate war as only a soldier who has lived it can, only as one who has seen its brutality, its futility, its stupidity.

General Dwight D. Eisenhower

World War II in Europe started in September 1939 and ended in May 1945. While every country in Europe was impacted by the war to a certain extent, the degree of involvement depended on many factors, including geography, political leaning, ethnic and religious composition, and changing circumstances. During the nearly six years of war, some countries were occupied, some were allied with Germany, some were opposed to Germany, some were neutral, some claimed to be neutral, some changed sides during the war, some were treated leniently by Germany, some were scheduled for total destruction by Germany, one was occupied for over five years, and several were occupied for four years. All of these variables created millions of European experiences and a variety of daily life stories.

Poland was the first country invaded and subjugated, and the following spring several countries in Western Europe were also invaded, defeated, and occupied. Yet the Nazi regime in Poland compared to Denmark or France was so different that investigating daily life in Warsaw tells us nothing about life in Copenhagen and little about life in Paris. In addition, establishing a supposed profile for Paris does not help us understand the life of a French farmer in the southern part of the country or a resident of Normandy near the northern coast. Further, any model we create in France will not enlighten us about the Soviet Union and certainly cannot prepare us for the brutality of life in Leningrad.

Daily Life in Nazi-Occupied Europe is divided into nine chapters, designed not to establish one daily life, but rather to give the reader a glimpse of the variety of lives experienced during the Nazi occupation. I believe that reading through the entire book provides a solid understanding of the European occupation experience, with all of its nuances and ambiguity. Every country was different, every year was different, and ultimately, every person was different.

This book focuses on the occupation, but each chapter includes information on the occupier—Germany—as well. The reason is clear: although Germany was not an occupied country, there is no war without the Nazis, and their adherence to fascist ideology is fundamental to any discussion of military conquest, life during the war, and the subsequent brutality that shocked the world. For these reasons, we might even say that the war started in 1933 when Hitler came to power.

Chapter 1 on Political Life describes the rise of the Nazis and their subsequent destruction of democracy in Germany. This chapter also deals with Hitler's diplomatic demands during the 1930s, as he slowly dismantled the provisions of the Treaty of Versailles. The chapter then looks at governments in several other countries at the time, including Poland, France, the Netherlands, and the Soviet Union.

Chapter 2 deals with Military Life; it is impossible to understand the occupation without an introduction to the rapid and devastating German conquests. This chapter examines many of the major battles of the war but focuses exclusively on the European theater. Nevertheless, World War II was genuinely a worldwide conflict in which events and battles in one area had an impact on the military situation across the globe.

Chapter 3 deals with Economic Life, paying special attention to Germany and the Soviet Union as the two major powers involved in combat on the continent. Economic problems in Germany affected plans for the upcoming war, the relationship between occupied countries and the war, and ultimately raised questions about Germany's prospects for winning. The end of this chapter examines daily economic life in the city of Leningrad, presented through children's diaries—their voices—that were recovered after the war.

Chapter 4 on Domestic and Material Life deals specifically with food, housing, family, women, and sexuality. The chapter focuses on a few countries where daily life experiences suggest the issues and struggles common in other occupied countries as well.

Chapter 5 on Intellectual Life looks at the impact of the occupation on the educational systems in several countries, including Germany, Poland, and France. As in previous chapters, Germany is discussed because its ideological racism established the basis for the educational systems imposed on most of occupied Europe. In addition, we look briefly at a number of brilliant scientists who were forced to leave Europe due to Nazi persecution. In several areas including science, Germany chose racial hatred over winning the war. Finally, this chapter will also examine Nazi art looting and the effort to recover lost masterpieces.

Chapter 6 deals with Recreational Life, but in this section we are forced to redefine what we mean by recreation within the confines of an ongoing war. Normally, songs, poetry, and the cinema might provide a lighthearted form of recreation, but under the occupation people wrote songs and poems that called for Germany's defeat. In the Soviet Union, beyond the area under German control, films as well as songs and poems adopted anti-fascist themes. The idea of recreation overlapped with the dream of overthrowing the oppressor and restoring life to normal.

Chapter 7 focuses on Religious Life and the controversies surrounding church collaboration and resistance. Churches preach morality and opposition to evil, and therefore it is obvious that even one church supporting the Nazis was one too many. This chapter asks why so many churches went along, sometimes enthusiastically, with the evil agenda of the occupier. At the same time, the chapter looks at examples of religious leaders who risked their own lives to help others.

Chapter 8 on Resistance examines the lives of resistors and collaborators, but also presents the difficulty in using those labels. While Nazi occupation was generally hated throughout Europe, not everyone was prepared to run off to the mountains or forest with a rifle to confront the enemy. For most people, the goal was survival for themselves and their family and establishing a life between the extremes of collaboration and resistance. This chapter also explores the high price that the Nazis extracted for any act of resistance.

Chapter 9 deals with the Holocaust, a subject that is easier to describe than to explain. The acts of brutality and savagery cannot be rationalized or dismissed as a result of particular circumstances; the actions were premeditated and intentionally cruel. This chapter describes the process of killing in graphic terms because the consequences of racial hatred are too important to treat superficially.

In the field of economics, discussions are sometimes organized around the concepts of macro and micro, that is government versus individual decisions on spending and related matters. To a certain extent, this entire book follows a similar dichotomy. In some chapters, you will read about governments and their political structures, diplomacy, and military policies. In other chapters, the focus will deal with individuals who were trapped in this war such as Anne Frank or Simon Igel (see Chapter 9) or famous French writers and entertainers who chose collaboration, resistance, or a position between those options (see Chapter 6). While each country and individual in occupied Europe was different and cannot be covered in detail, hopefully the focus on Poland and the Soviet Union in Eastern Europe and France and the Netherlands in Western Europe will open a lens into daily life in other countries as well.

Document recommendations are placed at the end of each chapter. For those readers interested in exploring primary sources, the brief list of documents concluding each chapter also includes a reference to a source—either a book or an online site—where the full document can be found.

The use of the asterisk (*) after a term indicates the inclusion of that item in the Glossary; the asterisk is applied only the first time that a word appears in each chapter.

I want to thank Dr. Nancy Sloan Goldberg for reading the entire manuscript. Our discussions of language as well as content greatly improved the text in every way.

INTRODUCTION

History shows that there are no invincible armies and never have been.
Joseph Stalin, radio address to nation, July 3, 1941

The Führer in Berlin expects that the armies will do their duty. History and the German people will despise every man who in these circumstances does not give his utmost to save the situation and the Führer.
Adolf Hitler, April 26, 1945, a few days before he committed suicide

World War II remains a pivotal event in the twentieth century. For twelve years, evil triumphed in the heart of Europe, and from that central location the pernicious ideology of the Nazis spread and attracted supporters throughout the continent. With its belief in racial superiority, fascism became popular in several countries in addition to Germany. Nevertheless, its aggressive agenda also provoked a strong reaction against it. While it took longer than some would have liked, a coalition of nations finally arose to fight back and ultimately destroy the aggressors.

During World War II, shifting alliances, changing borders, and the ebb and flow of military fortune made the concept of occupation fluid and evasive. For example, while the Nazi military occupied almost every country in Europe at some point, it controlled only one of them for the entire war. Poland suffered the longest domination—nearly six years—and paid for the experience with six million dead. The Soviet Union was neutral and not involved in the war for its first two years, but was attacked in the summer of 1941, partially occupied but remained mostly under the Soviet government, became a brutal battleground, and lost more people than any other country in World War II. Greece and Serbia were also invaded in 1941 and endured harsh occupations thereafter. Other countries in Eastern Europe, including Bulgaria, Croatia, Hungary, Romania, and Slovakia, were allied with Germany for most of the war. Italy was Germany's primary ally, at least until 1943 when Mussolini was removed from office and the German military rushed into Italy to slow down the Anglo-American advance. All of these factors have to be acknowledged to understand the nature of Nazi occupation at that time.

In Western Europe, the German spring offensive of 1940 led to the subjugation of Denmark and Norway—and a month later—Belgium, France, Luxembourg, and the Netherlands. While these countries were quickly defeated and subsequently required to sacrifice their own living standards to contribute to the German economy, the nature of the occupation regimes varied. A few other countries in Europe avoided occupation with proclamations of neutrality, but in most cases this status was ambiguous: Sweden traded with Germany, Switzerland provided banking services for the Nazis, and in Spain Franco met with Hitler and pledged support. Nevertheless, all three countries provided asylum for refugees escaping from the Nazis.

Clearly, there are a few hurdles to creating a single picture of daily life: the constantly changing map of occupied Europe, a variety of reactions to the Germans due to cultural differences across Europe, and the vastly diverse treatment of occupied countries according to Nazi racist criteria. Nevertheless, these difficulties do not detract from the importance of examining daily life across the continent. Understanding the life of a worker, farmer, soldier, priest, artist, writer, resistance fighter, or racial target is a challenge worth pursuing. For that reason, we will examine the search for food, the role of women, life inside a ghetto or a concentration camp, what some soldiers ate; identify priests who tried to protect those in danger as well as some who sided with the Nazis; view resistance actions from passive to violent; present famous writers and artists who

Introduction

tried to produce art in the midst of chaos; and look at the actions of men and women considered to be collaborators.

Certain overall patterns emerged across Europe. The first and most important was the universal and desperate search for food. Second was the constant threat of death. The Nazis refused to respect traditional lines between combatants and civilians. Their targeting of ordinary citizens, their use of forced labor, and their determination to destroy people they considered to be inferior introduced a level of brutality that shocked the world when its full extent was revealed.

The pattern of resistance and collaboration varied from country to country. In every area there were collaborators who supported the Nazis either out of conviction or self-interest. Some people believed in the Nazi mission to destroy other ethnic or religious groups, and some worked with the Nazis in exchange for food. Yet in almost every country under Nazi control, a small group of men and women refused to accept the verdict of military defeat. They risked their lives to organize and fight against huge odds and to preserve a semblance of dignity against evil. When faced with capitulation or continuing the struggle, a few chose struggle—their numbers increased as the war went into its second, third, and fourth years.

In every country there were a majority of onlookers or bystanders. These were people who disliked the occupiers but did not feel compelled, for a variety of reasons, to risk their lives by joining the resistance. They wanted to stay out of trouble and hoped that trouble did not come to them; they spent most days looking for food for themselves and their families. This last group included the largest percentage of the population throughout the continent.

Despite universal suffering, people sang songs and listened to music, wrote poetry and read literature, and wrote letters to family members or loved ones, all in the midst of the ruthless atrocities that Nazi occupation brought to their nation. In the face of brutality, these artistic expressions helped to preserve elements of humanity in a world that seemed to have abandoned all aspects of "civilization." The atrocities remain unimaginable and raise philosophical questions about the nature of human behavior itself. At the same time, the will to survive and to protect loved ones and family presents another side of social conduct. The tension between atrocity and survival brings us to our topic—daily life in the midst of chaos.

Finally, this book fundamentally asks us to consider what we mean by the term "civilization" used in the previous paragraph. Are

Nazis included in this term, since they are products of human society as much as believers in democracy or other values? Is "civilization" limited only to inventions, discoveries, and good deeds? The people who create might overlap with those who destroy through war and killing. Are we narrowing the reality of human history if we define "civilization" only in accord with positive actions and achievements? At the same time, how do we emotionally accept the humanity of members of the SS, the Einsatzgruppen, and other perpetrators of mass murder?

This book and others on the subject of war allow readers to choose what lessons they want to absorb. The Nazis exhibited one side of reality that has been judged as a war crime. Where did the brutality and sadism inflicted on others come from, and are those traits within all of us? Although Nazis demonstrated the worst aspects of human action, they still had the support of millions of people who fought for their ideology and their leader. Yet there were also millions of young soldiers who opposed this evil, thousands of kind people who helped those in danger, many more who shared food with a loved one or sometimes with a stranger, farm families who let people hide in their barns, and so many others who risked their own safety regardless of the danger. Perhaps more clearly than any other time in history, the confrontation between evil and good was made clear, and people were forced to choose.

This book on daily life under Nazi occupation tries to locate World War II between the extremes of total despair and human triumph. Either perspective is a valid response to the events that occurred from 1933 through 1945. There are many examples of atrocities too horrible to accept because we do not want to believe that people are capable of such acts. Similarly, there are also examples of heroism, selflessness, and bravery that we hope we might emulate if put in a similar situation. World War II forces us to consider our fears and hatreds as well as our humanity and capacity for caring.

Books on war always include statistics and numbers indicating how many people died or became prisoners. Often the numbers are so big they cannot be easily understood. To try to appreciate the individuality that each number represents, we need to go beyond lists of casualty figures; we want to visualize and create human beings as we process the numbers. Using the Soviet Union as an example, rather than saying that over twenty-five million Soviets died, we might try to count to twenty-five million and say "person" after each number: one person, two people, three people—until twenty-five million people, pausing for a couple of seconds to try to remember something personal about the daily life of each of those individuals.

As we try to comprehend the scope of this war, it is important to remember that Hitler came to power legally and that Nazi supremacy in Germany provides historical lessons about the fragility of democracy, the attraction of charismatic demagogues, and the power of propaganda to persuade those who want to believe in a message of division and hatred. At the same time, it is also necessary to recall the moments of bravery, heroism, and sacrifice that finally brought an end to the Nazi terror.

TIMELINE

1918	An armistice on November 11 at 11:00 A.M. ends World War I.
1919	The Treaty of Versailles is signed.
1922	Benito Mussolini is premier of Italy.
1923	Hitler attempts Beer Hall Putsch and is arrested.
1924	Hitler is sentenced to five years in prison; he writes *Mein Kampf*.
1929	The stock market crashes, and the Great Depression starts.
1932	Nazi Party wins most seats in Reichstag.
1933	President Hindenburg appoints Hitler as chancellor of Germany.
	Reichstag passes Enabling Act, giving Hitler emergency powers.
	Dachau opens as Germany's first concentration camp.
	The German secret police, the Gestapo, is established.
	Book burning takes place in Berlin.
	The Nazi Party is declared Germany's only legal political party.
1934	President Hindenburg dies, and Hitler assumes the positions of president and chancellor. His new title is Führer.

	The German military takes their oath to Hitler rather than the constitution.
1935	Germany announces rearmament.
	Germany imposes the Nuremberg Laws, declaring that German Jews are no longer German citizens. The laws define German Jews according to ancestry and then limit German Jews in terms of occupations.
1936	Germany remilitarizes the Rhineland.
	The Olympics are held in Berlin, and Jesse Owens wins four gold medals.
1938	Germany and Austria unite (Anschluss).
	Hitler, Mussolini for Italy, Chamberlain for Britain, and Daladier for France meet in Munich and agree to give the Sudetenland to Germany. Neither Czechoslovakia nor the Soviet Union is consulted.
	Kristallnacht (Night of Broken Glass) takes place in Germany.
1939	Hitler demands the return of Danzig from Poland.
	The western Allies guarantee Polish independence.
	Foreign Minister Ribbentrop and Foreign Minister Molotov sign the Nazi-Soviet Nonaggression Pact. Soviet neutrality is assured if Germany attacks Poland.
	German army invades Poland.
	Britain and France are at war with Germany.
	Poland is occupied by Germany and the Soviet Union.
	The Soviet Union moves to control the Baltic States: Estonia, Latvia, Lithuania.
	Soviet army attacks Finland.
1940	The Soviet-Finnish War (Winter War) ends with territorial adjustments in favor of the USSR.
	German forces invade Denmark and Norway. Denmark surrenders the same day. In Norway the pro-Nazi Quisling encourages the German action.
	British forces land in Norway.
	Germany invades Luxembourg, the Netherlands, Belgium, and France.
	Prime Minister Chamberlain resigns and is replaced by Winston Churchill.
	The Netherlands surrenders.
	Belgium surrenders.

More than 300,000 Allied troops are evacuated from Dunkirk. Churchill vows to continue fighting.

Norway surrenders.

Mussolini declares war on Britain and France.

World War I hero Pétain takes over in France.

France surrenders to Germany.

Vichy becomes the capital of Pétain's government.

British ships sink the French fleet at Mers-el-Kebir in Algeria.

The Luftwaffe begins the bombing of Britain. The English call it the Blitz.

The Warsaw Ghetto is established. Nearly half a million Jews are confined within the walls.

1941 U.S. Congress passes the Lend-Lease Act, allowing the president to send military assistance to other nations.

German forces invade Yugoslavia and Greece.

Rationing of food is imposed in the Netherlands.

Stalin ignores the German military buildup on his border. Operation Barbarossa, the code name for the German invasion of the USSR, begins. The three-pronged attack sends Army Group North toward Leningrad, Army Group Center toward Moscow, and Army Group South toward Kiev.

Smolensk falls to the Germans. The Red Army loses 300,000 men.

Anti-Jewish measures and executions increase throughout occupied Europe.

The nearly three-year siege of Leningrad begins. Hitler orders the city destroyed.

Kiev, the capital of Ukraine, falls to the Germans, and the Red Army loses another 600,000 men.

More than 30,000 Jews are murdered outside of Kiev at Babi Yar in two days.

The Wehrmacht moves toward Moscow. Moscow does not fall.

Japanese planes torpedo U.S. battleships at Pearl Harbor. More than 2,000 Americans are killed.

President Roosevelt asks Congress for a declaration of war against Japan.

Germany declares war on the United States.

1942

The Wannsee Conference is held in a suburb of Berlin. The Nazis plan to eliminate all European Jews in what they call the "Final Solution."

French Jews are deported to concentration camps.

President Roosevelt issues Executive Order No. 9066 for the internment of Japanese Americans.

Czech commandos shoot Reinhard Heydrich in Prague. Heydrich dies from his wounds, and the Germans take revenge by destroying the Czech village of Lidice.

An Allied attack on Dieppe in northern France is a failure, indicating that an invasion of France will need more planning.

The Vichy government arrests about 7,000 Jews for deportation to German camps.

British General Montgomery defeats the Germans under General Rommel at El Alamein in Egypt. The victory assures Allied control of the Suez Canal.

Fierce fighting takes place near Stalingrad.

1943

Roosevelt and Churchill meet in Casablanca in Morocco. They agree to invade Sicily and Italy, and that they will only accept "unconditional surrender" from the Axis powers.

Hitler promotes General von Paulus to field marshal, but the German general surrenders to the Russians at Stalingrad. After losing more than 100,000 in battle, the Wehrmacht loses another 100,000 who become prisoners of war. The Soviet victory at Stalingrad is often considered the turning point of the war in Europe.

Vichy France establishes Service du travail obligatoire (STO) to send workers to Germany.

Sister and brother Sophie and Hans Scholl at the University of Munich and leaders of the White Rose resistance, one of the few groups to oppose the Nazis on moral grounds, are captured and put to death by guillotine.

The Jewish ghetto in Kraków, Poland is liquidated.

The German liquidation of the Warsaw Ghetto is met with military resistance. German general Stroop has difficulty controlling the ghetto.

In Belgium on the same day, resistance fighters attack a train that is moving Jews to Auschwitz. More than 200 Jewish prisoners escape from the train.

The Germans burn the Warsaw Ghetto street by street, killing most of the remaining resistors.

The largest tank battle of the war is fought at Kursk. The Germans call it Operation Citadel, but the Germans cannot replace their losses or keep up with Soviet tank production.

The Allies invade Sicily (Operation Husky).

Mussolini is removed as premier in Italy.

Denmark is placed under direct German military control. This action coincides with the order to arrest Danish Jews, but the Danes help over 7,000 Danish Jews escape to Sweden.

The Allies invade Italy.

A rebellion in Sobibór concentration camp kills several SS officers but fails to free all the prisoners.

The Tehran Conference brings Roosevelt, Churchill, and Stalin to Iran and elicits a commitment to invade France in May–June 1944. Eisenhower is chosen as the commander of the Normandy invasion code named Overlord.

1944 After nearly three years, the siege of Leningrad ends.

The Allies liberate Rome.

D-Day landing (Operation Overlord) takes place in Normandy on June 6.

Germans massacre the townspeople of Oradour-sur-Glane in France.

Colonel von Stauffenberg plants a bomb to assassinate Hitler in the headquarters at Wolf's Lair. Hitler escapes and orders all plotters to be killed.

Soviet forces liberate Majdanek concentration camp.

The Polish Home Army begins "Operation Tempest," an uprising to liberate Warsaw. The lack of Soviet aid and Hitler's determination to destroy Warsaw doom the Polish forces.

With the Polish Uprising defeated, the Germans begin the large-scale massacre of Polish civilians—thousands are killed.

The French resistance helps to liberate Paris.

General de Gaulle and his supporters celebrate the liberation of Paris with a march along the Champs-Elysées.

In the Netherlands, railway workers go on strike, and the Germans retaliate by halting food shipments to the western part of the country. The winter of 1944 is cold and harsh, and the lack of food leads to approximately 20,000 deaths.

Churchill visits Stalin in Moscow and agrees to a Soviet-British division of Eastern Europe.

Hitler launches the Battle of the Bulge; SS troops execute captured American soldiers.

1945

The Red Army enters Warsaw.

The Red Army enters Auschwitz concentration camp.

Roosevelt, Churchill, and Stalin meet in Yalta, Crimea, USSR to discuss the end of the war.

German pastor Dietrich Bonhoeffer is executed on the personal order of Hitler.

American forces liberate Buchenwald concentration camp.

President Roosevelt dies. Harry Truman becomes president.

The British liberate Bergen-Belsen concentration camp.

Italian partisans execute Mussolini in Milan.

American forces liberate Dachau concentration camp.

Hitler commits suicide.

Joseph Goebbels and his wife commit suicide after poisoning their six children.

German soldiers shoot into a crowd celebrating the Dutch liberation in Amsterdam.

German general Alfred Jodl signs the German surrender in Reims, France.

Victory day in Europe is proclaimed.

German general Wilhelm Keitel surrenders to the Red Army in Berlin.

Victory day in the USSR is proclaimed.

A trial of leading Nazi officials opens in Nuremberg in November.

GLOSSARY

The Glossary is intended as a resource for the reader who seeks a quick definition of terms used in this book. Proper names are not included here. Items are marked with an asterisk (*) the first time they appear in each chapter.

Anschluss: union between Germany and Austria banned in Treaty of Versailles but carried out in 1938.

Appeasement: policy of compromise with Hitler that is associated with Neville Chamberlain and pursued primarily by Britain and France.

Arbeit Macht Frei: slogan on concentration camp gates meaning "Work makes you free."

Aryan: the term that Hitler used for the "superior" German race. This "race" does not exist.

Auschwitz: located near Kraków, Poland, this was the largest concentration camp.

Babi Yar: a ravine near Kiev where the Germans executed over 30,000 Jews and a total of 100,000 people in 1941.

Belzec: a concentration camp in Poland.

Bergen-Belsen: a concentration camp in Germany where Anne Frank died of typhus.

Blitz: the British name for the bombing of London by the Luftwaffe in 1940.

Blitzkrieg: German for lightening war or a fast-moving offensive form of warfare.

Buchenwald: a concentration camp in Germany.

Bulge, Battle of the: Hitler's last major offensive on the western front. After initial success, the Germans were stopped.

Carpet Bombing: practice of laying down a carpet of bombs to hit a target in the area.

Casablanca Conference: meeting between Churchill and Roosevelt in 1943 in Morocco. The demand for "unconditional surrender" by the Axis powers was its best known outcome.

Champs-Élysées: avenue in Paris from Arc de Triomphe to Place de la Concorde; the route that de Gaulle walked to celebrate the liberation of Paris.

Collateral Damage: term for unintentional casualties, especially of civilians.

Collaborator: person who worked with or helped occupiers.

Dachau: the first German concentration camp. It is located near Munich.

Degenerate Art: term used by Nazis for art they did not like, especially various modern art forms.

Drancy: internment or transit camp near Paris for Jews in France before they were sent to concentration camps in Poland or elsewhere.

Dunkirk: Allied troops (mostly British) left the continent in a massive ship rescue operation in May 1940 as Germany consolidated its grip on France and Belgium.

Einsatzgruppen: mobile killing squads who executed over a million people in Eastern Europe and the Soviet Union.

Enigma: the German code machine that confounded the west until the code was broken at Bletchley Park near London.

Exodus: in France the mass refugee movement south to escape the German invasion.

Final Solution: German name for the elimination of Europe's Jewish population; planned at the Wannsee Conference.

Four-Year Plan: Modeled on the Soviet Five-Year Plan, a German attempt to prepare the economy for war through long-range planning.

General Government: name used for the Nazi occupation government in Poland.

Ghetto: a walled-in area in a city where Jews and others were held before being sent to a concentration camp. Most infamous ghettos were in Polish cities such as Kraków and Warsaw.

Holocaust: destruction by fire; deliberate murder of Jews in WWII.

Kolkhoz: a collective farm in the Soviet Union.

Kristallnacht: in November 1938, an organized attack on Jewish businesses and religious places in Germany.

Kursk: largest tank battle in the war. In summer of 1943, Germany hoped to reverse the defeat at Stalingrad.

Lake Ladoga: lake on one side of Leningrad that was used to bring supplies into the city. The lake froze in the winter, allowing trucks to access the city.

Lebensraum: German for "living space" and a reference to Nazi plans to remove the populations of Poland and the Soviet Union to make way for German settlement.

Lend-Lease: U.S. legislation in 1941 allowing the "lending" of military supplies to Allies. Britain and the Soviet Union were the largest recipients of American aid.

Lidice: town in Czechoslovakia destroyed by the Germans in retaliation for Heydrich's assassination in Prague in 1942.

Luftwaffe: German air force.

Maginot Line: French concrete and fortified trenches built between the wars along the border with Germany.

Majdanek: a concentration camp near Lublin, Poland.

Manhattan Project: secret U.S. project to build an atomic bomb. The effort proved successful, and two bombs were dropped on Japan in August 1945.

Mein Kampf: *My Struggle* or Hitler's autobiography that outlines his political program.

Milice: pro-fascist French police.

Molotov Cocktail: glass bottle filled with flammable liquid and thrown at target. Named as an insult toward Soviet foreign minister (as in "here is a cocktail for Molotov").

Monuments Men: Allied unit commissioned to recover stolen art.

Munich Pact: 1938 appeasement giving Czechoslovakia's Sudetenland to Germany.

Nazi-Soviet Nonaggression Pact: 1939 agreement between Stalin and Hitler that gave Stalin territory in Eastern Europe in exchange for Soviet neutrality.

Nuremberg Trial: trial of leading Nazi Party officials for war crimes.

Operation Barbarossa: German code name for the invasion of the USSR in 1941.

Operation Citadel: German code name for tank battle at Kursk in 1943.

Operation Overlord: Allied code name for invasion of Normandy in June 1944.

Operation Reinhard: German code name for building more concentration camps.

Operation Tempest: code name for the uprising in Warsaw in 1944.

Operation Torch: Allied code name for the invasion of North Africa.

Operation Typhoon: German code name for the attack on Moscow in 1941.

Oradour-sur-Glane: a village near Limoges, France, that was destroyed by German troops in 1944.

Ravensbrück: a concentration camp in Germany mostly for female prisoners.

Reichstag: name for German parliament and also the building in which it meets.

Righteous Among the Nations: designation by World Holocaust Remembrance Center of Yad Vashem in Israel for those who saved Jews in World War II.

Roma and Sinti: ethnic groups commonly called Gypsies in Europe.

Samogon: Russian homemade alcohol or moonshine.

Scorched Earth: Russian policy of burning farms and fields to destroy resources before the enemy obtains control of them.

Service du travail obligatoire (STO): the compulsory and unpopular program that sent French workers to Germany.

Sieg Heil: Nazi salute meaning "Hail Victory."

Sobibór: a concentration camp in Poland.

Social Darwinism: misreading of Darwin by Nazis to justify struggle of the fittest between races.

S.S.: Nazi elite military units known for their loyalty to Nazi ideology and for their brutality toward others.

Stalingrad: crucial Soviet victory over Germany in 1943. Considered the turning point of war in Europe.

Sudetenland: Czech territory given to Hitler at Munich Conference in 1938.

Tehran Conference: Allied summit in 1943 that set date for D-Day for spring of 1944.

Theresienstadt: a concentration camp in Czechoslovakia.

Treaty of Versailles: treaty ending World War I. Hitler was determined to destroy the provisions of Versailles.

Ustashe: pro-Nazi, pro-Catholic, ultra-right-wing party in Croatia.

Vélodrome d'Hiver (Vel d'hiv): a former bicycle stadium in Paris where Jews were held until sent to Drancy and then to concentration camps.

Vichy: capital city of the French collaborationist government under Pétain.

Wannsee Conference: meeting in January 1942 in Berlin suburb to plan the killing of all of Europe's Jews.

Warsaw Ghetto: the largest ghetto in Europe confined 400,000 people under brutal conditions. Most of the inhabitants were sent to concentration camps. This was also the site of a heroic uprising in 1943 against Nazi oppressors.

Wehrmacht: the German army.

Weimar Republic: democratic government in Germany between World War I and 1933.

Yalta Conference: Allied summit (FDR, Churchill, Stalin) in February 1945 to discuss the fate of Germany, trials for war criminals, the war with Japan, creation of United Nations, and other postwar issues.

1
POLITICAL LIFE

My good friends, for the second time in our history, a British Prime Minister has returned from Germany bringing peace with honour. I believe it is peace for our time. We thank you from the bottom of our hearts. Go home and get a nice quiet sleep.
Prime Minister Neville Chamberlain, September 30, 1938

I have many times offered Great Britain and the British people the understanding and friendship of the German people. My whole policy was based on the idea of this understanding. I have always been repelled. I had for years been aware that the aim of these war inciters had for long been to take Germany by surprise at a favorable opportunity. I am more firmly determined than ever to beat back this attack. Germany shall not again capitulate.
Chancellor Adolf Hitler, September 3, 1939
(two days after Germany invaded Poland)

INTRODUCTION

Before exploring daily life related to topics such as economics, domestic and material life, intellectual life, recreation, resistance, and genocide, it is important to examine political life in Germany between the wars as well as other events that contributed to the second great war of the twentieth century. How did the world move from seeking peace in 1919 to preparing for another war barely twenty years later? That question serves as a connection to the personality of Adolf Hitler and a series of political and economic crises, including the creation of the Weimar Republic,* the development of fascism, the Great Depression, and finally the rise of the Nazi Party.

At the end of World War I, most western leaders considered the prospect of another European war to be unimaginable. Trench warfare had revealed the destructive power of new weapons such as the machine gun, poison gas, grenades, artillery, and more. As a result of the increasing lethality of these weapons, the Great War of 1914–1918 had devastated large areas in Europe and left millions of people dead. Throughout the 1920s and 1930s, governments in England, France, and other countries viewed diplomacy and compromise as the best way to resolve conflicts, leading many nations to sign a meaningless pledge promising not to use war to settle disputes in the future. This utopian treaty ignored history and reality, and all the countries that signed the Kellogg-Briand Pact in 1928 would become belligerents in World War II a decade later. The agreement depended solely on the good will of its signers, meaning that even one violator would nullify the entire concept. Unfortunately, more than one violator arose, yet it was the chancellor of Germany who more than any other leader wanted war and prevented compromise. Hitler's goals were not achievable without war, but the west did not understand his motives or objectives until it was too late.

WEIMAR REPUBLIC

In November 1918, the wartime government of Germany collapsed, and Kaiser Wilhelm II (1859–1941) fled the country. On November 11 an armistice ended the war, and moderate politicians serving in the German Reichstag* (parliament) took power. These new leaders confronted two immediate problems: one was creating a democratic system of government to replace the monarchy, and the other was negotiating a treaty to end the war that the German people could accept. Neither item was resolved successfully.

The establishment of a new governmental system took place in the city of Weimar in 1919, when a constitution for a republic was written. The Weimar Republic was a parliamentary system, but it had several weaknesses that led to its unpopularity and eventual demise. The primary weakness, not necessarily the fault of the constitution, was a lack of a national consensus on Germany's future. The country was split into many political factions, including those on the far right and far left that rejected democracy and sought power for themselves. The Catholic Center Party and the Social Democratic Party, neither of which produced strong leaders or ever won a majority of seats in the Reichstag, held the center of the political spectrum. As smaller parties proliferated, Germany endured a series of weak coalition governments. Finally, and fatally, the Weimar Republic was unable to create sustained economic growth sufficient to reassure the middle class that democracy could provide the security that the German people desired. With domestic enemies on the right and the left conspiring to destroy it, the Weimar Republic did not have time to build popular support committed to the preservation of democratic institutions.

TREATY OF VERSAILLES*

In 1919, Allied leaders met in Paris to draft a treaty that would solve the problems that had caused the war in 1914. Their task was impossible from its inception; each of them arrived at the conference with different aims. While Allied goals in general were committed to curtailing German military power, there was no consensus on how to achieve that objective and certainly no plan on how to meet German expectations for a lenient treaty. As representatives of the losing side, German delegates were given little input into negotiating the provisions of an agreement that in its final form limited the size of the German military, stripped away some territory from Germany, affirmed that Germany accepted responsibility for the war, and established the basis for reparation payments to help rebuild France and Belgium. German delegates had no choice but to sign a treaty that they knew would be unpopular in Germany, and not surprisingly opposition developed quickly and helped the nationalistic right grow stronger. Many veterans argued that Germany had not really lost the war, and therefore the treaty was the work of foreign governments, democrats, socialists, Jews, and others who had "stabbed Germany in the back" as part of a conspiracy to weaken and destroy their country.

ADOLF HITLER

Hitler (1889–1945) was a German soldier in the Great War, where he served as a runner at a time before modern forms of communications were available to all military units. His job was literally to carry messages between trenches, and it was dangerous work. He was wounded before the end of the war, so he left the conflict at a time when the German army appeared to be holding its positions in Belgium and France. When he was told in a military hospital that Germany had surrendered, he could not believe it and more importantly, like many other German veterans, refused to accept Germany's defeat. He was convinced that the country had been betrayed by cowardly politicians.

After the war, Hitler joined other veterans who lived in a cloud of nostalgia—in a world centered on German military prowess. His fiery speeches soon elevated him to the leadership of a group of discontented veterans, and collectively they called themselves the National Socialist German Workers Party (Nazi was an acronym of the syllables in German). Their goal was to restore Germany to its "glorious" past.

Hitler wanted power. When he attempted to seize power illegally in Munich in 1923, he was arrested and put on trial. He used the trial to expound on his ideas, and several newspapers published his long speeches and thus provided free publicity and political exposure for his ideas. Many veterans and nationalists agreed with much of his program, as did the judge who gave him a light sentence, which meant he served it in a comfortable jail cell with access to friends and party members. In prison he dictated his thoughts to one of his comrades, Rudolph Hess (1894–1987), who organized Hitler's rants into the book *Mein Kampf** (*My Struggle*).

MEIN KAMPF

In *Mein Kampf*, Hitler outlined both his view of the world and his plans for the future. He saw the world in terms of struggle, not between species or individuals or even nations, but between races (Social Darwinism).* Immersed in nineteenth-century German romanticism and mythology, he claimed that all Germans belonged to a so-called "Aryan race,"* descendants of tribes of blond, blue-eyed warriors who should and would dominate the world. According to his view, the "Aryan" race needed to expand beyond the borders of Germany, and that this nearby land—called living space or *lebensraum** in German—could be found in Eastern Europe and Russia. Conquest to the east fit well with the other side of Hitler's racial views. He claimed that the "superior Aryan" race was being challenged by Jews, Slavs (Poles and Russians), and other "inferior" peoples who lived in the territories east of Germany. For Hitler the struggle was inevitable and only one "race" could win. All the other groups had to be destroyed in a war that would resolve this racial conflict forever.

Hitler had a long list of races, religions, and nationalities he hated and wanted to destroy. He saw enemies of the German people everywhere he looked. For example, both communism and democracy, although opposed to each other, were considered enemies of Germany. In addition to Poles, Russians, and Jews, he viewed Roma and Sinti,* homosexuals, people with disabilities, Jehovah's Witnesses, and many others who were not blond and blue-eyed as inferior and therefore suitable for extermination. Eventually his racist theories would lead to the deaths of millions of people in the war and the Holocaust.*

Mein Kampf became a best seller in Germany, and the royalties helped to pay some of Hitler's expenses after he was released from prison. Donations to the party from wealthy supporters also paid for his life style. Nevertheless, the Nazi Party remained a small political party throughout the 1920s.

ELECTIONS IN 1932

When the Depression hit Germany in 1929, many people lost both their jobs and their faith in the Weimar Republic. The government seemed unsure of what actions to take to confront the crisis, and extremist parties gained strength as a result. The Nazi Party benefited from government uncertainty and stalemate. In the last election before the Depression, the Nazis had received only 2.6 percent of the vote (12 seats), but in 1930 their vote total increased to 18 percent (107 seats).

Elections for president and parliament were scheduled for 1932, and the Nazis were prepared to take advantage of both. In the presidential election, former World War I general Paul von Hindenburg (1847–1934) ran for a second seven-year term, but because of his age he did not actively campaign; he relied on his reputation and fame. Hitler decided to run against him and traveled the country making speeches, while the Nazi propaganda department plastered small towns and rural areas with posters and radio broadcasts announcing the Nazi program. Despite these efforts, President Hindenburg was reelected by a substantial margin. At the same time, Hitler had spread his message throughout the country and received millions of votes even in his losing campaign. Some observers noted the contrast between the aged Hindenburg, who seemed to represent the nineteenth-century Prussian aristocracy, and the energetic Hitler who appeared to have ideas about a new Germany retaking its place in European affairs. No longer an obscure politician, Hitler had emerged as a major force in German politics.

Almost three months after the presidential election had given the Nazi Party national publicity, elections for the German parliament or Reichstag were held. The Nazi Party received the highest number of seats of any party in Weimar Republic history. More than thirteen million votes amounted to 37 percent of the total, nearly double the second-place party. Although their 230 seats did not give them a majority, they had enough representatives to block any other party from governing without them. Germany's Communist Party took 14 percent of the vote, suggesting that a majority of Germans, 37 percent for the Nazis plus 14 percent for the communists, had voted for parties that opposed the Weimar Republic and democracy.

While another Reichstag election at the end of the year saw a decrease in Nazi votes (33.1 percent and 196 seats) and an increase in communist votes, half of the electorate again voted for the two parties opposed to democracy. The Nazi Party still controlled enough seats to prevent a governing coalition from acting without its support. Early in January 1933, the government faced further deadlock and inaction. Advisors around Hindenburg miscalculated, thinking they would be able to control Hitler, and they urged the elderly president to appoint Hitler to office. On January 30, 1933, a triumphant Hitler emerged to become the new chancellor. Some foreign observers did not understand the meaning of this development. A *New York Times* article announced: "Hitler Puts Aside Aim to Be Dictator" and the paper's editorial the same day assured readers: "There is thus no warrant for immediate alarm" (*New York Times*, January 31, 1933, 3, 16).

When Hindenburg appointed Hitler as chancellor, the Nazi leader had accomplished his first goal—attaining power. He immediately moved to realize two additional objectives simultaneously—to destroy the Treaty of Versailles and to replace democracy with Nazi dictatorship. Due to the weakness of the Weimar Republic and the inaction of the western powers, he was successful in both areas. His triumph was short-lived, however, as he ultimately brought destruction to himself, Germany, and Europe.

END OF DEMOCRACY IN GERMANY

The fragility of German democracy was quickly revealed. When democratic institutions were challenged and undermined, neither German politicians nor the German people defended the Weimar Republic. Almost immediately a suspicious fire destroyed the Reichstag building, and the Nazis blamed communists and introduced a bill in parliament suspending the constitution and giving Hitler emergency powers to govern. This Enabling Act needed a two-thirds majority to pass, and only a coalition of the Catholic Center Party and the Social Democratic Party could have blocked this legislation. The Catholic Center Party, fearing communism more than dictatorship, capitulated and voted in favor of the bill. In other words, one of the founding parties of the Weimar Republic voted to abolish democracy. The other political party, the Social Democratic Party, voted against the Enabling Act, and some of its members were sent to Germany's new prison camp at Dachau* (near Munich) while others fled or were killed. Before the summer was over, Hitler completed his assault on democratic institutions and abolished all political parties except the Nazis.

BOOK BURNING

One of the most frightening early actions of the Nazis was the staging of a book burning (see also Chapter 5) in front of prestigious Humboldt University in Berlin in 1933. The location was chosen to signal the termination of free thinking and the end of the open exchange of ideas. Books by various authors considered to be subversive for their support of democracy, socialism, or peace were confiscated and thrown on the pyre by enthusiastic young Nazi supporters.

The destruction of democracy was nearly complete after only a few months of Nazi rule, with the end coming the following year when President Hindenburg died and Hitler combined the positions of president and chancellor. There was no significant opposition to this action. The German army accepted a political deal that eliminated its domestic rivals. From 1934 on new military recruits swore allegiance not to a constitution but to Hitler himself—the Führer: "I swear by almighty God this sacred oath: I will render unconditional obedience to the Führer of the German Reich and people, Adolf Hitler, Supreme Commander of the Wehrmacht,* and, as a brave soldier, I will be ready at any time to stake my life for this oath" (Jewish Virtual Library, 2019). The swastika replaced the German flag, and the Nazi salute "Sieg Heil"* (Hail Victory) became the new greeting.

REARMAMENT

Having completed one of his major objectives with the destruction of German democracy, Hitler started the assault against his second target, the Treaty of Versailles. Although he knew that there was sympathy in the west for revising the treaty, Hitler intentionally ignored Britain, France, and the League of Nations (Germany quit the League in 1933). He was making it clear that he did not accept the validity of the treaty and therefore did not have to negotiate his way out of it. Instead, he counted on western weakness to allow him to move unilaterally and without punishment for his behavior.

In 1935, Hitler challenged the west when he announced German rearmament, including the creation of an army, air force, and navy. He gambled correctly when he predicted western inaction; in fact, he was rewarded immediately when the British signed a Naval Pact with Germany that accepted the new German navy as long as it did not challenge British naval superiority. For the British, who saw German rearmament as unstoppable, preserving their own navy as the world's largest satisfied their national goal. Hitler had no problem promising not to build a larger fleet since he never intended to keep his word anyway.

Abandoned by the British as a result of the Anglo-German Naval Treaty, the French government decided to seek an ally other than England. In this case, France returned to the policy that saved it from defeat in World War I. In 1914, France was allied with Russia, and the Franco-Russian alliance in the Great War compelled the German army to split its forces and fight in the west and in the east simultaneously. The result was stalemate and trench warfare. Therefore, when England accepted German rearmament in 1935, France decided to copy its own World War I diplomatic model and enquired about a deal with Soviet Russia.

Fortunately for France, the Russians were also worried about Germany, especially because Hitler's belligerent speeches were loaded with attacks on communism and the Soviet Union. Although the Soviet Union proclaimed its revolution as the first step toward the end of capitalism and the creation of socialism, in the 1930s the Soviet Union had practical reasons to accept a western alliance. Stalin feared the Nazis and German aggression, and his foreign minister Maxim Litvinov (1876–1951) encouraged him to consider an agreement with western powers, even a capitalist one such as France. After German rearmament, Russia responded positively to the French diplomatic overture, and the two countries signed a defensive alliance pledging support if either was attacked. France and the Soviet Union then included Czechoslovakia in their defensive pact as a warning to Germany.

Stalin understood that all of his economic gains could easily be destroyed if his country remained isolated and confronted Germany alone. At that moment, France and the Soviet Union shared a common need, and while they did not ultimately trust each other, they were brought together by fear of Hitler's intentions. The reality was that neither France nor Russia actually wanted to fight Germany, and both hoped that the act of having a treaty would deter Hitler from further aggression. Their treaty was similar to a high-stakes bluff in a game of poker, but Hitler loved to gamble on the world stage, and he was not intimidated by the other side.

In 1936, he sent the new German army into the demilitarized Rhineland, a strip of territory between the Rhine River and the French border intended to serve as a buffer zone between Germany and France. Although this was a unilateral violation of the Treaty of Versailles, Hitler calculated that the west would not react and he was right. Hitler counted on western weakness and their fear of conflict.

APPEASEMENT*

In 1937, Neville Chamberlain (1869–1940) became the prime minister in London. Believing that Hitler was a politician like all others, with demands but limited goals, he pursued a policy of negotiation and deal-making with the German leader. The policy was called appeasement, which for Chamberlain meant accommodation and compromise. Chamberlain wanted peace, but he had the wrong negotiating partner in Hitler who wanted war. Chamberlain was not unintelligent, but he did not perceive until it was too late that Hitler was using diplomacy only as steps toward his ultimate goal. Today the word appeasement has a new meaning—giving in to a dictator—and Chamberlain has the reputation of a failed prime minister.

AUSTRIA

In early 1938 Hitler was ready to strike again, and this time his target was Austria. Hitler portrayed the aim of bringing all German speakers into one state—the Third Reich—as reasonable. Since many Austrians were either pro-Nazi or at least sympathetic, the union, known as Anschluss* but banned by the Treaty of Versailles, was accomplished without too much difficulty. Hitler was welcomed with a triumphant parade in Vienna.

CZECHOSLOVAKIA AND THE MUNICH PACT*

Hitler's next objective, Czechoslovakia, was more difficult and almost led to war. Following his victory in Austria, he demanded a section of Czechoslovakia called the Sudetenland,* where a German-speaking population lived peacefully within a democratic state. Hitler falsely claimed that the Sudeten Germans were oppressed and insisted that the Czech government cede the territory to Germany. Czechoslovakia refused, but as the summer of 1938 went by Hitler increased the bellicosity of his demands and threatened war.

Built in Munich after the Nazis came to power, the Führerbau (Führer's Building) housed Hitler's office on the second floor. On September 30, 1938, after signing the Munich Pact there, Hitler left the building with (left to right) Göring, Mussolini, and Count Ciano (Mussolini's Foreign Minister and son-in-law). The Munich Pact ceded the Sudetenland to Germany without the approval of the government of Czechoslovakia. (The Illustrated London News Picture Library)

Facing Hitler's October 1 deadline of capitulation or war, Britain and France started to distribute gas masks in their capital cities. Benito Mussolini (1883–1945), the dictator of Italy, suggested a summit meeting to resolve the issue, and Chamberlain and Premier Edouard Daladier (1884–1970) of France agreed to meet in Munich to work out a settlement. At the end of September, the three leaders (Mussolini, Chamberlain, Daladier) all arrived in Germany to appease the Führer. Hitler fabricated news reports claiming that Czechs were killing Germans in the "disputed" territory, and he even threw tantrums demanding a deal or war. After several days of discussions, Chamberlain's policy of appeasement was implemented, and the Sudetenland was ceded to Germany. The Munich Pact is considered one of the most infamous agreements of the twentieth century.

Chamberlain and Daladier returned to London and Paris as heroes for saving the peace, but the Munich Pact that they signed had disastrous consequences: first, four great powers had assumed the right to order a small country to move its border without the agreement of that helpless nation; second, no one asked the League of Nations to play a role, confirming the uselessness of that institution; third, France had demonstrated bad faith by not adhering to its treaty with Czechoslovakia; fourth, the Soviet Union, despite its treaty with France and Czechoslovakia, had not been invited to Munich. The consequences of Munich would haunt Europe for a long time, as Hitler was more determined to pursue his expansionist agenda, and Stalin saw the betrayal by France as a reason to seek another alliance that might protect the USSR. Everyone in Europe would pay in blood for the crime of Munich.

Before Chamberlain left Munich, he asked Hitler to sign a document on British-German friendship, and the German chancellor who was celebrating his Sudetenland triumph readily agreed. The statement read: "Anglo-German relations is of the first importance for the two countries and for Europe. We regard the agreement signed last night and the Anglo-German Naval Agreement as symbolic of the desire of our two peoples never to go to war with one another again. We are resolved that the method of consultation shall be the method adopted to deal with any other questions that may concern our two countries, and we are determined to continue our efforts to remove possible sources of difference and thus to contribute to assure the peace in Europe" (*The Guardian*, October 1, 1938). Chamberlain viewed appeasement as a successful policy, while Hitler saw it as another step toward the end of the Versailles Treaty and the future war for "Aryan" supremacy.

DANZIG, POLAND

In March 1939, Hitler violated the Munich Pact. Already in possession of the Sudetenland, Hitler sent the German army to occupy the rest of Czech territory, and the defenseless government in Prague had no alternative but surrender. In the meantime, with German encouragement, a pro-Nazi government in Slovakia announced its independence from the Czech state. Moving quickly in order to create a new crisis and keep the west off-balance, Hitler demanded that Poland's port city of Danzig be turned over to Germany. Chamberlain now understood that Hitler had lied to him both at Munich and in the subsequent Anglo-British friendship statement. With the policy of appeasement in shreds and faced with this new German threat, England and France issued a declaration of support for Poland's independence and territorial integrity. The Polish government, with British and French backing, had no incentive to enter into talks with Germany on the Danzig question.

The British and French guarantee of Polish sovereignty meant that the European crisis had entered a new phase: Britain and France both pledged to defend Poland, and if Hitler refused to compromise, then war was inevitable. In that scenario, everyone wondered what Stalin would do.

STALIN

Stalin felt betrayed by the Munich Pact that had delivered the Sudetenland to Hitler. Despite Soviet treaties with France and Czechoslovakia, France had not asked that a Soviet representative be included in the Munich meeting. The policy of appeasement not only betrayed the sovereignty of Czechoslovakia, but it also destroyed the French-Soviet Mutual Defense Pact. Hitler walked away from Munich with the Sudetenland, while Stalin watched from Moscow as he lost his allies. With an aggressive Germany demanding the city of Danzig from Poland, war was coming, and Stalin wanted to protect his own country. He sent a signal to the other European powers by firing his pro-western foreign minister Litvinov and replacing him with V. Molotov (1890–1986), one of his staunchest supporters. This message suggested a new start for Soviet foreign policy, as Molotov did not have the pro-western reputation that Litvinov had. This change came just in time for Hitler's next action—war with Poland.

NAZI-SOVIET PACT

Hitler had no intention of backing down despite the British-French guarantee for Poland. At the same time, he understood that fighting a two-front war as in 1914 would be a problem for Germany. He wanted to avoid Soviet intervention in Poland if possible, and he ordered his foreign minister, Joachim von Ribbentrop (1893–1946), to contact the Soviet government about a deal to keep Russia neutral. Since Hitler wanted to attack Poland by September, Ribbentrop had to finish talks with Molotov as soon as possible. With this deadline in mind, the German foreign minister visited Moscow in the third week of August 1939 and offered territory in Eastern Europe in exchange for Soviet neutrality. For Stalin, this was an excellent offer, as he could stay out of the war and reap the benefits of German aggression throughout Eastern Europe. Ribbentrop was willing to give Stalin whatever the Soviet ruler requested in terms of territory, as Hitler did not care what any treaty said as long as it helped him achieve his immediate goals. At another time, Germany could always reclaim whatever it had ceded.

The Nazi-Soviet Nonaggression Pact* was controversial at the time it was signed and remains so to this day. Western observers called it an agreement between dictators, a betrayal of the west, and Stalin's permission for Hitler to go to war. Soviet commentators claimed that it was no worse than Munich and other examples of appeasement, and that Stalin had every right to forge a bargain that considered Soviet interests over British-French needs.

Despite the Soviet argument that the pact between Hitler and Stalin was just another compromise, there was a significant difference between this pact and previous forms of appeasement. Appeasement under Chamberlain, despite its failure, was intended to keep the peace, while the Nazi-Soviet Pact was clearly permission for Hitler to go to war.

There is no question that the pact helped both dictators but hurt the west. Certainly, the overall winner was Hitler, who started the war that he wanted by attacking Poland without fear of Soviet intervention and without worrying about fighting a two-front war. The major victim of the pact was Poland, which had assumed that British-French help was imminent and believed that it had no reason to discuss German demands regarding Danzig. Britain and France can also be viewed as losers in this calculation, as they had issued empty guarantees to Poland with no way to get men and supplies across the continent to stop a German attack. Not only had they not prevented the German invasion, but they also found themselves at war with Germany without Soviet help.

It is especially interesting to note that Stalin emerged from the situation as both winner and loser. On the positive side for Stalin, he received promises of territory in Eastern Europe without going to war. The Soviet economic buildup of the 1930s and industrialization achievements would not be in jeopardy as the western powers fought against Germany on their own, and Stalin at the same time had no objection to the European nations destroying each other while he watched from afar. In addition, Stalin had his revenge against France. As Stalin famously announced in a 1939 speech warning the west, he would not be responsible for pulling their "chestnuts out of the fire." Nevertheless, Stalin was also a loser as a result of the pact. He did not recognize that Hitler was using him and would betray their pact later.

The German invasion of Poland began on September 1, 1939. Britain and France declared war on Germany on September 3.

POLITICAL LIFE OF POLAND

In the late eighteenth century, Poland disappeared from the map of Europe for the next 100 years. Three powers, Austria, Prussia, and Russia, divided Poland among themselves at a time when Poland was powerless to defend itself. Nevertheless, the dream of a Polish national state lived on in popular memory. There were several rebellions in the nineteenth century against Russia, but the uprisings were always suppressed. After World War I, the breakup of the German and Austrian empires and revolution in Russia allowed the Treaty of Versailles map-makers to draw boundaries for a reborn Polish state. In order to give the new country a seaport, the German city of Danzig was added to the territory of Poland.

Like many new nations in Eastern Europe after World War I, Poland struggled to establish a stable government. It fought a war against Soviet Russia during 1919–1920 and successfully acquired additional territory in the east. In the 1920s the country was an unstable democracy, as politicians argued about how to create one national identity. Finally disgusted with instability, the military hero Marshal Józef Pilsudski (1867–1935) seized power in May 1926 and ruled as a military dictator for nearly ten years until his death.

Bordered by Germany and the Soviet Union, Poland was in a precarious situation in terms of foreign policy. Pilsudski signed nonaggression pacts with both countries, but Poland could survive only as long as the two powerful neighbors respected Polish independence. Hitler cancelled his pact with Poland a few months before the invasion on September 1, 1939. While German newspapers claimed that Germany was defending itself against Polish military attacks on German civilians, this blatant Nazi aggression was obvious to other countries. Germany invaded its neighbor with over one million men and new weapons that included dive bombers called Stukas and tank divisions called panzers. These new weapons allowed Germany to introduce the term blitzkrieg* or lightning war to the world. Britain and France had promised to defend Poland, but neither country had any realistic way to get troops across Europe to help. On September 3, 1939, Europe would be at war for the second time in only twenty years.

The Polish army had no chance against the modernized Wehrmacht and Luftwaffe.* After only one week, the Germans were outside of Warsaw. Soon it was clear that continued resistance would only mean more civilian deaths from German shelling and bombing. Warsaw and the rest of the country surrendered on October 6, and the Polish government left for exile in London.

Germany annexed part of western Poland, while the southeastern section came under direct Nazi rule. Designated the General Government,* this area included the major cities of Warsaw and Kraków. It was treated like a colony under the dedicated and cruel Nazi Hans Frank (1900–1946). Within the new capital of Kraków, Hans Frank made Wawel Castle, traditional home of Polish kings, his headquarters.

In addition to the calamity of the German invasion, Poland lost its eastern part to the Soviet army on September 17 in accordance with the Secret Protocol of the Nazi-Soviet Nonaggression Pact. For Poles, it was another partition similar to that one in the late eighteenth century, and the country disappeared from the map after only twenty years of independence.

Both the Nazis and Soviets mistreated the local population, carrying out executions and mass murders, especially of Polish intellectuals and Polish Jews.

In a brutal act of terror, the Soviet police drove at least 20,000 Polish military officers and intellectuals into Katyn Forest, shot them, and buried them in mass graves. No one was safe in Poland during this war.

OCCUPATION OF POLAND

Unlike other European nations, the Poles never established a collaborationist government that supported the Nazis. As the first country overrun, Poland faced the longest occupation of any nation in Europe. It was a punishing five and a half years before the Red Army drove the Wehrmacht back toward Germany. The war brought suffering, murder, execution, torture, and death in battle and in concentration camps. The Nazis killed 17 percent of the population, or six million out of thirty-five million Poles. Of the six million dead, half were Polish Jews and half were Polish Catholics.

Hans Frank implemented Hitler's racial policies of extermination without hesitation. In interviews with German newspapers, Frank even bragged about the execution of Poles. Since the Nazis considered all Poles, Catholics and Jews, to be inferior, German soldiers had no hesitation in shooting or torturing regular citizens. Sometimes Wehrmacht troops would burn down an entire village or round up hostages and shoot everyone in public executions. The Germans had total control, and they accepted no limitations on their own behavior.

POLITICAL LIFE OF FRANCE

During the 1930s, the French population was divided politically, and the lack of agreement on the direction of the country resulted in hesitant leadership. Without political consensus on fundamental issues such as church–state relations, education, and foreign policy, the Third Republic produced weak and indecisive governments. Some historians have argued that this political discord was just as important as France's military situation in explaining its defeat in 1940. When the Germans invaded in 1940, France had about the same number of tanks and planes as Germany, but France was overwhelmed and collapsed in a matter of weeks.

At the beginning of the war, France was the hope of much of non-Nazi Europe. More than Britain, which considered itself to be separate from the continent, France stood for values that democratic Europeans admired and viewed as the alternative to the Nazis.

Despite all of its problems and the arguments that the French had among themselves, the country still symbolized democracy, liberalism, and cultural freedom. As a result, the defeat of France had significant implications. With Russia neutralized, France was believed to be the only land power with a chance to keep Germany under control, but instead France surrendered and was occupied after only six weeks. The political, military, and psychological impact of the fall of France cannot be overstated.

VICHY

Following the armistice between Germany and France in June 1940, the Germans divided France into different sections: the northern part of the country under direct military occupation by German troops and a so-called free zone that included the southern half (about 45 percent) of the country under a French administration led by Marshal Philippe Pétain (1856–1951). Pétain's capital city was at Vichy,* about 220 miles south of Paris.

As leader of the Vichy government, Pétain believed that France had become too liberal and even decadent after World War I, and he saw in Germany a country that was hard working and disciplined. He hoped that an alliance with Germany would lead to a conservative regeneration of French civilization. In July 1940, the French National Assembly, made up of both the Senate and the Chamber of Deputies, voted itself out of existence and granted authoritarian powers to Pétain. The vote was an overwhelming 569 to 80. It was the termination of the Third Republic and the beginning of a pro-German puppet regime in the southern section of France. The Vichy government adopted the slogan "Work, Family, Fatherland" and pursued policies that encouraged women to remain in the home, favored the Roman Catholic Church, and discriminated against Jews.

It is worthwhile to reflect on the context of the end of the democratic Third Republic in France. Between the end of World War I and the early stages of World War II, at least three democratic systems disappeared from Europe: Italy, Germany, and France. It may be surprising that all of the autocratic leaders who came to power in these countries did so legally. Benito Mussolini (1883–1945) was named premier in 1922 by the Italian king, Hitler was appointed by President Hindenburg to become chancellor in 1933, and the parliament of the French Republic voted to turn power over to Marshal Pétain in 1940. None of these takeovers took place illegally or through a seizure of power. One of the lessons of the World War II era remains the fragility of democracy and the possibility that people can tire of their system and vote their own rights and freedoms out of existence.

France was politically divided when it entered the war, and it was physically divided along the demarcation line between north and south during the occupation. Although France was not treated as harshly as Poland, most French people wanted their independence returned. While a part of the population wanted to give Pétain a chance to revitalize the nation, the majority avoided politics and tried to stay out of trouble with the authorities. Most people hoped to find enough food to feed their families while waiting for liberation. A minority joined the resistance, but as the war continued active resistance increased in numbers and effectiveness. While the resistance was never as large as the French later claimed, it proved effective against the Germans at the time of the Normandy landing in 1944.

THE NETHERLANDS

The Netherlands had been neutral in World War I and hoped to remain so in World War II as well. Despite restating its policy of official neutrality and refraining from any aggressive acts toward Germany, the Netherlands found itself under attack on May 10, 1940. The small Dutch army could not resist Germany's overwhelming military force for more than a few days. The country was overrun, and the Dutch government surrendered to prevent further damage and death. The royal family quickly escaped and spent the war years in London as a government-in-exile.

Despite their victory, the Germans unnecessarily bombed the city of Rotterdam, an action that targeted civilians. The German military violated international law that forbids the intentional killing of civilian populations. While the bombings of Warsaw and Rotterdam took place early in the war, eventually the genocide against Jews, Roma, and many other groups made the Nazi war against civilians one of this war's major themes.

After the shock of the initial invasion, the country seemed to recover fairly quickly. Amsterdam, occupied on May 15, did not suffer a lot of physical damage. Most aspects of daily life returned, including transportation in the cities, schools, and entertainment venues. Nevertheless, hopes for a return to a normal existence soon vanished, as the Germans ordered all windows to be covered at night to prevent Allied planes from seeing their targets; the blackout was enforced by the Dutch civil defense units patrolling the streets. Other changes quickly followed. One was a night-time curfew, and another was censorship of newspapers and the radio. Bookstores were emptied of their history books and international literature and filled with Nazi propaganda. Nazi posters went up attacking Jews and Bolsheviks, and often these two groups were shown as being part of one international conspiracy.

OCCUPATION OF THE NETHERLANDS

German occupation governments varied from country to country. Some countries such as France had their own collaborationist government, while others like Belgium were placed under German military control. In the Netherlands, the pro-fascist National Socialist Movement (NSB in Dutch) was never a very large party, but it welcomed the Nazi takeover. The NSB leader, Anton Mussert (1894–1946), hoped to be appointed as the dictator of the country, but the Nazis gave him a meaningless title—leader of the Dutch people—and then chose the Austrian Nazi Arthur Seyss-Inquart (1892–1946) for that position. Seyss-Inquart was a loyal Nazi who had advanced through government postings in Austria and Poland until he arrived in the Netherlands, where he enthusiastically carried out persecution of Jews and other minorities.

POLITICAL LIFE OF USSR

There were two revolutions in Russia in 1917: the first started with demonstrations and strikes that forced Tsar Nicholas II to abdicate; the second was led by the Bolshevik Party (later Communist Party) under the leaders V. Lenin and L. Trotsky. Lenin promised to take Russia out of World War I, and he did so by signing a peace treaty with Germany that ended the war but surrendered vast territories to the Germans. At about the same time, a civil war devastated an already-weak economy and resulted in famine in 1921. The government desperately sought an economic plan that would encourage growth but also adhere to communist doctrine.

For the next decade, this economic problem was central to Soviet political life. Members of the Communist Party debated whether to support an economy that combined elements of capitalism and socialism rather than total government ownership and centralized control in all areas. The first option was implemented by Lenin in response to the desperate economic situation in 1921, but his death in 1924 opened the subject to argument among his potential successors. Both Trotsky and Stalin were among the contenders to succeed Lenin, but by 1927 Stalin had outmaneuvered Trotsky and sent him into exile.

Stalin moved to tighten his hold on the country. He introduced a Five-Year Plan for industry that centralized all decision making in Moscow; government agencies decided what would be produced, how much of it, and where factories would be built. The structure favored heavy industry, such as steel plants, hydroelectric dams, trucks, machinery, and mining; it did not emphasize domestic goods. Soviet industrialization in the 1930s was designed to make the country a major world power that the west would be reluctant to disturb.

The other aspect of Stalin's economic policy was the collectivization of agriculture. Stalin ordered all peasants to give up their private land, animals, and tools, and move onto collective farms where their former goods would be owned by the collective farm itself. The peasants would share all of those items to bring greater equality in the countryside, but peasants hated the idea. The Russian countryside was thrust into chaos, especially in Ukraine, but eventually the policy was slowed down to prevent even greater agricultural disaster.

One aspect of Stalin's rule was a massive propaganda campaign designed to create the belief that Stalin was the greatest leader in world history. The so-called cult of personality involved naming cities, towns, mountains, schools, and eventually 70,000 places after him.

Soviet foreign policy in the 1930s cannot be understood without reference to the economic progress under the Five-Year Plans. In 1939, Stalin saw a chance to take revenge on the west and protect his country at the same time; the Nazi-Soviet Nonaggression Pact gave him what he needed.

When the war started, Stalin was in a very advantageous position. His country was assured peace and could pursue its territorial and economic goals without fear of outside interference. On September 17, 1939, the Red Army rolled unopposed into eastern Poland, and two months later the Soviet Union presented Finland with demands that led to the Winter War. Shortly thereafter, the Soviet Union occupied and annexed the Baltic States of Estonia, Latvia, and Lithuania, followed by a part of Romania. At that moment, it looked as if the Nazi-Soviet Pact was delivering all the promised territories to Russia with little effort.

Of course, Stalin could not celebrate for long, as Hitler was preparing to violate Soviet neutrality (see Chapter 2). Despite the military devastation in the early days of the German invasion in 1941, the Soviet government responded quickly. The day after the Wehrmacht offensive started, the Soviet government organized a military high command committee called *Stavka* that included Stalin and several of his closest aides and important generals.

In events we will explore in more detail (see Chapters 2 and 3), the first few months of war were a disaster for Russia. Nevertheless, the Soviet side had an advantage that was not apparent immediately—while other countries had to create centralized political and economic structures to confront the wartime emergency, the Soviet Union was already centralized as a command economy.

POLITICAL LIFE OF BELGIUM, GREECE, YUGOSLAVIA

Neutral Belgium was invaded on May 10, 1940, as part of Germany's spring offensive. After two and a half weeks, King Leopold III (1901–1983), without consultation with the Allies or with his government officials, surrendered to Germany. While the king faced house arrest, the Nazis placed the country under a military governor who ran the government for four years. Not unlike the occupation in other countries, Belgium suffered from rationing and shortages. The Nazis also implemented their anti-Semitic program, and almost 29,000 out of 70,000 Jews were killed.

Greece was a monarchy under King George II (1890–1947), and the country was divided between pro-Allied and pro-German factions. Mussolini in Italy had already occupied Albania, and in the fall of 1940 he demanded the stationing of his troops in Greece. When the Greeks rejected the Italian dictator, Mussolini invaded. The Greek army pushed the Italians back, and Hitler decided to bail out his ally. The German invasion of Greece in April 1941 achieved its goals quickly, but this action had important results: first it revealed Mussolini as more of an impediment to Germany than an asset; second Hitler had to postpone the invasion of the Soviet Union to defeat Greece; and third the Nazis imposed a harsh occupation regime on the Greeks. King George of Greece moved first to Crete and then to Cairo for the duration of the war. Toward the end of World War II, a civil war between communist and monarchist factions resulted in a return of the monarchy, but it was abolished in 1973. In a global perspective, the delay in the timing of the invasion of the Soviet Union may have been the most important result of the events in Greece.

Like Greece, Yugoslavia was invaded by Germany in 1941 and split into several parts, including Croatia and Serbia. Croatia established a pro-Nazi government (Ustashe)* that committed atrocities against all minorities, including Serbs, Jews, and Roma. The Croatian state killed at least 300,000 Serbs, 30,000 Jews, and another 30,000 Roma. Serbia became embroiled in its own civil war even as the larger war raged in the Balkans. Serbian communists fought Serbian monarchists at the same time that they both fought Germans and defended themselves against the brutal Croatian Ustashe.

CONCLUSION

Shortly before signing the Treaty of Versailles in 1919, Germany had won two wars and had imposed treaties on other countries. The first was in 1871 following the Franco-Prussian War, when Germany forced France to pay reparations and surrender two provinces. The second was in 1918 when Germany took a large amount of territory away from Russia. One year later, Germany was the loser, and it had to sign the Treaty of Versailles that led to reparation payments and territorial losses by Germany. In comparison to the treaties that Germany imposed on its enemies previously, the Treaty of Versailles was not harsh. Nevertheless, some Germans never accepted defeat, including a small group of veterans whose leader was a charismatic speaker with an extremist program.

Throughout the 1920s, Hitler continued his efforts to expand the base of his party, using a message that blamed others—Jews, democracy, communism, and the Weimar Republic. His goal was to destroy all of those systems when he had complete power.

The rise of Hitler is also the story of the decline of Germany. In the early 1930s, the country was suffering from the Depression, and the political system was too weak to address the economic situation with decisive action. The president (Hindenburg) was old, and the political establishment was far more afraid of communism than of fascism. Hindenburg appointed Hitler to be chancellor in January 1933.

The Depression is often cited as the reason for Hitler's rise to power. While high unemployment and economic dislocation were serious in Germany, the same issues existed in the United States, Britain, France, and other countries, none of which turned to fascism to solve their problems. The United States had an election in 1932, chose a president from the other political party, and had a smooth transition from Herbert Hoover to Franklin Roosevelt in 1933. The Depression is not a sufficient explanation for German support for the Nazi Party.

As mentioned earlier in this chapter, Hitler had two immediate goals, and he accomplished both of them: he destroyed German democracy, and he dismantled the European consensus that was opposed to another large war. Leaders from other countries negotiated with Hitler and assumed that they had the same objective—a compromise that would avoid armed conflict. Hitler's goal was the opposite—pushing western powers until they had no choice but war. He won decisive diplomatic victories before he arrived at his objective in Poland.

The war that Hitler brought the world continues to confound our sense of right and wrong, good and evil, and normative and abhorrent behavior. How could an entire nation engage in widespread brutality, racism, and mass murder? It does not matter now that not every single German believed in the message of Adolf Hitler because there were enough Germans who did, and with them a sufficient number of supporters all over Europe as well. It was not that Hitler disguised his aims and came to power promising one policy and then pursuing another; everyone knew exactly what he represented, and yet millions of people accepted his goals and carried out crimes in his name.

At the end of the war, a few German leaders were put on trial at Nuremberg,* where testimony revealed details about the genocide central to the Nazi program. The leaders who were convicted were certainly guilty of war crimes, crimes against peace, and crimes against humanity, yet they primarily gave the orders that were carried out by husbands and sons and thousands of others who in other times might have been normal neighbors. Why did they participate in atrocities? After the war, how did they melt back into society and resume a regular life? These questions may always remain, frustratingly, unanswered.

FURTHER READING

"Adolf Hitler: The Fuehrer Oath." Jewish Virtual Library. https://www.jewishvirtuallibrary.org/the-fuehrer-oath. Accessed April 18, 2019.
"An Anglo-German Pledge." *The Guardian*, October 1, 1938.
Beevor, Anthony. *The Second World War*. New York: Little, Brown and Co., 2012.

"Hitler Puts Aside Aim to Be Dictator." *New York Times*, January 31, 1933, 3, 16.

Paxton, Robert O. *Vichy France*. New York: Columbia University Press, 1972.

Roberts, Andrew. *The Storm of War: A New History of the Second World War*. New York: HarperCollins, 2011.

Sontheimer, Michael. "Germany's WWII Occupation of Poland: When We Finish, Nobody Is Left Alive." *Spiegel Online*, May 27, 2011. https://www.spiegel.de/international/europe/germany-s-wwii-occupation-of-poland-when-we-finish-nobody-is-left-alive-a-759095.html. Accessed November 7, 2017.

Weinberg, Gerhard L. *A World at Arms: A Global History of World War II*. Cambridge, UK: Cambridge University, 1994.

2
MILITARY LIFE

The war against Russia will be such that it cannot be conducted in a knightly fashion. This struggle is one of ideologies and racial differences and will have to be conducted with unprecedented, unmerciful and unrelenting harshness.

Adolf Hitler, March 1941

The Red Army and Navy and the whole Soviet people must fight for every inch of Soviet soil, fight to the last drop of blood for our towns and villages . . . onward, to victory!

Stalin, July 1941

INTRODUCTION

The most shocking statistic from World War II is not the number of military personnel who were killed, an estimated 20–25 million and still the largest of any war in history. The figure that continues to horrify is the 50–55 million civilians who died—twice the number of military deaths. In one sense, that is all that is needed to know about daily life during this war—every day was a life and death struggle for civilians under Nazi occupation. Whether civilians served in the army or not, they survived day by day, fearing for their own safety and the safety of their families.

Every war kills people in uniform, and in every war innocent civilians are also victims of the fighting. However, the dead in World War II were not merely "collateral damage,"* but rather people who were intentionally starved, shot in the head, hanged, gassed, and killed in ways we still find hard to comprehend. World War II was unique because from the first day to the last Germany and its allies violated all treaties, conventions, and understandings about how wars are supposed to be fought. The Nazi agenda was driven by its racist theory and focused on the destruction of innocent civilians even more than on winning the war.

The casualty numbers in different countries also reveal the horrific nature of Nazi cruelty. In Poland, for example, 250,000 soldiers died, but there were six million other deaths that resulted from the Nazi campaign against the population. In Yugoslavia, most of the one million dead were nonmilitary, and in Greece and Czechoslovakia, ten times more civilians than soldiers died. All Nazi institutions, including the S.S.,* Gestapo, and Wehrmacht,* killed to intimidate the population, but Nazi racism meant that Eastern Europe suffered more casualties than Western Europe. The Soviet Union lost the most people of any country in the war—between twenty-five and thirty million, of whom ten million were in the military.

1938

Throughout the 1930s, Hitler often ignored the cautious advice of his generals as he gambled on risky diplomatic demands, including rearmament, occupation of the Rhineland, Anschluss* with Austria, and control of the Sudetenland.* He was successful in every case due to the west's policy of appeasement.* At Munich in 1938, after being given the Sudetenland, Hitler also started the process of Czechoslovakia's fracture and the unravelling of the French-Soviet alliance. His campaign against the Treaty of Versailles* was almost complete.

HITLER DEMANDS DANZIG

Hitler took small pieces at a time. First he moved his army into the remainder of Czechoslovakia, with Slovakia spun off as a Nazi ally. The British and the French decided that it was time to resist German aggression, and they announced that they would fight to defend Poland. This western pledge created an opportunity for

Hitler, who demanded that the Polish port of Danzig be turned over to Germany. For the German leader, this situation had developed perfectly—if the west backed down and pressured Poland to surrender the port city, Hitler would have another diplomatic victory. If the west decided to fight, then he would have his war. In the midst of these developments, Stalin further strengthened Hitler's position when the Soviet leader fired his pro-western foreign minister, M. Litvinov, and replaced him with V. Molotov. The scene was set for another Hitler victory.

NAZI-SOVIET NONAGGRESSION PACT*

As discussed in Chapter 1, Stalin knew that Hitler needed Soviet neutrality in order to avoid a two-front war; he also knew that Hitler wanted war. As a result, when German foreign minister Ribbentrop arrived in Moscow in the third week of August 1939, Stalin made significant territorial demands in Eastern Europe; Ribbentrop agreed to all of them. For Stalin, this was a way to acquire territory while watching the western countries fight among themselves. For Hitler, the concessions to Stalin were easy to grant as he felt that all treaties could be ignored when it was convenient. As mentioned in Chapter 1, the Nazi-Soviet Nonaggression Pact was Soviet appeasement with one major difference from the previous variety: British and French appeasement was intended to prevent war, while Stalin readily accepted neutrality because he knew it would lead to war.

WAR: POLAND

The rest of the world understood the likely result of the nonaggression pact, and several world leaders exchanged letters urging restraint and encouraging peace. No one, however, had a specific plan other than asking Hitler to behave himself—not exactly a proposal with a chance of success.

In Germany, official propaganda accused the Poles of attacking Germany and harming German civilians. These were false claims to try to cover up the reality of German aggression that started on September 1. Two days later, Germany ignored a British-French ultimatum that demanded withdrawal from Poland by 11:00 A.M. The diplomacy of Britain and France ended in disaster. They had hoped to prevent a German invasion rather than fight a war, but they had failed on both counts. They had no way to move their

Members of an elite SS division, these German soldiers take a break as they approach Pabianice in Poland in September 1939. Located near the city of Łódź, Pabianice had a Jewish population of about 8,000, all of whom were moved into a ghetto before being sent to Chelmno concentration camp. (Library of Congress)

armies across Europe in support of Poland, and in any case they were not prepared to engage Germany in battle.

An official state of war did not change the reality in Poland itself. Isolated and fighting alone, the Poles mounted the best defense possible under the circumstances; nevertheless, their defeat was inevitable. Germany introduced a fast-paced offensive style of war that journalists called lightning war or blitzkrieg.* Polish forces were overwhelmed, and in just over two weeks Nazi soldiers were in Warsaw; on September 17, Stalin took half of the country in the eastern sector. Poland, which had been partitioned in the late eighteenth century by Russia, Prussia, and Austria, was reborn in 1919 at Versailles. Only twenty years later, Poland was partitioned again and disappeared until 1945.

PHONY WAR

All sides used the winter of 1939–1940 to prepare for the battles that they knew would come in the spring. The relatively quiet months from October to March have been called the Phony War (Phoney in England) or *Sitzkrieg* (sitting war in Germany) or *Drôle de guerre* (strange war in France). Despite this label, there was some action in Scandinavia. Stalin took the opportunity to pressure Finland to cede territory to Russia, but when Finland refused, Stalin attacked in November 1939. It might seem obvious that November, December, and January would be the worst months to fight in

Finland due to the cold, but Stalin was overconfident and did not expect strong resistance. He miscalculated, and the Finnish army gave the Red Army a tough fight. Finns fought on skis in white camouflage, and they made a weapon famous: gasoline in a bottle stuffed with a rag, set on fire, and thrown at a target intended as a "cocktail" for Molotov* (Soviet foreign minister). Despite this brave Finnish defense, Stalin won the Winter War, and the border near the city of Leningrad was adjusted in Russia's favor.

SPRING OFFENSIVE

Anyone bored by the Phony War and awaiting action in the spring was not disappointed. The first move came in April, when Germany invaded Denmark and Norway. While the attack on Denmark lasted only one day, the fighting in Norway continued for two months. The British intervened and sank a large number of German ships, but ultimately the Allied effort there had to be abandoned.

The offensive against the Netherlands, Belgium, and France started on May 10, the same day that embattled British prime minister Chamberlain resigned and was replaced by Winston Churchill (1874–1965). Churchill could not have come into office at a more difficult time, as the Germans were overrunning all of Western Europe. The Netherlands fell in four days, but not before the Nazis bombed Rotterdam despite the Dutch surrender.

BATTLE OF FRANCE

France was the anchor of the western alliance on the continent. Hitler and his tank commanders planned a daring thrust through the Ardennes Forest, a region that the French believed was impenetrable. German tanks were able to traverse the small roads that crossed the forest, and they emerged in France in a lightly defended area. French training manuals anticipated a frontal German assault and a stalemate like the previous war; for this reason the best French troops were waiting in their concrete trenches named for the former defense minister André Maginot.* The Wehrmacht largely ignored the Maginot Line, leaving French units sitting in bunkers while their country lost battles everywhere. Once the original French plan went awry, their generals did not have a quick backup response. In the middle of these French problems, the Belgian king, without checking with his own government or allies, surrendered his army and thus exposed the flank of the Allied forces. The British realized that in order to preserve their own army for the future, their forces would have to be evacuated. Churchill ordered seaworthy ships and boats to sail for Dunkirk* to rescue the stranded army, and between May 26 and June 4, close to 340,000 troops, including 100,000 French soldiers, were saved.

The Dunkirk evacuation included good news and bad news. On the positive side, the heroic ship rescue raised the morale of many people in Britain as well as the soldiers who had been saved to fight again another day. On the negative side, as Churchill honestly told his people, you do not win wars by running away. In addition, France was only a couple of weeks from surrender.

FRANCE SURRENDERS

France was in trouble—the population was fleeing west and south (called the "Exodus")* to escape the German advance, while the government was in disarray with no military plan in place. In an attempt to rally the nation, several World War I generals were brought into the government, including Marshal Philippe Pétain (1856–1951), the hero of Verdun in 1916. Pétain believed that France should accept German armistice terms and follow Germany's example—a conservative social program with traditional values of family (women stay home), hard work (the state is supreme over the individual), and patriotism (Pétain knows best). Unfortunately, he also adhered to another part of the German example—racism and anti-Semitism.

Due to the military disaster, Pétain's policy was adopted. France signed the armistice after only six weeks of battle, and the country was divided between the north under direct Nazi occupation and the south under the government formed by Pétain in the city of Vichy.*

By the summer of 1940, Hitler controlled almost all of Europe, either through occupation or alliance. Only Britain held out against Germany, and while Britain alone was not a threat to Germany's European empire, Hitler wanted to force Britain out of the war.

BATTLE OF BRITAIN

Although Hitler drew up a plan for the invasion of England (Operation Sea Lion), the German navy was not large enough to carry a landing force across the English Channel. Instead, Hitler turned to his air force, the Luftwaffe,* and started the bombing of

RAF (Royal Air Force) bases and then civilian targets. The ensuing Battle of Britain was an air battle that raged for three months, with the British Hurricane and Spitfire taking on the German Messerschmitt. Eventually the Germans could not sustain their loss of planes and pilots, and Hitler decided to turn his attention elsewhere; he made plans to attack the Soviet Union.

TROUBLE IN THE BALKANS

Mussolini was more trouble than he was worth as an ally. Everywhere Italy invaded, its army stalled and needed German assistance. Whether it was North Africa, southeastern France, or the Balkans, the Wehrmacht had to deploy troops to save Mussolini from embarrassing defeat. Mussolini's invasion of Greece in October 1940 was not successful, and by the spring of 1941 had turned into a disaster for Italy. In April 1941 the Wehrmacht intervened in Greece and invaded Yugoslavia as well. Once again the true nature of German policy was revealed when the bombing of Belgrade killed 17,000 civilians. Both Greece and Yugoslavia quickly surrendered, and Yugoslavia was split along ethnic lines. Croatia became a fascist state under the extreme racist Ustashe* organization; it engaged in the brutal killing of Serbs, Jews, and Roma.* The other part of Yugoslavia, Serbia, descended into civil war, but one of those factions was led by Josip Broz, known as Tito (1892–1980), and it became one of the most effective anti-Nazi guerrilla movements in the war.

SOVIET UNION

In *Mein Kampf*,* Hitler wrote that his goal was the destruction of the Soviet Union. Following his successful campaigns in Poland and Western Europe, he felt that the time was right to push toward that objective. In December 1940, he told the Wehrmacht to prepare for Operation Barbarossa* in the spring of 1941. The largest German army ever assembled, eventually over three million men, began to deploy along the Soviet border. The target date was May 15, 1941, but due to events in the Balkans that was postponed for five weeks.

A fatal flaw in Hitler's plans was his overconfidence and belief in his own genius. He thought that invading the Soviet Union would lead to another quick victory such as that in Poland or France. In June 1941, the German army moved rapidly into Soviet territory, but within a few months the invasion slowed down. The Germans had miscalculated on several items: they did not anticipate the resistance of the Red Army, they never solved the logistical problems related to the size of the Soviet Union, and they were not prepared for the prolonged economic consequences of the engagement that they faced. The Soviet Union surprised Germany by mobilizing far more men and resources than Hitler expected. By the autumn of 1941, the Wehrmacht's advance to the east had slowed down, and it soon became apparent that winter supplies would be needed.

The Soviet High Command (Stavka) turned out to be surprisingly responsive to the situation. While Stalin remained the final authority on all actions, he found and listened to the advice of a few officers he trusted, especially Marshal Georgy Zhukov (1896–1974). In the emergency situation created by the invasion, Stalin appealed to old-fashioned Russian patriotism and allowed more freedom for the church. Toward the end of the war, when the military threat was over and the Wehrmacht was in retreat, he reinstated prewar policies and rescinded the rights that had mobilized the population. Winning was everything, but unlike Hitler, Stalin was successful.

INVASION

It seems impossible for Germany to move three million men and not be detected during that process, but the invasion on June 22, 1941, came as a surprise to the Soviet government. Actually, Stalin's own spies as well as western leaders had warned him that Germany was planning an attack, but Stalin did not order his military to take preventive measures. He considered alerts coming from the west to be a form of disinformation intended to start a war between Russia and Germany. Stalin accepted Hitler's excuse that the large troop movements along the border were intended to hide those soldiers from British bombers. When the attack came, Soviet forces were unprepared to deal with the initial invasion, and the Wehrmacht advanced quickly into Soviet territory.

Operation Barbarossa envisioned a three-pronged offensive: with Poland as its starting point, Germany's northern army crossed the Baltic States and aimed for Leningrad, the central army went through Belarus toward Moscow, and the southern prong headed for Kiev in Ukraine and oil resources near the Caspian Sea. A Romanian army allied with Germany launched a simultaneous attack into Ukraine.

The invasion was at first a great success for the Nazi regime. The German army had complete control of the air and quickly rolled deeply into Soviet territory. The German advance appeared to be unstoppable, so Stalin issued Order No. 270, a no retreat order, forcing his military to stand and fight regardless of the circumstances. The result was tremendous manpower losses for both sides—more than a million men in the Soviet army before the end of the year and half that number for the Germans. The situation appeared to be a disaster for the Soviet Union, but the larger Russian population was able to provide new recruits while the Wehrmacht had a more difficult time replacing some of its best front line troops.

Although the Germans moved quickly, the Soviet Union was so large that even constant advances left them far from their goals. Due to the size of the Soviet Union, every successful battle brought the German army new problems. They took control of vast territories that had to be administered; they captured hundreds of thousands of Soviet soldiers who had to be dealt with in some way; and most of all they had to feed and resupply themselves. Every day took them further away from their food and armaments supplies. Russian peasants did not make it easier for them. As the civilian population retreated, they burned their own lands to prevent the Germans from finding food or shelter. This scorched earth policy* was copied from the previous time that Russia was invaded—in 1812 when Napoleon attempted what Hitler was trying in 1941.

The economic resources that Germany already controlled were sufficient for a four-month struggle in Russia but certainly not enough for the four-year war that took place. The challenges of war with the Soviet Union were insurmountable, and Germany could not overcome the difficulties created by resistance, distance, and climate.

REACTION

When the invasion started, the Soviet government appeared to be in disarray. In Moscow, Foreign Minister Molotov announced the invasion on the radio, but many people wondered why Stalin had not spoken. In order to spread panic, the Germans dropped leaflets on Moscow claiming that Stalin was dead. On July 3, Stalin finally addressed the nation, with an appeal to all citizens to defend traditional Russian values. For the Soviet Union, this was not just another war—it was a national crusade to save Russian civilization—it was the Great Patriotic War. Observers agree that the feeling of patriotism throughout the country was very powerful.

The hundreds of thousands of men who were called up or volunteered overwhelmed the system. Food, uniforms, and weapons were all in short supply. The medical system could not handle the number of casualties, and the lack of hospitals (and field hospitals) and medicines cost many lives among soldiers and civilians.

Stalin's no-retreat and stand-and-fight policy also led to many deaths. Soldiers who did not have guns, bullets, or food had little choice but to leave the front lines, but if caught they were accused of treason or desertion and many were executed. Large Soviet armies that might have pulled back were destroyed or captured. By the end of 1941, the Germans had taken 2–3 million Soviet prisoners. Cruel as it may sound, Soviet soldiers who died on the battlefield may have been better off than those taken prisoner. The Germans violated every international code on caring for prisoners. Soviet prisoners were starved, tortured, and even used for target practice. Thousands were required to perform hard labor with minimal food provided—literally worked to death. For Germans, the death of Soviet or other prisoners of Slavic ethnicity was an extension of the vicious racial policy that Nazis imposed throughout Europe. As a result, of the 5.7 million Soviet prisoners controlled by Germany, approximately 3.3 million or more than 50 percent died in captivity (German-Russian Berlin-Karlshorst Museum, 2019).

Some historians argue that Stalin's stubborn position against retreat had the long-term positive effect of wearing down the German military. In addition, slowing down the German advance meant that German armies would eventually face autumn rains that turned dirt roads to mud, to be followed by a harsh winter that the Wehrmacht was not prepared for. The German army expected a quick victory, but like Napoleon they did not succeed.

In addition to the chaos along the front lines of battle, Soviet civilians found themselves facing a desperate situation. Artillery and bombing destroyed cities, the countryside, and the economy. Millions of civilians fled east, but millions also fell quickly under Nazi occupation. The consequences were deadly, as Nazi racial policy targeted Slavs, Jews, Roma, and other groups—and resulted in premeditated and systematic genocide.

It seems remarkable that after these first few months of chaos and defeat, the Soviet army was able to reorganize itself and turn the war around, one of the most amazing military transformations in history. It took place just in time to save the Soviet Union and changed apparent Nazi victory into the eventual destruction of Germany and the Nazi regime.

Three of the most famous battles of the war were fought over cities targeted by the Wehrmacht: Leningrad, Moscow, and Stalingrad.* In all three cases the German army was not victorious. The Nazis inflicted enormous punishment on people and territory, but in the end they did not accomplish their goals. They surrounded and starved Leningrad, but it did not surrender; they approached the outskirts of Moscow, but they did not occupy the city; and they largely destroyed Stalingrad but did not conquer it and lost a huge German army in the process.

LENINGRAD

The siege of Leningrad lasted for more than 870 days, and in that time span over a million people died in the city. In January 1944 Leningrad was freed from the grip of the German blockade.

The situation would have been worse if not for Lake Ladoga,* Europe's largest lake that provided the connection between the city and the rest of Russia. The winter of 1941–1942 was extremely cold, and while temperatures of fifteen to thirty degrees below zero (Centigrade) made everyday life difficult, it also meant that the lake was frozen solid, allowing trucks to cross it. During that winter, this "Road of Life" allowed half a million Leningrad inhabitants to escape the city and also provided a path for bringing food and supplies into the city.

In the desperately cold weather, people burned everything they could find including furniture and books; they also ate whatever they could catch including dogs and cats. The absence of cats led to an increase in the rodent population, and toward the end of the siege, cats were shipped back to the city in order to bring the rat population under control.

People could not survive on dogs and cats forever. Most important was the production of bread, but the rationing system mandated the highest amount of calories for the army—that is 500 grams (just over one pound) of bread per day for soldiers. Inhabitants who did not work in war industries received 125 grams each day, barely enough to stay alive. More than 90 percent of the one million deaths in the city were from starvation, diseases, and ailments associated with the lack of food. Many people also endured psychological trauma, including children who became orphans and then had to fend for themselves in a dark and difficult world where survival was all that mattered. These young people were robbed of their childhoods. In terms of the total number of casualties,

In 1941, Germany invaded the Soviet Union with three armies, all of which sliced through Russian forces and drove toward major cities. As the Northern Army Group approached Leningrad, the entire city population was mobilized to prepare for the German onslaught. In this photo, Russian women are shown digging antitank trenches to the south and west of the city. Leningrad subsequently endured a three-year siege before the Soviet army forced the Germans to retreat. (Library of Congress)

a relatively small number, about 18,000 residents, died from bombings or artillery attacks.

MOSCOW

Counting on a quick victory over Soviet forces, the Wehrmacht did not bring winter clothing for its soldiers or cold-weather lubricants for its guns. The Wehrmacht hoped to capture Moscow in Operation Typhoon* before winter, but Soviet resistance kept the German army outside the city. In November, winter arrived, and by December temperatures were as much as thirty degrees below zero. Perhaps 100,000 German soldiers suffered from frostbite, and 15,000 of those cases resulted in amputations. German trucks and tanks would not start, and rifles often froze as well. The Russians were better equipped for the cold weather, dressed in white uniforms as camouflage and carrying properly lubricated weapons.

Several factors helped the Soviet army: the first was the command of General Georgy Zhukov (1896–1974), one of the best generals in World War II; the second was the ability of the Soviet army to deploy large reserve forces from Siberia as soon as the Soviet government learned that Japan was not going to attack Russia; the third was Hitler's refusal to listen to his own generals; and the fourth was the cold weather. All of these together allowed the Red Army to hold Moscow. As the first major land battle that the Wehrmacht did not win, Moscow should be considered one of the turning points of the war.

STALINGRAD

The Wehrmacht was far from defeated. Hitler ordered an attack on Stalingrad, and Stalin countered by ordering no retreat from the city. The ensuing struggle lasted for months, dragging on into the winter of 1942–1943, leaving the Wehrmacht exposed without supplies. The German air force no longer had the ability to deliver promised food and equipment, and as a result German General Friedrich von Paulus (1890–1957) asked Hitler for permission to retreat. Hitler refused, and to prevent von Paulus from taking this action on his own, Hitler promoted him to field marshal; no German field marshal had ever surrendered. With his starving, freezing, and surrounded army about to be destroyed completely, von Paulus capitulated. According to many sources, Hitler was less concerned about the army of 300,000 men than the fact that von Paulus did not commit suicide.

NORTH AFRICA AND ITALY

The prize in North Africa was the Suez Canal and control of the eastern end of the Mediterranean Sea. Whoever controlled that area would have access to the Middle East and its oil resources. The Italian army was already in Libya in 1940 when it moved east toward Egypt, but the British were able to halt that advance; when they pushed Italy back, Germany intervened. The confrontation in the desert raged throughout 1942, with two crucial battles at El Alamein in Egypt. The British prevailed in one of the decisive engagements of the war, keeping the Suez Canal and oil fields in Allied hands. Shortly thereafter the first American landing of the war took place in Tunisia. In 1943, victory in this part of Africa (code named Operation Torch)* allowed President Roosevelt and Prime Minister

Churchill to meet in Casablanca* in Morocco, where they reached two important agreements: the invasion of France would take place in 1944, and they would accept nothing less than unconditional surrender from the enemy.

The Allies also decided to invade Italy. Anglo-American forces landed in Sicily at the southern tip of Italy, followed by the invasion of Italy itself. Facing defeat, the Italian government dismissed Mussolini, placed him under arrest, and switched sides to join the Allies. Rather than allowing the Allies to march through Italy without a fight, Hitler rushed troops to block the Allied advance. The ensuing battles were difficult and included an infamous mistake by the Allies. Assuming that the Germans had fortified an ancient monastery called Monte Cassino, the Allies bombed the historic treasure and only later discovered that its destruction had not been necessary. Finally, Allied troops entered Rome, but that victory in the first week of June 1944 was quickly overshadowed on the front pages of newspapers by the landing in France on June 6.

FROM STALINGRAD TO D-DAY

For several months in 1942 Nazi press coverage of Stalingrad had predicted victory, but early in 1943 the battle disappeared from German newspapers as if it had never taken place. Details of the defeat were not published due to censorship under the occupation, but Europeans knew how to read between the lines. Those living closer to London also heard the news on BBC radio, and word spread quickly from person to person. The information raised the morale of Europeans and encouraged the growth of resistance forces in every country. Suddenly it seemed that the invincible Nazis might lose the war.

Hoping to retake the offensive in the Soviet Union, Hitler and his generals planned an attack that led to the largest tank battle in history. At Kursk,* Operation Citadel* was intended to stop Soviet momentum after Stalingrad and retake the initiative. The Soviet side was prepared, and the confrontation involved thousands of tanks and mine fields stretching for miles. Eventually the battlefield was littered with twisted metal hulks burning in the summer heat. To this day, no one knows how many men died and how many tanks were destroyed, but most importantly the Wehrmacht was unable to stop the Soviet advance to the west.

The Wehrmacht retreated through the same villages and towns they had ravaged in their advance, and as they moved, they torched the same landscape that was already in ruins. The Red

Army unleashed massive artillery attacks on German positions, but this destruction was of their own countryside. The result was further devastation and death—a country destroyed once when the Germans invaded and again when the Germans retreated. Slowly the Red Army liberated the occupied sections of its country and revealed the brutality of German rule. Kiev was taken in November 1943, and with it came the discovery of death pits dug by the Germans such as Babi Yar* (see Chapter 9). The city of Odessa was freed from Romanian rule, uncovering the reality of another genocidal occupation. Finally, in January 1944, the three-year siege of Leningrad was lifted, but the city was still littered with corpses awaiting burial when the ground thawed.

The Soviet defense and ultimate victory cost the country an extraordinary number of dead—twenty-seven million total, including eight to ten million soldiers and the rest civilians caught in the vortex of battle, starvation, disease, or genocide. The Soviet Union lost more people than any other country involved in the war and literally saw an entire generation wiped out in the sacrifice against Nazi brutality.

D-DAY

As the Soviet army pounded German lines in the east, the western Allies prepared for Operation Overlord,* the invasion of northern France. The landing on June 6, 1944, came late in the war, but there were good reasons for the date of the attack. The Allies first had to secure control of the Atlantic Ocean, which meant developing weapons that could counter German submarines or U-boats. Only then could the troop transports bring American soldiers safely to Britain. A second requirement was the destruction of the Luftwaffe to assure Allied air supremacy, and this was largely accomplished by 1944. A third challenge was the need for secrecy, a daunting problem when trying to accumulate thousands of ships, landing vehicles, tanks, jeeps, ammunition, and men—all without German detection. The Allies used a variety of techniques to deceive the Nazis about where and when the invasion would occur, and in the end they were successful.

On the French side of the English Channel, the Germans built up the beaches with fortified concrete bunkers and armed them with artillery and machine guns that could sweep the beach. They also placed spikes, mines, and sharp posts under the water to make the landing as difficult as possible.

In June 1944, the weather was stormy, but the Allies feared that further delay would work to Germany's advantage. A brief break in the forecast during June 5–6 was sufficient for the invasion to proceed, and late on the night of June 5 Allied paratroopers floated down over parts of Normandy. In the early morning of the sixth, thousands of ships crossed the Channel; the liberation of Western Europe had begun. The fighting was intense everywhere, but the American landing beach code named Omaha proved to be the best defended by the Nazis and the most difficult to take. Despite all the obstacles, the first day was a success and the Allies had returned to France for the first time since Dunkirk—after four years of Nazi occupation.

The plan was to secure Normandy and then turn east and drive toward Germany. The Allies faced the logistical problem of feeding and supplying their own troops, and while the distances were not as great as the Germans faced in the Soviet Union, in France most of the supplies had to come across the English Channel by ship or plane.

For the Allies, the next targets were bridges across the Rhine River into Germany. British field marshal Montgomery argued for a plan to surprise the Nazis and take the bridges with paratroopers, and Eisenhower agreed to the proposal. In September 1944 Operation Market Garden dropped American and British paratroopers in the Netherlands, but the assault failed when the attackers were dropped in the wrong place; the Germans were not taken by surprise and the paratroopers suffered heavy losses (later made into the movie *A Bridge Too Far*). As a result of this failure, Allied forces again faced the prospect of fighting for every mile of territory in northern France as well as across Belgium and the Netherlands until they reached the German border. The fighting remained fierce as the Wehrmacht held its ground.

Allied armies approached Germany in December 1944, but Hitler decided on a major offensive that he hoped would turn the tide of battle. Allied troops were camped near the German border in one of the coldest Decembers on record, but rather than wait until spring, the Nazis planned a surprise attack that resembled their offensive through the Ardennes in 1940. With tanks and troops massed on the German side, they caught the Americans off guard, just as the French had been four years earlier. The Germans came through the same forest and pushed about one hundred miles into American defenses. The bulge* in U.S. lines gave its name to the battle. Once again logistics played a key role as the fighting continued for a month; finally, American air power and additional troops rushed to the area halted this last German offensive. Victory could not erase the high price of 75,000 American casualties.

Early 1945 brought the Allies into Germany from both sides—Americans, the British, and others from the west and Soviets from the east. With victory in sight, the Allies had diplomatic issues to discuss, and the three Allied leaders—Churchill, Roosevelt, and Stalin—met in Yalta in the Soviet Union. President Roosevelt, elected to his fourth term in 1944, was not well, but he agreed to make the long and strenuous trip as a show of goodwill toward Russia. The Big Three resolved several important issues: the Soviet Union would join the war against Japan three months after Germany's surrender, Germany would be divided into zones of occupation, Nazi leaders would be put on trial for war crimes, the United Nations would be created to replace the League of Nations, and Poland would hold elections to establish a democratic government. In reality, Stalin considered Eastern Europe to be part of a Soviet buffer zone against future German aggression, and he never intended to allow Poland to hold democratic elections. When the war ended, Poland and the other countries in Eastern Europe came under Soviet domination for the next forty-five years.

Three months after the Yalta Conference, the war was over. President Roosevelt did not live to celebrate the Allied victory, as he died from a cerebral hemorrhage on April 12. Fascist leaders died more violently shortly after the American president: on April 28 Mussolini was captured trying to escape from Italy and partisans shot and hanged him; on April 30 Hitler committed suicide, and his body was burned by his aides; the next day Minister of Propaganda Joseph Goebbels and his wife poisoned their own six children and then committed suicide themselves. Germany surrendered the next week.

OCCUPIED COUNTRIES

Throughout Europe, pro-Nazi regimes were overthrown and collaborators* arrested. In Eastern Europe, the Red Army was in control and made plans to install pro-Soviet governments. Poland's government-in-exile was pro-western, but Stalin's supporters set up a rival, pro-communist government. The west hoped, idealistically, for a fair election and a coalition government, but Stalin was determined that Poland would have a pro-Moscow regime. Pro-western leaders were arrested, and the communists "won" a rigged 1947 election. In other parts of Eastern Europe, the Soviet takeover occurred in stages: Bulgaria and Romania held elections in which communists won while non-communists were arrested; in Hungary and Czechoslovakia non-communists won elections, but in both cases communists joined the government, took control of the police and security forces, and steadily removed non-communists from power. Germany was partitioned by the Allies, so East Germany was acknowledged to be under Soviet control.

Western Europe remained pro-western, but not without some anxiety on the part of the United States. In France and Italy, communist parties were popular because of their role in the resistance, and in free elections the communists received 20–25 percent of the votes. The United States decided to help these countries with an economic rebuilding program intended to undermine communist support—the Marshall Plan and the NATO alliance. Both efforts were successful, and the previously occupied nations—Denmark, Norway, the Netherlands, Belgium, France—all stayed pro-western. Italy and Spain had been fascist during the war, but they also retained pro-western governments, with democracy in Italy and the fascist dictator Franco in Spain.

WEAPONS

World War I was fought with machine guns, poison gas, and grenades, and also witnessed the first tanks and air planes. Twenty years later, these weapons had been improved and made more lethal, but remnants of the past carried over into the start of World War II—many German infantry units still relied on horses to pull weapons and supplies into Poland and the Soviet Union. As the war progressed, all nations worked to improve their existing weapons and to develop new ones. The advances were remarkable. Producing jeeps and trucks to replace horses was one challenge; bringing these vehicles across the Atlantic Ocean in sufficient numbers to supply American troops as well as Lend Lease Allies (Lend-Lease) was perhaps even more remarkable. By the end of the war, discoveries and inventions had occurred in unexpected areas such as medical and computer technology and ultimately in the realm of physics—and even created an atomic bomb.

Weapons: Germany

When Hitler announced rearmament in 1935, Germany had the advantage of rebuilding its military almost from scratch, allowing for the production of new weapons designed for offensive warfare. It also introduced innovations in the conduct of warfare. While France built the Maginot Line to prepare for trench warfare (with better machine guns), Germany planned for fast-moving tank (panzer) divisions supported by infantry and air cover. The concept of blitzkrieg or lightning war was a new weapon itself that took much of Europe by surprise.

The tank was introduced in World War I but was improved greatly during World War II. The best tank combines armor, firepower, and speed; adding armor and weight can make a tank safer, but it also reduces speed. The German Tiger was well armed, solid, and fast enough to be among the best tanks deployed in the war. The problem for Germany was not the quality of the Tiger but Germany's inability to build enough of them to compete with the United States and the Soviet Union.

While several countries were training paratroopers, Germany was the first to use them in combat. Creating special units of men dropped from air planes who then fought like infantry was an innovation that Germany used effectively in Norway, Belgium, and Crete.

Germany built several new air planes. The Stuka dive-bomber was used in the invasion of Poland and other early campaigns. It was notorious for the sirens that blared as it attacked, intended to instill fear among the target population. The Stuka was followed by the Messerschmitt Bf 109, one of the best fighter planes in the war. The most famous battles involving the Bf 109 took place in 1940 in the Battle of Britain. The Spitfire was Britain's answer to the German plane, and experts still argue about which one was superior. Germany also produced the Focke-Wulf 190, a mass-produced single-seat fighter used in the invasion of the Soviet Union, but eventually the Russians also mass-produced their own plane—the Ilyushin—to counter the German air force. Germany could not keep up with American and Soviet factories as the war progressed, a factor crucial to eventual Allied victory. In addition, the Luftwaffe was expected to operate on too many fronts at once—ordered to bring supplies to the vast spaces of the Soviet Union while defending German factories from Allied bombing. Despite his promises to Hitler, Hermann Göring could not keep up with all of these commitments simultaneously.

Germany also experimented with rocket-bombs such as the V-1, launched from the continent toward London shortly after D-Day. Because the V-1 made noise as it approached, the British called it a "buzz bomb"; but people learned that if the sound stopped it meant the bomb was on its way down. A few months later, German scientists introduced the first ballistic missile, known as the V-2. Approximately 3,000 of these weapons were used against civilian targets in London and cities in Belgium, resulting in 9,000 deaths. The weapons were built by forced labor, but the scientists who designed them, rather than being condemned for the deaths they caused, were highly prized by the United States and the Soviet Union after the war ended.

Finally, Germany built a submarine fleet that patrolled the Atlantic Ocean and destroyed thousands of tons of Allied supplies. The U-Boats (short for undersea boats or Unterseeboot in German) operated in "wolf packs" and attacked western shipping effectively, until new technology allowed Allied convoys to find and destroy the submarines. Reducing the submarine threat in the often-underrated Battle of the Atlantic was essential before the Allies could invade France.

Weapons: Soviet Union

Partisans

There were several unique weapons in operation in the Soviet Union. The first, of course, was the large Red Army, with estimates indicating that more than thirty million soldiers served in the Soviet military during the war. In addition, thousands of men and women driven from their villages and homes and caught behind enemy lines formed fighting organizations of partisans. Regular army soldiers who had been separated from their military regiments also formed guerrilla units to harass the Germans. The Nazis became increasingly frustrated by these partisan attacks. In 1942, German forces (sometimes Wehrmacht and sometimes SS) launched over twenty sweeps through Belarus, but they were more successful killing ordinary villagers than in finding partisans. The numbers indicate the difficulty of trapping partisans in the vast wooded and forested areas of Belarus: Germans killed 30,000 partisans but also 350,000 civilians; at the same time the partisan population grew steadily in 1942 from 30,000 to over 90,000.

The Soviet government preferred all aspects of the war to be centrally controlled, and at first did not support partisan warfare. Eventually the partisans proved valuable in operating behind German lines where they disrupted German communications and destroyed Wehrmacht supplies. Eventually the Soviet government recognized the important potential of partisan units and ordered the Red Army to treat them as regular soldiers and share guns and ammunition, and also coordinate military actions against enemy targets.

Some estimates put the number of partisan fighters at 500,000, but while that may sound high, there were at least two factors to consider: the cruelty of the Nazi occupation and the size of the Soviet Union. The Nazis were fighting a race war that terrorized the local population, and of course people ran away if they could. In cities like Kiev or Odessa, subject to German and Romanian terror, respectively, teenagers had an incentive to escape. In addition, all through Ukraine, Jews who were not killed in the initial roundup also fled to the forests and joined with others to survive. After 1943, with some modern weapons supplied by the Red Army, partisans were able to launch effective attacks against the Germans.

Partisan units lived a hard life in the forests, fighting both Germans and winter weather. In 2008, the film *Defiance* told the story of the Bielski brothers. Based on true events, the film deals with the mostly Jewish fighters whose families had been killed by the Germans and who had no choice but to hide and band together in the woods. Eventually, they organized an extensive operation that included stockpiles of hidden food, a bakery, tailors, carpenters, and a gun repair shop. They even had their own doctor and nurses. As Jews escaped the Nazis and moved into the forests, they brought whatever skills they had in civilian life to the partisan operation. The Bielski brothers, despite tremendous difficulties, survived the war with perhaps a thousand other members of their unit. Overall, guerrilla units provided an important weapon in the Soviet war effort.

Katyusha

Lacking traditional artillery, the Red Army developed a weapon that was cheap to produce, highly mobile, fired from the back of a truck, and devastating in its destructive power. The official name was BM-13, but Russian soldiers called it "Katyusha" after one of their favorite songs. German soldiers named it "Stalin's Organ" due to the whistling noise it made in the air. Whatever it was called, this multiple rocket launcher was effective and gave the Red Army a lethal weapon that could be moved quickly if necessary. It was first used at the Battle of Smolensk in July 1941, and as the war continued it became one of the Soviet army's most important weapons. Later in the war, Katyusha rockets were mounted on American trucks (Studebakers) that were shipped to Russia as part of Lend-Lease.

T34 Tank

Another Soviet weapon was the T-34 tank. Mass-produced during the war, this tank combined speed, armor, and firing capability. Germany also turned out high-quality tanks such as the Panther and the Tiger, but Soviet assembly lines eventually out-produced German industry. Both the Soviet and German tanks were excellent, but as the Battle of Kursk demonstrated, quantity as well as quality was crucial to victory.

Women

"Women" may not sound like the name of a new weapon, but in the Soviet military, women were deployed in unique ways. In every country, women replaced men in factories and on farms but usually were not allowed to participate in combat. Due to heavy losses in the first months of the war, the Soviet army accepted women for specific and specialized combat roles, especially as snipers and as pilots. In both areas, they excelled and won many honors and medals.

It takes special mental as well as physical skill to serve as a sniper, and the Soviet Union produced some of the world's best in its training schools. A successful sniper had only one goal—shooting Germans and counting "kills." Some of the Soviet women had so many kills that German snipers were assigned by the Wehrmacht to hunt them down.

Aliya Moldagulova (1925–1944) was sixteen-years-old when she escaped the siege of Leningrad and was sent for sniper training. She had seventy-eight kills and was named a Hero of the Soviet Union before her death from battle wounds in 1944.

Lyudmila Pavlichenko (1916–1974) was one of the best and most famous snipers in the world. Although she studied for an academic career in her native Ukraine, Pavlichenko volunteered for the army as soon as the war started. She was deployed in Odessa, but when that city fell she moved to Sevastopol; after only one year of war she had over 300 kills. In one battle, a German sniper killed two Russian snipers, and Pavlichenko was assigned to find him. Their personal duel went on for almost twenty-four hours, each one waiting for a clear shot. They spotted each other at the same time; she fired a second faster and got the kill. Wounded in battle, Pavlichenko spent time in a hospital and when healed was sent to the United

States on a goodwill visit. She visited President Roosevelt, and the American press gave her the nickname of "Lady Death."

At the age of forty-six, Nina Petrova was the oldest female sniper in the Soviet army. She ran up 122 kills before she died in car accident just one week before Germany surrendered.

Some snipers had specialties, and Roza Shanina was famous for firing two rounds in rapid succession and hitting both targets, a so-called doublet. In nine months as a sniper, she had fifty-nine kills, received the Order of Glory, and was nicknamed the "Invisible Horror of East Prussia" in the Soviet press. She was killed early in 1945 at the age of twenty.

Russian female pilots were so fierce that Germans called them "Night Witches" (Nachthexen). Marina Raskova (1912–1943) was a well-known pilot before the war, and she organized and trained three all-female regiments that included women as pilots, mechanics, and bomb loaders. They earned their German nickname by flying at night, but mostly by their fearless attacks on German lines. The pilots won twenty-three "Hero of the Soviet Union" awards. Raskova was killed in 1943 and buried with full state honors.

After losing over a thousand planes in the first days of the German invasion, the Soviet Union recovered its productive capacity and built effective fighter planes. Most importantly, the plane they manufactured was not complicated or difficult to mass-produce, allowing 37,000 to be put in action before the end of the war. The Ilyushin and Yak-3 were both considered easy to use in combat and generally equal to enemy planes.

Weapons: British

Britain was not occupied by Germany and is not a major topic in this study, but several British weapons were essential to the outcome of the war.

Radar, short for Radio Detection and Ranging, uses radio waves to detect objects and measure distance. Developed by British scientists and military, it was a crucial factor in defending Britain during the German bombing of the island.

The role of code breaking during the war was so highly classified that information about it remained secret until recently. The 2014 film *The Imitation Game* finally told some of the story of how Britain broke the Enigma code.* Enigma was the name of the machine that looked like a typewriter but used a rotor system to change the code on a regular basis. Alan Turing (1912–1954) worked with a team of mathematicians in Hut 8 at Bletchley Park near London, and the information they provided was important in the Battle of the Atlantic—helping Allied convoys avoid German U-boats.

Weapons: America

Although the United States was not an occupied country, the atomic bomb is part of any discussion of weapons. Funded by the federal government under extreme secrecy, the Manhattan Project* turned theoretical physics into the reality promised by Einstein's formula. Shortly after Germany's surrender, the first atomic bomb was tested successfully in New Mexico. President Harry Truman, who had learned of the plan to create a bomb only after the death of President Roosevelt, approved the bomb's use. Two atomic bombs were dropped in the war, one on Hiroshima on August 6 and the other on Nagasaki on August 9, 1945. The destructive power of the bombs, combined with the Soviet declaration of war against Japan on August 8, led to the rapid surrender of the Japanese Empire. (See Chapter 5.)

Conclusion on Weapons

Weapons are usually considered to be tools—guns, tanks, planes, and ships—and people like to argue about which ones were the best. For example, was the German Tiger better than the Soviet T-34? Is the Messerschmitt Bf109 superior to the Spitfire? The answer is always both yes and no. Who is driving the tank and flying the plane? How many tanks are on the battlefield on each side? Which side has sufficient reserves and can resupply their forces quickly? Who is giving the orders and devising the strategic and tactical plans? Tanks and planes are pieces of equipment, and they were controlled by humans who may be experienced, who might have a better plan than the other side, who may have the ability to improvise if the plan falls through, and who might perform in battle at a level beyond the expectation of their weapon. While both sides had effective weapons and dedicated soldiers, victory was sometimes determined by unexpected factors including better officers, the element of surprise, incredible combatants like Soviet snipers, and possibly pure luck. Even in modern warfare Carl von Clausewitz (Prussian military theorist 1780–1831) is still correct: "Everything in war is very simple, but the simplest thing is difficult." Despite having well-made weapons and carefully thought-out plans, a military unit might be delayed by a storm and all its trucks and resupplies end up stuck in the mud, or in Russia, in the snow. A soldier with a fine weapon but no gloves is in trouble at thirty degrees below zero.

For final victory, you need exactly what the Allies brought together—they had more men and women, better leadership, high morale, the ability to keep several fronts going simultaneously, and production at a pace that the enemy could not rival. Occasionally they had some luck as well.

CONCLUSION

World War II was truly a global war, and all theaters of battle were crucial to the final outcome, including the battle for the Atlantic and submarine warfare, bombing campaigns designed to cripple the enemy's productive capacity and destroy morale, and the struggle throughout the Pacific area. Both the German and Japanese militaries were well-trained and tough adversaries, but they both underestimated their opposition, which after 1941 included Britain and its Commonwealth, the Soviet Union, the United States, and resistance to the occupation in both Europe and Asia. For the first three years of war, the German army won almost every battle, but eventually a united allied coalition was able to engage Germany on several fronts simultaneously and push to victory. Germans fought to defend every mile of territory under their control, and at no point was the struggle easy. At war's end, cities all over the continent, from Leningrad and Stalingrad to Warsaw and Caen, lay in ruins. It was time for Europeans to put as much effort into rebuilding as they had into destruction.

FURTHER READING

German-Russian Berlin-Karlshorst Museum Archives, 2019. http://www.museum-karlshorst.de/.

Myles, Bruce. *Night Witches: The Untold Story of Soviet Women in Combat.* Chicago: Academy Chicago Publishers, 1990.

Overy, Richard. *Why the Allies Won.* New York: W.W. Norton, 1997.

Sontheimer, Michael. "Germany's WWII Occupation of Poland: When We Finish, Nobody Is Left Alive." *Spiegel Online*, May 27, 2011. https://www.spiegel.de/international/europe/germany-s-wwii-occupation-of-poland-when-we-finish-nobody-is-left-alive-a-759095.html. Accessed November 7, 2017.

Wright, Gordon. *The Ordeal of Total War, 1939–1945.* Prospect Heights, IL: Waveland, 1997.

3

ECONOMIC LIFE

> Every gun that is made, every warship launched, every rocket fired signifies, in the final sense, a theft from those who hunger and are not fed, those who are cold and are not clothed.
> President (former general) Dwight D. Eisenhower,
> April 16, 1953

INTRODUCTION

Germany's invasion of the Soviet Union was Hitler's biggest mistake, not just militarily, but economically as well. It was the Soviet ability to withstand the massive attack that led the way toward eventual Allied success. Many observers expected a German victory, since the German army had never lost a battle and the Soviet army was large in numbers but somewhat in disarray; nevertheless, the Red Army absorbed devastating blows until the Wehrmacht was thrown onto the defensive and eventually crushed. To understand how this dramatic transformation took place, this chapter is going to look at the German economy before the war, German military plans that were related to its economic situation, and the economic response on the Soviet side that ruined Hitler's dreams of a world empire. In the process, we will examine aspects of economic life that applied to all the occupied nations of Europe: the mobilization of workers, forced labor, trade, supply, and the spread of crime.

This chapter explores two additional topics. During the war, the city of Leningrad (St. Petersburg today) lost a million people due to a three-year siege maintained by the Wehrmacht. Within the city, children suffered both physical and psychological damage, but like Anne Frank in Amsterdam, many recorded their experiences in diaries. These personal eyewitness accounts, some written by survivors and some by children who perished, provide unique insight into the trauma of life and death under horrific conditions.

The chapter also discusses Germany's prospect for victory. Since the Allies won, it is easy to assume that they were destined to win without looking closely at the possibility of western defeat. World War II was difficult from beginning to end, and changing just a few variables might have led to a different and tragic conclusion.

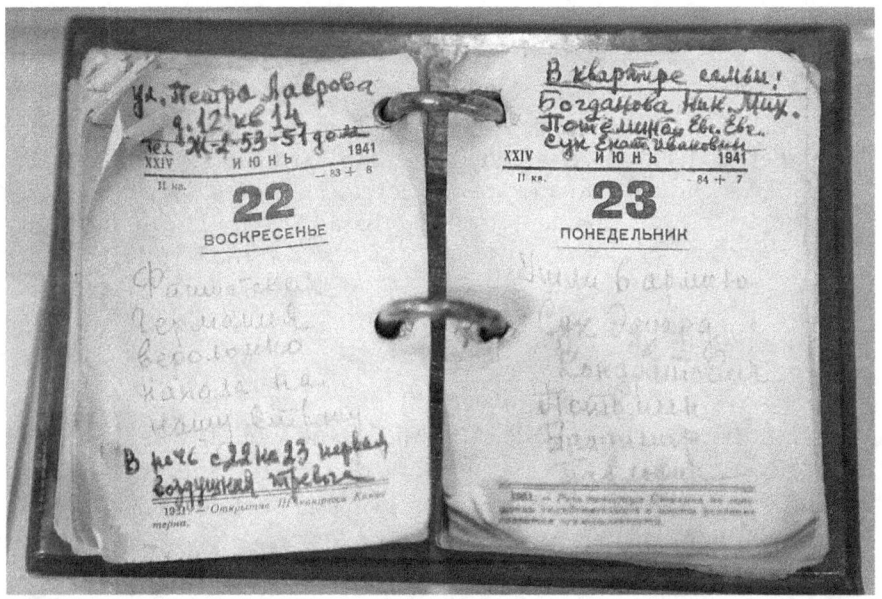

Leningrad diaries, whether kept by children or adults, all told the same story. As food slowly disappeared, personal accounts focused on the shrinking rations and the slow starvation and deaths of family members. Some people dreamed about food while others reported in a straightforward manner the reduction of the bread allotment and the death of a relative. A few diaries just stopped in mid-sentence. Many Russian war museums have diaries on display. (Alexander Demianchuk\TASS via Getty Images)

IRRATIONAL ECONOMICS

Economic planning is generally based on rational principles or mathematical models of production, consumption, distribution, and supply and demand. Nazi economic policy was unique in that it was built on irrational assumptions related to nationalism, ideology, power, and race. Germany's embrace of aggressive nationalism, militarism, and an expansionist foreign policy was linked to a belief in a struggle between races. For the Nazis, this supposed battle placed one nonexistent race—the "Aryan"* or pure Germanic race—against all others, especially Jews, and in this fight to the death there could be only one winner. In looking forward to this inevitable war, Germany was motivated less by economic gain than by vicious racism. Rather than a realistic calculation of the costs of economic conquest and exploitation, war for Nazi Germany provided a path toward the extermination of its enemies. Once that objective had been enshrined as a national policy, the government devised an economic plan to accomplish that goal.

After Germany went to war, it continued to act irrationally and against its own interest. Rather than encouraging friendship in other countries, the Nazis engaged in policies of discrimination, brutality, torture, and repression that made Germans disliked in Western Europe and hated in Eastern Europe. Developing economic cooperation was not as important to Germany as carrying out its racist agenda.

As a result, economic life in Europe under Nazi occupation brought the Gestapo, the SS, the mistreatment of local populations, the war against civilians, starvation, and other horrors rather than brilliant planning. There is no question that some countries suffered more than others both militarily and economically, and clearly Eastern Europe was punished to a greater extent than Western Europe. Nevertheless, every occupied nation suffered from Nazi racism and genocidal policies.

GERMAN ECONOMICS, RACISM, WAR PLANNING

There was a wide gap between German planning and implementation. Racism, economics, and war were inseparable elements in the Nazi program. For Hitler, each one of these concepts led logically to the next: he had to destroy certain racial groups; to eliminate those racial groups Germany had to win the war that it did not win in 1914; to win the next war Germany had to prepare its economy for a major conflict. The occupation and economic exploitation of conquered countries in Europe would then make it possible for Germany to accumulate the resources that it needed to destroy the rest of its enemies. All of these concepts were connected.

After 1936, Germany was quickly and permanently on a virtual war footing, as its second Four Year Plan* sought a self-sustaining economy. A massive building program brought full employment and increased support for the Nazis; some neighboring nations even saw German success as a model for their own development and order. All resources in Germany were devoted to the militarization campaign. The rapid mobilization also helped Hitler's diplomatic offensive, as increasing German strength led western powers to recognize the difficulty of resisting Germany's demands.

Throughout the 1930s, Hitler contradicted his own military when they urged caution. He preferred to gamble, confident that a militarized Germany gave him the muscle necessary to back up his threats. He had one major advantage in this area—he embraced the eventual necessity of going to war, while western political leaders were determined to avoid a repeat of the horror of 1914–1918. While Hitler played on this western reluctance with skill, he also knew that Germany had additional economic deficiencies he had to address. Germany had coal resources, but it lacked rubber and oil, leading the Nazis to invest in synthetic rubber and fuel. At the same time, Hitler cultivated a friendship with Romania, an oil-rich country that was also antagonistic toward the Soviet Union.

All of these actions were part of a process. Hitler planned a diplomatic offensive to extract concessions from the western powers before risking a general war. He challenged the west with his aggressive diplomatic demands, and he achieved easy victories. Hitler's diplomatic success bought time to strengthen the German economy and army.

BLITZKRIEG* AND ECONOMICS

Given Germany's economic limitations, the military tactic of blitzkrieg or lightning war was central to German success. The idea was to attack, move quickly, and win without depleting supplies. Each fast conquest would provide new resources that would replenish equipment before the next attack. For Germany, economic success and military success were linked together. Every small conflict would allow Germany to extract economic wealth from its neighbors and build for the future.

Militarily the invasion of Poland was successful, but economically it did not provide the resources necessary to finance the next invasion. Germany gave priority to its hatred of Polish Catholics and especially of Polish Jews, and therefore sacrificed possible economic exploitation in favor of racial cleansing. Poland never became a major supplier of resources for the German armed forces.

GERMANY MOVES WEST

Germany still needed the economic boost that was supposed to come with occupation and exploitation, and the invasion of the wealthier nations in Western Europe in the spring of 1940 was part of this scenario. Blitzkrieg tactics against several countries were successful, allowing the German military to remain well supplied during the conquests of Denmark, Norway, Belgium, the Netherlands, Luxembourg, and France. The surprisingly rapid defeat of France was a major prize that positioned Germany to extract resources needed to wage a longer war.

Germany did not have a blueprint for the economic integration of western countries into its military plans. In theory, the German army would take what it needed from factories and farms despite the lack of a coherent strategy for full economic integration. Hitler and the Wehrmacht did not address the logistical problems that win and lose wars. In the nineteenth century Napoleon's soldiers were expected to forage for food, but a twentieth century army needed an industrial supply system that converted foreign industry into resources that in turn maintained a pipeline to the army. The Nazis hoped to use the economic resources of most of Europe to keep the German military in the field, but their failure to understand modern economics led to long-term disaster when Hitler decided to invade the Soviet Union.

WAR WITH THE SOVIET UNION

The invasion of the Soviet Union in June 1941 seemed to go well at first, but Germany's rapid advance disguised several problems. The Wehrmacht had three primary targets but succeeded in taking only one of them. Neither Leningrad nor Moscow was captured; Kiev was occupied, but the rich agricultural lands in Ukraine never provided the expected economic boost to the German economy;

instead continuous battle drained resources and disrupted German plans. The war in the east would cost more than it returned.

Germany's ability to utilize the economic resources of western Russia and Ukraine was disrupted by the resistance of the Red Army and partisans. Many Ukrainian peasants disliked the collective farm system (*kolkhoz*)* and other Soviet policies. Rather than offering liberation and freedom from these practices, the Wehrmacht refused to abolish or even promise to change the system and instead mistreated the population. Once Ukrainians realized that Hitler was not going to fulfill their desires, and in fact was worse than Stalin, they had no reason to switch sides and fight for the brutal invader. Germany's policies that condemned Ukrainians to treatment as inferior prevented them from finding an economic or other reason to support the Nazi invader.

As the struggle in the USSR continued, Germany faced a war of attrition and had to restructure its economic plan for an extended battle. Hitler was responsible for all final decisions despite his limited patience and lack of interest in long-term planning. His failure to insist that the military and economic experts consult regularly was a major error. The continuation of the brutal war drained German supplies until two of his best economic advisers, Fritz Todt (1891–1942) and Albert Speer (1905–1981), finally convinced Hitler to make some necessary adjustments; by then it was too late.

DEFEAT IN RUSSIA AND OCCUPATION POLICIES IN EUROPE

As the war with the Soviet Union continued far beyond Germany's original expectation, its occupation policies throughout Europe became more desperate and brutal. For the Nazis, occupied territories were to serve basically as colonies, providing raw materials and cheap labor, but they underestimated the populations of the defeated countries. The longer German occupation continued, the greater the resistance occupied peoples of Europe displayed. Germany faced a different type of two-front warfare: Soviet power in the east and rising hostility in the west.

OCCUPATION: FORCED LABOR

The combination of continuous conscription and losses in the war created a labor shortage in Germany. By 1942, Germany was fighting on so many fronts that its labor needs were almost impossible to fill. Germany attempted various methods in the occupied countries to deal with this situation: recruitment of voluntary workers by offering incentives such as extra pay and food for their families, round-ups of unwilling workers sent to Germany as forced labor, and slave labor made up of various minority populations that were expendable from the Nazi perspective. For the first category, German propaganda promised good jobs with high salaries and increased food rations, and some workers responded by going to Germany voluntarily. Germany became so dependent on this labor that 30 percent of its workers in armaments and aviation plants were foreign. Other workers were trapped when army trucks blocked a street to prevent escape and soldiers herded everyone into the back of the vehicles before taking them to German factories. Half-starved prisoners had neither the motivation nor the strength to perform heavy labor, and the Germans did not care whether these workers lived or died, as they were simply replaced by other victims.

The first country that was exploited in this way was Poland, with about 100,000 Polish workers in Germany working mostly in agriculture. Half a year later, in the spring of 1940, there were over one million foreign workers in Germany, with a large number of prisoners imported from defeated nations. After the surrender of France, another one million prisoners were added to the German labor supply. German racism even affected how labor was employed: French prisoners were more likely to be used as skilled labor, Polish workers were kept in agriculture, and Russians were sent into mines without enough food to maintain their own weight. Eventually, five million Soviet prisoners were used as forced labor, but most of them were mistreated and did not survive the war.

FRITZ SAUCKEL

In 1942 Fritz Sauckel (1894–1946) was put in charge of the Nazi Ministry of Labor to find a way to compensate for the drain on the German labor supply, increasingly desperate due to the war in the Soviet Union. He was an early member of the National Socialist Party and a close friend of both Göring and Martin Bormann. A dedicated Nazi, he was ruthless in the employment of slave labor for German industry.

Wehrmacht losses seemed to be irreplaceable, and Göring moved Sauckel into this position and gave him total control over the occupied countries. Sauckel's innovation was the setting of quotas for each country, and he then ordered local Nazi officials to meet those numbers or suffer the consequences. In an attempt to increase productivity, he stepped up the punishments for those who lagged behind in their output. He also increased propaganda aimed at the recruitment effort throughout Europe.

Workers rounded-up in occupied countries had to be shipped to Germany, but since the military had priority on transportation, the Labor Ministry used old railway cars or run-down trucks that subjected its human cargo to harsh conditions. Prisoners transferred from concentration camps experienced deplorable conditions, similar to the packed trains without food, sanitation, or ventilation that they had already endured when going from ghetto* to camp. If they didn't die on the train, they soon died from insufficient food and a calorie intake that did not equal what they expended every day at work. During his trial at Nuremberg,* Sauckel listed five million foreign workers in Germany, with only 200,000 of them being voluntary. The numbers are unreliable as

Despite desperate Soviet resistance, the German army occupied Minsk, the capital of Belarus. In August 1941, SS chief Himmler visited the Shirokaya Street prisoner camp holding about 2,000 captives. This photo captured the compelling moment of an inmate staring at the Nazi official. Later that day, Himmler watched as 100 Jewish prisoners were executed. (National Archives)

Soviet prisoners (perhaps five million) and other slave workers often were not counted.

Heinrich Himmler was in charge of the concentration camp system, and he considered those prisoners to be SS property. His plan was to use the inmates to produce goods needed by the SS, but his racism made his efforts counterproductive as he starved and worked his labor force to death.

ECONOMIC LIFE: SOVIET UNION

Despite its many problems and limitations, the Soviet Union had an economic advantage when the war started. As economic planning was essential to the Soviet system, it already had a command economy in place. While other nations had to create a wartime economy and turn private industries into government operations, the Soviet Union did not experience a change or transition in any fundamental sense. The only problem was moving people and factories to the east away from German control or destruction. Remarkably, the Soviet authorities were able to transfer sixteen million workers and over 2,500 plants or factories to the east beyond the reach of the Germans. The result was a factory system that rivaled and even surpassed other European countries in military production.

CRIME: SOVIET UNION

Vodka and homemade moonshine called "samogon,"* cigarettes, and food were popular items on the black market. As the war progressed, captured or abandoned German equipment provided valuable items for trade. After nearly four years in the Soviet Union, the German army had accumulated a lot of goods of all kinds, some brought from Germany and some stolen from Russians. As the Wehrmacht retreated in the last year of war, it had to leave much of this equipment behind, and many of the items were suitable for barter—weapons, canned food, beverages, or even clothing removed from dead soldiers. Any product "liberated" from a German was officially the property of the Soviet state, but in the chaotic conditions of war these goods provided valuable trade material. For Soviet soldiers, German guns, knives, helmets, clothes, shoes, and boots were always in need. The source—an enemy corpse—was irrelevant.

Theft and petty crime were punishable offenses, but in practice there was little time to deal with minor infractions. Many crimes were not reported since they reflected badly on officers and party officials and could lead to a political investigation that no one wanted. A modest amount of stealing was almost universal and tolerated. It was common knowledge that officers would under-report casualties in order to continue to collect the rations of dead soldiers. The most serious crime was desertion, which was always dealt with harshly.

As revenge for German destruction of the Soviet Union, Russian soldiers took whatever they could when they arrived in Eastern Europe or Germany in late 1944 and early 1945. Those countries were richer than Russia, and soldiers felt that they were owed some compensation. The Soviet government anticipated this possibility by issuing regulations in 1944 that proclaimed all captured items the property of the USSR or Red Army. Accordingly, the Red Army dismantled and shipped German factories to the east. Captured German soldiers and technicians were sent along to help reassemble the factories. Despite the prohibition against looting, Soviet officers were allowed to mail German trophy material back home. The amount permitted depended on rank, with generals allowed sixteen kilos a month, officers ten kilos, and soldiers five kilos. Anything that could be packed in a box was considered fair game. Food was most popular, but warm clothing was also in demand. In some parts of the USSR the postal service was overwhelmed by boxes loaded with captured German booty.

AGRICULTURE: SOVIET UNION

The problems with Russian agriculture went back many centuries. Historically, Russia was located too far north to succeed as an agricultural country, yet farming was the traditional economic system in the country. Temperatures are colder, and the growing season is shorter than in England or Scandinavia, and in addition, the Russian rainy season coincides with the fall harvest rather than spring planting when it would be beneficial to farmers. As a result, Russian peasants never produced a significant surplus of food.

Due to all of these natural problems, the daily life of a Russian peasant was a grueling ordeal. They were poor. Russian governments encouraged communal farming as opposed to individual

Economic Life

private farming so peasants could share scarce tools and animals. In the 1930s, Stalin's government forced all peasants to join collective farms. Many peasants resisted, and thousands were sent to Siberia as a punishment. In some parts of the country such as Ukraine, the regime punished the population by confiscating grain and allowing millions to starve.

In the summer of 1941, the Wehrmacht advanced rapidly and overran farms in western Russia and Ukraine. The timing of the invasion disrupted the Russian farm season, and as they advanced, Germans stole crops and animals whenever possible. Many Russian peasants fleeing east burned their own lands (scorched earth)* rather than allow the Germans to seize the benefits of their production. Despite these activities, the Nazis soon controlled most of Ukraine, known as Russia's breadbasket.

At first, Germany expected Ukraine to provide an agricultural surplus for both the Wehrmacht and the German population at home. That plan could have worked if Ukraine had surrendered on the first day of the German invasion, thereby leaving all the land intact, neatly planted, and waiting for the fall harvest. Instead, the Soviet Union never surrendered, meaning that Ukrainian fields became battle zones, destroyed by bombing, pummeled by artillery, and trampled by soldiers and tanks. The harvest could not provide the surplus that Germany had anticipated.

German capture of this territory meant less food for the Russian people and army. Where the countryside was occupied by Germans, food resources were taken by the Wehrmacht, leaving Soviet citizens to survive as best they could—trading, bartering, stealing, engaging in black marketeering, or any other way possible. Where the countryside was occupied by Soviet forces, the Red Army also confiscated agricultural produce. Unfortunately for civilians, battle lines continued to shift, leaving territory between the armies ruined and displaced peasants with nothing.

The turning point came in 1943, when the Soviet army held the line at Stalingrad* and started to push the Germans back to the west. As the Wehrmacht withdrew, it burned again the very farms that had been burned in 1941 by retreating Russians. By the time German troops moved out of Russia and into Eastern Europe on their way back to Germany, the Russian countryside was a disaster. Almost everything had been destroyed at least once. Farms, buildings, houses, and all other structures were mostly rubble. By 1945, the Soviet Union was faced with the highest death count of any country in the war, vast expanses of ruined land, and a rebuilding project that seemed overwhelming.

FOOD: SOVIET UNION

Every country under the occupation suffered from food shortages, but not many countries were hit as hard as the Soviet Union. Providing enough food for both the largest army in the war and the civilian population was nearly impossible. The highest level of rations went to the military, leaving civilians with ration coupons that did not guarantee that an item was available in a store. The government tried to convince people that foods not normally consumed were tasty and healthy. For example, a pound of squirrel was promoted as having more calories than a pound of pork; the only problem was that you had to catch several squirrels to obtain a full pound.

Adding to the food shortage was the lack of farm laborers, most of whom had been drafted. Farms, barns, and roads were in ruins, and many fields were covered with dead bodies, land mines, and other explosives. Even if farm workers could be found, the land would not be ready for planting in the spring.

TRADE AND SUPPLY: SOVIET UNION

During the war, traditional trade routes were disrupted and even meaningless. Soviet factories produced mostly military goods for the front and neglected items for civilian consumption. Rather than trade, it makes more sense to think about supply lines—how the central government was able to move supplies from factory to battle zone or from farm to a starving city.

American Aid

One exception to the bleak situation was the supply line that brought war material and food from the United States to northern Russia. After the United States entered the war, it became an ally of the USSR and recognized that Russia's survival was crucial to America's war effort as well. As a result, Lend-Lease* aid was sent from the United States to the Soviet Union in amounts second only to what the United States sent to Britain. While the United States exported about $50 billion in such aid overall, with over $31 billion going to Britain and its empire, the Soviet Union received more than

$11 billion in Lend-Lease assistance. In addition to locomotives, tanks, trucks, and jeeps, the USSR received crucial food items such as spam, sugar, and flour that helped feed the Red Army. Convoys had to evade German submarines lurking in the Atlantic Ocean or waiting near German-controlled Norway. The voyage was long and treacherous, and many ships were victims of German U-boats. In addition to the "Arctic Convoy" route, other supplies were sent from Alaska to Siberia or around South Africa to Persia (Iran) and then to southern Russia. American aid played an important role in the Soviet war effort, both economically and politically to reassure Stalin that the United States supported the Soviet struggle against Germany. At the same time, some Americans have forgotten that Soviet industry was out-producing German factories by the end of the war. Lend-Lease supplied important food and vehicles for the Soviet Union, but ultimately the Red Army and Soviet factories earned their victory in battle and productive capacity.

INDUSTRY AND LABOR: SOVIET UNION

As the Germans overran large parts of western Russia, the government had to draft and rush millions of men to the front in order to slow down the German offensive. At the time of the invasion, the Red Army consisted of more than five million men, but within ten days of the attack another five million had been added to the military ranks. The massive draft numbers had an impact on the industrial and agricultural work force. Every man sent to war was one man removed from the labor force. The number of available factory workers decreased by more than 10 percent, while more than 30 percent of farm workers were no longer available. This meant that the factories and farms lost their best workers to the armed forces, just as the pressure to maximize production increased. All of the able-bodied men sent to the military needed first-rate equipment and a high-calorie diet. The situation seemed out of control; skilled workers were replaced by the unskilled or others unfit for the military—those above or below draft age, those with little education, teenagers, people with disabilities, the retired, and women who had to fill skilled positions.

How could the government deal with all of these crises at the same time? In a centralized system such as the Soviet Union, the government treated laborers as if they were in the army. One month after the invasion, local party authorities were given the power to move workers as needed. As in the military, absenteeism could be treated as a criminal offense, similar to desertion. In early 1942, men between sixteen and fifty-five and women between sixteen and forty-five were mobilized. Later the same year farm workers and fourteen-year-old teenagers were similarly mobilized. With these decrees, the government was able to assign eighteen million workers wherever they were needed. For all laborers, the factory day was made longer and vacations were cancelled. The Soviet centralized command system thus used its power over the population to draft soldiers as well as workers to deal with the emergency.

Saving factories from German takeover was another area where the government moved into action. After the invasion, Soviet industrial production fell by 50 percent overall, including the loss to German control of 50–60 percent of coal, steel, aluminum, and railway lines. These losses meant that the Soviet Union had to fight the war from a shrinking industrial production base. Rather than surrender to this disaster, the Soviet government ordered the relocation of factories to the east. Soviet workers were told to dismantle machines and ship them to the Urals and Siberia, out of reach of the Wehrmacht. The emergency movement of factories continued despite the cold winter of 1941–1942. Hundreds of factories were moved to safe areas far from German control. Gun factories in Moscow and armaments factories in Leningrad were moved to the Urals, an area that had already benefited from intense industrial investment during the Five Year Plans in the 1930s. The transferred machines found a home in recently constructed industrial enterprises. This massive transfer of assets and productive capacity was successful, and eventually Soviet production recovered and surpassed that of Germany.

According to the Soviet government, the population demonstrated its patriotism by making financial contributions to the national cause. The "Defense Fund of the Motherland" was supposedly a voluntary charity that raised over seventeen billion rubles for weapons, collected over four billion rubles in war bonds, and took in almost two billion rubles in jewelry donations. With these funds the government paid for thirty thousand tanks, two thousand planes, eight submarines, and other equipment as well. A popular slogan was "All for the front, all for the victory!" (Museum of the Great Patriotic War, 2019).

URBAN LIFE: LENINGRAD

Survival in the cities depended on where the city was located—in a war zone or behind the lines. Cities such as Smolensk and Kiev were taken by the Germans, and the populations struggled under Nazi occupation for several years. In the south on the Black Sea, Odessa was occupied by Germany's ally, Romania, and Romania devastated the city and carried out vicious attacks on the Jewish population. Other cities such as Stalingrad remained just beyond German control but became battlegrounds and were completely destroyed. In the north of Russia, Leningrad withstood a German siege of three years, providing a good example of life in a city that was not occupied but was also not free of the war. Leningrad provides a microcosm of an urban environment during the war.

Keeping the city of Leningrad supplied during the war was certainly one of the greatest economic challenges faced by the Soviet Union. While all of the Soviet Union experienced varying degrees of deprivation and shortages, no place suffered more than Leningrad. The city, built on order of Peter the Great and originally named St. Petersburg, had been the capital of Russia from the early eighteenth century until after the Russian Revolution. Following the death of Soviet leader V. I. Lenin (1870–1924), the name of the city was changed to Leningrad; after the collapse of the USSR in 1991 the city would reclaim its original name of St. Petersburg.

Because of the city's important role in Russian history from Peter I to Lenin, as well as its fame as the birthplace of the revolution, Hitler wanted to conquer Leningrad and planned a gala celebration with champagne after the city was captured. His plan was unsuccessful, although he was able to condemn the city to three years of hardship and starvation that killed nearly one million inhabitants, including 200,000 children.

In June 1941 everyone listening to the radio heard Foreign Minister V. Molotov (1890–1986) announce and denounce the German invasion. Immediately the Leningrad city soviet (council) ordered the mobilization of all men between sixteen and fifty-five and all women between sixteen and forty-five. The mobilization did not mean military service for all, but it did mean that everyone in those age groups was eligible for assignment by the city: civil defense, digging anti-tank trenches, working in a defense factory, or any other required position determined by city authorities.

The German army never occupied Leningrad, but the Wehrmacht surrounded it on three sides and established a blockade to prevent food or supplies from entering the city. The first winter was horrible, with sub-zero temperatures and rapidly disappearing food reserves. The ration for the city was set at twenty-eight ounces or less than two pounds of bread per day for workers (compared with almost three pounds in other parts of the country) and one pound for children. Due to the effectiveness of the blockade, the ration, already insufficient, had to be cut five times during the war, eventually dropping to twelve ounces per day for workers and four ounces for everyone else. As the ingredients for bread grew increasingly scarce, a loaf often included a variety of items: flour, cellulose, flour dust, and other random fillers. All household necessities as well as food were rationed.

Citizens of Leningrad survived any way possible, eating anything they could buy, steal, or catch. Starvation was extensive, and rumors of cannibalism circulated. Even family pets disappeared: dogs, cats, mice, and all other forms of animal life became part of the food supply. Soon leaves and the bark of trees were consumed as potential sources of nourishment. Nothing could stop the relentless search for food. Cold, shelling, disease, and starvation left the city with piles of bodies to bury, but solidly frozen ground made burial almost impossible; the spring thaw simply revealed the decay and rot all around city (for a fictional view of the war in Leningrad, see the historical novel *City of Thieves* by David Benioff).

The only area around Leningrad that was not under German control was Lake Ladoga,* located to the east of the city and generally out of range of German artillery. It became the most famous supply line in the Soviet Union. The only way in or out of the besieged and starving city was across this lake. In winter the lake would freeze and provide about twenty inches of ice thickness, sufficient to allow trucks to cross, bringing food, military supplies, and evacuating the wounded from the city. In the summer goods had to be delivered by ferry and boat. In all seasons the supply lines were tenuous and treacherous. Despite massive losses during the three-year siege, the city of Leningrad survived due to this heroic supply effort. Only in January 1944 when the siege was ended did the city begin a slow recovery from the pitiless ravages of war.

LENINGRAD DIARIES

As a result of the siege, the children of Leningrad were forced to confront adult concerns and issues of life and death at a young age. They were not free to attend school, play outside, talk at leisure with their parents, or go on vacation. A childhood of love and security became a childhood of uncertainty and psychological trauma.

The diaries of young adults in the city of Leningrad confront us with the horror they lived every day: no heat, no electricity, no hot water, and limited food. They reveal a twisted world: stepping over dead bodies in the streets, hearing neighbors fighting or screaming or losing control or even dying, and watching their parents slowly starving. In every situation, we wonder what the psychological impact was when a child assumed the burden of adulthood while still so young.

Some of the diaries of children and teenagers were preserved by relatives or found after the war. They were collected and published in 2016 in a powerful book called *Children of War: Diaries 1941–1945*. The best way to understand the desperation in the city of Leningrad is to read the words of the children themselves, and the following section uses summaries with a few direct quotations from the diaries as well.

Tanya Savicheva (*Children of War*, 21)

Eleven-year-old Tanya Savicheva left a brief and emotionless diary that simply listed the name, date, and time of death for those around her. After several brothers and sisters, she recorded Grandma, then two uncles, and finally "Mama." Tanya was alone for short time before she died in 1944 of intestinal tuberculosis.

Yura Ryabinkin (*Children of War*, 51–54)

The diary of Yura Ryabinkin discusses the artillery bombardment of the city and the subsequent mobilization of the population for defense. As the terrible winter of 1941 set in, Yura's main topic changes to food. He reports that his mother's legs are swollen and he is battling a lice infestation. By mid-December his family is out of cereal, and Yura acknowledges that "all my strength is leaving me, ebbing away, drifting away."

Tanya Rudykovskaya (*Children of War*, 57–64)

Tanya Rudykovskaya was nine years old at the time of the invasion, and she wrote in her diary every day and detailed every bit of food she had to eat no matter how small. When lucky, the family had some coffee, a bit of bread, and a sardine. Occasionally, there was soup. Early in 1942 she reported that "PAPA DIED." One week later the family had run out of bread.

Lera Igosheva (*Children of War*, 73–77)

Fourteen-year-old Lera Igosheva recognized that her life would never be the same after the war started. The arrival of Germans on the outskirts of the city brought artillery and air plane attacks that made the ground shake. She tried to be brave. As the weather grew colder in the autumn and winter, she increasingly wrote about the shortage of food. She reported that she was dreaming about food and someday being able to eat everything she wanted. Nevertheless, the family was desperate. One night her father came home with a cat, and Lera at first felt disgusted by the thought of it. Although they avoided looking in each other's eyes, the entire family was soon eating together. They were not upset when another cat was served for dinner, but it was not long before Leningrad faced a problem with rodents as the cat population dwindled.

As the winter of 1941–1942 continued to punish the city, Lera recorded the lack of firewood and her freezing apartment, the intermittent electricity and running water, and other hardships as well. Finally, the problems became more personal. Her father died in January 1942.

Gayla Zimnitskaya (*Children of War*, 97–103)

Like Lera, Gayla Zimnitskaya was also fourteen years old at the time of the invasion. Her diary begins early in the winter of 1941 and focuses on two subjects: German bombardment and the desperate food situation. Her description of the artillery attacks provides a good indication of the terror she felt when her apartment started to shake from the impact. As she moved toward the air raid shelter she saw wounded children and teachers being carried on stretchers toward the ambulances. The air raid shelter provided protection from the bombs, but it was without heat or food; her family remained underground listening to the moaning of the wounded and waiting for the all-clear to sound.

The most important issues involved food. Just as winter started, Gayla reported another reduction in the bread ration. In December a neighbor knocked on the door, dropped to her knees, and begged for food for her starving children. Gayla's mother opened all her cabinets to reveal only empty shelves. Eventually, death came to Gayla's family as well: "Aunt Lyola died without saying another word. She was so sweet and beautiful and only thirty-five years old."

The lack of food and growing numbers of dead from starvation led to family members turning against each other. Moral standards disappeared, and survival instincts took over. Gayla's neighbor asked her to hide her bread ration because her husband was eating all the food himself, including the share for the two daughters. Normal codes of morality had been destroyed; the war changed people in ways no one could have predicted.

Gayla confronted another surprise when she helped her friend take her father's body to the cemetery. The friend had paid with her bread ration—more precious than money—for a grave to be prepared, and despite the freezing temperatures Gayla and her friend placed the coffin on a sledge and pulled it along the icy streets. They were weak from lack of food, and pulling the sledge was difficult. Despite a German air attack they made it to the cemetery where they found only unburied corpses in crude body bags. There was no prepared grave, no markers, and no one in the office to talk to or inquire about the situation. There was really nothing to enquire about—it was clear that whoever worked at the cemetery was trading false promises of gravesites for food. The friend's father was left in the pile with all the other bodies.

Lena Mukhina (*Children of War*, 177–192)

Seventeen-year-old Lena Mukhina sounded patriotic and enthusiastic when she wrote that Hitler made a grave error by invading Russia. She started to lose her determination during the long winter. By January Lena herself was losing strength, and the next month she revealed that "yesterday Mama died. I'm all alone now."

Mayya Bubnova (*Children of War*, 211–219)

Mayya Bubnova was an eighth grader who reacted to the invasion with strong feelings of patriotism. She criticized those people who thought of their own safety before the nation itself and volunteered to work in a factory at night in order to help destroy the fascist invaders. She was excited to be part of the war effort and happily mentioned every Soviet victory or advance against the Germans. During the cold January of 1942, she reported a temperature of minus thirty Celsius. Despite the cold and lack of food, she continued to praise the brave soldiers who were pushing the German army back. By the end of January, she noted a temperature of minus forty—so cold that people froze to death if they sat down for a rest. Nothing worked well in such cold weather—water did not flow, the electricity was off so they could not listen to the radio, and food was so scarce that she had to stand in line from three in the morning until one in the afternoon to get her ration of bread. Despite all the problems, Mayya proclaimed that the sacrifices were worth the effort to save the Motherland.

Diaries: Conclusion

It is impossible to imagine the reality of the lives of children in Leningrad during the war, and that is why it is so valuable to have these diaries that allow the children to speak for themselves. Childhood trauma is a major theme of World War II in all countries, but few nations suffered to the extent that the Soviet Union did. While these diaries describe life in one city, they provide essential testimony that remind us of the impact of war on children and families.

The siege of Leningrad represents only one example of the widespread brutality and cruelty exercised by the German military in the Soviet Union. Nazi aggression was not restricted to Leningrad, and all citizens of Russia were subjected to ruthless oppression. More than four million Soviet civilians were sent to Germany as slave workers, and over a million of those were children. Of the fourteen million Soviet civilians who died in the war, more than one million were children. The Nazis did not distinguish between children and adults in their war against civilian targets.

The Karlshorst Museum in Berlin reports that the German shelling of Leningrad often persisted for eighteen hours a day. What did that noise do to domestic life? Did people become so used to the sound that they carried on their daily business and ignored it or did they suffer from shell shock? When they left their apartment in the morning after a night of shelling, how frightening was the prospect of seeing victims lying in the street? German shelling killed 18,000 people during the blockade. Did the living become psychologically immune to the sounds and sights of death?

Each of these questions asks about the psychological impact of the war on Leningrad, but they apply to other cities as well. Domestic life implies a family and some sense of order and tranquility, yet those ingredients were missing in Leningrad, Odessa, Kiev, Stalingrad, and many other villages and towns. Is it possible to calculate the stress level and the trauma that existed in these places every day? For those who survived the war, how does one determine the different paths that their lives took as a result of those experiences? It may be safe to assume that anyone who lived through Leningrad suffered from posttraumatic stress disorder after the war.

WHY DID GERMANY LOSE, AND WHY DID THE ALLIES WIN?

These two questions are related to each other, but the answers are not easy to discern. Was it possible for Germany to win World War II? For almost three years starting in 1939, Germany won almost every battle. Its land empire in Europe stretched from the Atlantic Ocean to beyond the Black Sea, and its military machine seemed unbeatable.

An interesting book that deals with this question is *Why the Allies Won* by Richard Overy. He looks at some of the military factors but also focuses on economic issues that limited Germany's prospects for final victory. On the military front, Germany was hurt when the Allies took control of the oceans and opened effective bombing campaigns over Germany (and Japan). Looking at the economics of war, Overy points out the serious consequences of Hitler's failure to streamline the German economy. Various agencies and bureaucracies competed with each other but also created inefficiencies and duplications that slowed down weapons development. Although Germany was ahead of the western economies in its military buildup in the 1930s, the Allies adapted and caught up after the war started. By the last years of the war, the United States and the Soviet Union were both out-producing Germany. Once the economic advantage shifted, the west had the upper hand. Germany could not fight in North Africa, Italy, France, and the Soviet Union at the same time.

Western victory depended on more than economics. Western countries did not have an obsessed racist like Hitler as a leader. His megalomania left no room for advice from others. At times he ignored significant issues and then insisted on making decisions without all the facts he needed. He never acknowledged any mistakes. Even Stalin, who also concentrated power in his own hands, listened to some of the military experts around him. Despite these factors, could Germany have won the war?

INEVITABLE?

Looking back at historical events and knowing what already happened, it is not difficult to find the many reasons why an event turned out the way it did. For example, some people might argue that American independence from Britain after 1776 was inevitable, or that the North winning the Civil War was similarly predetermined. Nevertheless, many observers at the time did not think that the colonies could defeat England or that Lee would lose to Grant. Knowing what happened in 1945 is one thing, but was that outcome inevitable? Was it possible for Germany to win World War II? If we look at the map of Europe in May 1941, it seems that Germany had already won the war. On the continent, every country was either an ally of Germany, occupied by Germany, or neutral. While Britain is not on the continent of Europe and was not occupied, few experts believed that Britain could defeat Germany by itself. Even British prime minister Churchill did not think England could beat Germany.

In May 1941 the map of Europe indicated a probable German victory, and yet one month later Hitler's army invaded the Soviet Union and everything changed. At the end of the same year Japan bombed the American naval base in Hawaii, bringing the United States into the war. By January 1942, the Wehrmacht had been stopped outside of Moscow, and Britain was no longer alone but part of an alliance with the United States and the Soviet Union. The German conquest that seemed inevitable in May became improbable only a few months later.

Despite the grand western alliance, the war lasted four years after May 1941. Economic power and production proved to be major factors in determining the eventual victor in this struggle. Could Germany harness the economies of the countries under its occupation? Could the United States make a rapid shift from a peace-time to a war-time economy? Could the Soviet Union hold out against the invasion and produce enough guns and tanks to survive? The answer to these questions was not immediately clear. What if Germany added the production of each country it occupied to its own economy? If Germany had successfully coordinated the economic output of all conquered countries, the result would have been a powerful economic base for the Nazi regime. What went wrong?

Theoretically, a military planner could take the size of the German economy and then add the productive capacity of Poland and France to calculate the future power of the German empire. Using prewar figures, this method would add $3 billion for Poland and $12 billion for France to Germany's $18 billion economy. Other countries that Germany occupied could have contributed even more wealth to the Nazi regime: $2 billion each from Austria and

Belgium, $3 billion each from Czechoslovakia and the Netherlands, $1 billion each from Denmark and Greece, $0.5 billion from Norway, and $1.5 billion from Yugoslavia, adding $30 billion to the German economy (including Poland and France). In reality, however, this notion was unrealistic and made German war planners more optimistic than they should have been. Just as Poland was largely devastated by the German invasion and its economy worth far less than $3 billion to the German occupiers, the same conclusion was true in almost every country occupied by Germany: in the process of invading, Germany destroyed much of the industry and farmland that Germany needed to win the war. The reality of the occupation never lived up to the expectation.

Total war was every country's fate in World War II, but mobilizing all the economic resources necessary to fight this war was more difficult than anyone had imagined. For Germany, ideology remained an obstacle to rational economic planning, as the eradication of "inferior races" used assets that could have been deployed for the war effort itself. The Nazis spent a lot of resources rounding up, transporting, and killing Jews, Roma,* and other ethnic targets. The agriculturally rich Ukraine was damaged so severely that the Germans struggled just to feed their own army, leaving little surplus to ship to Germany. As Russians retreated, they carried out a scorched earth policy, burning and leaving a deserted economic landscape for the Nazis. None of the occupied territories delivered its prewar productive value to the Germans.

Hitler ignored the lesson of the Great War—avoid a two-front war—when he ordered the attack on the Soviet Union in June 1941. His commitment to ethnic cleansing was closely linked to the campaign in the Soviet Union. Germany wasted economic resources pursuing their policy of genocide in Russia and throughout Eastern Europe. The Nazi plan to clear the land of minority groups before they had won on the battlefield contributed significantly to their ultimate failure.

FURTHER READING

Benioff, David. *City of Thieves*. New York: Plume, 2009.

Children of War: Diaries 1941–1945. Translated by Andrew Bromfield, Rose France, and Anthony Hippisley. Moscow: Argumenty I Fakty, AIF Kind Heart Charitable Foundation, 2016.

Glantz, David M. *The Battle of Leningrad 1941–1944*. Lawrence: University Press of Kansas, 2002.

Museum of the Great Patriotic War, Moscow. https://victorymuseum.ru/.

Klemann, Hein and Sergei Kudryashov. *Occupied Economies: An Economic History of Nazi-Occupied Europe, 1939–1945*. London: Berg, 2012.

Milward, Alan S. *War, Economy and Society 1939–1945*. Berkeley: University of California Press, 1979.

Werth, Alexander. *Russia at War 1941–1945*. New York: Carroll & Graf Publishers, 1964.

4

DOMESTIC AND MATERIAL LIFE

Go through your wardrobe; Make-do and mend.
—British propaganda poster

We can do it!
—Rosie the Riveter; American propaganda poster

A clear plate means a clear conscience; Don't take more than you can eat.
—British propaganda poster

INTRODUCTION

This chapter explores topics related to domestic and material life, including food allowances, labor, housing, clothing, and birth rates. How did the occupation affect families, women, and children? With a large percentage of the male population in the military, what was the impact of the war on marriage and sexuality? A variety of sources from Poland, France, the Netherlands, and the Soviet Union create a composite snapshot of experiences shared by others. Oral history projects collected in the postwar period and diaries written during the war and recovered after 1945 are among the sources that provide insight into these issues.

What experiences did Europeans in occupied countries share? All of Europe's population was tormented by the absence of food and daily hunger. In addition, everyone dealt with the presence of foreign soldiers, accepted curfews and blackouts, learned where bomb shelters were located, heard Nazi propaganda, and had a general fear of attracting attention or getting into trouble. There were other commonalities—men were drafted into the army, women ran families on their own, women and teenagers worked in factories, birth rates were disrupted, and anxiety was pervasive across Europe.

Despite these similarities, it is not possible to create a single model that fits all of occupied Europe. The area under German control was too diverse both geographically and culturally to produce one universal response. It is not difficult to think about some of the categories that separated one experience from another: social status, class, nationality, religion, type of government, military situation, child, teen, adult, male, female, gay, ethnicity, rich, middle class, poor, married, single, urban, rural, in the army, farm or factory worker, healthy, ill, government official, Jew, Roma,* Catholic, Lutheran, Orthodox, and the list goes on almost without end. Further examination of these categories reveals that each person was physically, mentally, and psychologically different and experienced the occupation uniquely.

GERMANY

As discussed earlier in Chapter 2 (Military Life) and Chapter 3 (Economic Life), German military plans depended on short wars, at least until the theoretical completion of German economic integration with the rest of Europe had taken place. In the long run, Germany's success depended on its exploitation of the economies of occupied nations, especially in the wealthier west. The problem for Germany was that its economic shortages and needs increased beyond initial expectations as the war continued. Hitler was successful in establishing domination over Poland, and then Norway, the Netherlands, Belgium, Denmark, and France before he turned east again. It was the invasion of the Soviet Union that destroyed his plans, with the defeat at the Battle of Stalingrad* changing the economic as well as military landscape.

Hitler controlled almost all of Europe before June 1941, but his ambition, greed, and hatred overwhelmed rational planning. After the invasion of the Soviet Union, Germany's goal of creating an economic empire was soon destroyed. While the Soviet Union was wealthy in terms of resources, Hitler's motives for attacking

Domestic and Material Life

went beyond economics and military conquest and included racial genocide (see Chapter 9). Rather than adding to Germany's economic base as its previous conquests had done (sometimes only in theory), the war in the east simply drained resources away from Germany. According to the original plan, the economic exploitation of Poland and the Soviet Union would come later, only after the war was over and the local populations had been removed. At that time Germany's racial enemies would be eliminated and *lebensraum** would be available for German settlement and development. Due to sustained Soviet resistance, that time never came for Germany.

This examination of daily life will begin by looking at Germany's first victim and various aspects of the occupation of Poland. The racist agenda that was at the center of Germany's war explains most clearly Nazi actions in Eastern Europe.

POLAND

Nazi Policy

Nazi leaders such as Heinrich Himmler (1900–1945) of the SS, Joseph Goebbels (1897–1945) who was propaganda minister, and the sadistic Reinhard Heydrich (1904–1942) all planned to destroy the population of Eastern Europe and turn those territories into *lebensraum* for Germans. From the moment of their invasion of Poland, the Nazis demonstrated their disdain for Polish culture and for

The Nazi boycott of Jewish-owned stores in Germany started immediately after Hitler came to power in 1933. Stationing guards in front of these establishments was intended to intimidate potential shoppers. Two years later, in 1935, the infamous Nuremberg Laws stripped German Jews of their citizenship and other basic rights. The laws made it easier to separate and isolate German Jews from German Christians. (National Archives)

Poles as individuals. Immediately, Poles faced a curfew that kept them indoors from evening to morning. Violators could be shot on sight.

Himmler followed this action by reducing elementary education to four years before Poles were forced to go to work for the Nazis. According to this policy, Poles were to serve as future slaves for Germany and did not require education; they only needed to learn to obey German commands. Himmler ordered many Polish intellectuals, political leaders, university professors, and clergy, to be killed or sent to concentration camps. Approximately sixty thousand Polish intellectuals were executed at the beginning of the war.

Other actions intended to humiliate Poles followed quickly, including attempts to remove all artifacts of Polish history or cultural life. The Germans built a high fence around Kraków's monument to a Polish victory over the Teutonic Knights at Grunwald in 1410, because the Nazis could not tolerate a statue that commemorated a Polish victory over Germans. Brave Poles put flowers on the fence while the statue was being destroyed, but the demolition continued. This removal of Polish national monuments was part of a campaign to humiliate the population. To further this policy, Polish bookstores were closed and replaced by Nazi propaganda shops.

Serving as the capital city for Germany's occupation government, Kraków received special treatment in the attempt to "Aryanize"* the entire country. City parks, benches, and trams carried signs that read "For Germans Only." Germans even claimed the sidewalks; Poles had to stay to one side and get out of the way of any German coming toward them. Market Square (*Rynek Glowny*) in the center of the city was renamed Adolf Hitler Platz, a clear insult to Polish residents. Even the name of the city was changed from the Polish Kraków to the German Krakau. Everywhere the Polish eagle was removed and replaced by the swastika. Governor-General Hans Frank made plans to demolish some Polish neighborhoods and rebuild them in a Germanic style, but the war postponed his plans, and most of the projects were never carried out. Several changes were made on Wawel Hill where Hans Frank resided, but these took place in 1939 and 1940 before the war spread to other parts of Europe. While other building projects were postponed indefinitely due to cost, the Germans did find the time to maintain four prisons and Gestapo headquarters where torture was carried out. Similar policies were imposed on other parts of the country as well, and as the war continued relations worsened between Germans and Poles; Nazis never tired of reminding Poles who had the power.

Economics

Poland suffered under Nazi occupation because its German rulers intentionally imposed economic hardship on the population. The Nazis created economic and financial burdens such as a monetary exchange rate heavily in Germany's advantage, wiping out the savings of many Poles. While there were jobs in war-related industries, wages were kept low by German factory owners. As in every occupied country, the black market flourished, but despite the high prices and risk of arrest, many Poles relied on that option due to inadequate supplies allocated to legal shops. In effect most people saw their average calorie intake drop to one-third of its prewar level. Poor diets and nutrition led to falling birth rates, disease, and rising death rates for the old, young, and poor.

Food

While Poland was primarily agricultural and did not have a large industrial base, this economic reality was largely irrelevant to German planners who viewed Poland through a racial rather than an economic lens. Germany never counted on the Polish economy to supplement its war effort. According to Nazi racial concepts, Poland was expendable, meaning that the daily ration allowed for Poles was insufficient to keep the population alive. The impact of food shortages and the rationing system started immediately with the invasion in 1939, when it became clear that the German intention in Poland was never a fair food allocation but rather one of forced deprivation. Poles were allocated about 700 calories per day, which is about 25 percent of what is necessary—basically, a starvation diet. This low number is even more tragic since Germany imported Polish grain and potatoes, indicating that Poland grew enough food to provide a decent diet for its own population. The Nazis sent any surplus from Poland to Germany to maintain the calorie intake of German civilians. Despite this Nazi policy, we know that most Polish Catholics survived the war, suggesting that Poles did not rely solely on the official ration coupon for their daily

Stutthof (Sztutowo in Polish) was a concentration camp 22 miles east of Danzig (Gdańsk) and was established by the Nazis immediately after the conquest of Poland. At first a camp for political prisoners, it increasingly held more Jewish inmates. In 1945, when the Soviet army approached, prisoners were subjected to a forced march to the ocean in freezing conditions and machine gunned as they entered the frigid water. (United States Holocaust Memorial Museum, courtesy of Panstwowe Muzeum Stutthof)

food intake. It was not uncommon for Poles to leave the larger cities and move in with relatives in the countryside where food was more readily available.

The situation was diametrically opposed for two other groups in Poland. Germans in Poland had special privileges, with all the food they wanted without worrying about ration coupons. The second group was Polish Jews who were given 185 calories per day, a starvation allowance, and since they were locked in the ghetto* they could not go to the countryside or use the black market as some Polish Catholics did.

Kraków Ghetto

Hans Frank (1900–1946) was a dedicated Nazi who planned to kill all Polish Jews and many high-ranking Polish Catholics as well. Immediately after setting up their government, the Germans imposed restrictions on the daily lives of Jews, but as always they started with what seemed to be petty restrictions in order to limit any negative reaction. Some of these initial impediments included wearing of armbands or patches identifying their religion and posting notices on their shops warning non-Jews not to buy there. Jews were not allowed to visit parks or ride on trams. Any German could choose any Jewish person randomly on the street and make them perform difficult or humiliating labor. Nazis enjoyed torturing religious Jews by cutting their beards and defacing their holy symbols. These actions, perhaps minor compared to what came later, were intended to isolate the Jewish population, identify them as different, and begin the process of dehumanization that culminated in the concentration camps.

Initially, Hans Frank ordered 50,000 Jews out of Kraków on short notice without providing a place for them to go. Thereafter, Otto Wächter (1901–1949), the governor of the Kraków District of the General Government,* took over the implementation of the policy, and in March 1941, he ordered the remaining 15,000–16,000 Jews in the city to move into a ghetto. As a special act of cruelty, the Nazis forced the Jews to build a wall around the ghetto that resembled tombstones, giving the impression to those living inside that they were within a cemetery. The ghetto had four heavily guarded gates so a few Jews with the proper papers could go in and out to their jobs.

Moving Jews to the ghetto was the continuation of the plan to isolate and dehumanize the Jewish population. Dehumanization meant taking away their dignity as humans and treating them like animals. The Nazis made people crowd into small apartments without running water or sanitation. With three or four families in one room, it is not a surprise that so many died of epidemics such as typhus.

Despite the desperate conditions, Jews tried to create a community that provided entertainment, including a few cafés and clubs with singers and musicians. An empty factory became a concert hall, and a small restaurant called "Polonia" was set up. There were few jobs so people just sat together on the sidewalk, knitting or playing chess.

The "Eagle Pharmacy," run by Tadeusz Pankiewicz (1908–1993) and a small staff, none of whom were Jewish, tried to provide a little relief from the oppressive atmosphere. Pankiewicz received special permission to keep his pharmacy open after the ghetto walls went up, and he did his best to provide medicine for an increasingly ill population. The many acts of kindness dispensed along with medications were not forgotten, and Tadeusz Pankiewicz was recognized as "Righteous Among the Nations"* after the war.

Despite this small sign of humanity, German cruelty was apparent everywhere. One synagogue was turned into a storeroom for plastic body bags needed for all the dead bodies in the ghetto, and an ancient Jewish cemetery was filled with trash. In the ghetto, some Jews lost religious faith, while others found prayer to be comforting. Rabbis continued to conduct services and teach lessons. Religious or not, everyone in the ghetto learned the "Kaddish," the traditional prayer for the dead.

In April 1940, Governor-General Hans Frank made his intentions clear: "I am planning, if possible, to free the city of Kraków of the Jews and to undertake a major operation of displacing the Jews, as it is absolutely unacceptable that thousands of Jews hang about and live in the city that has been mercifully granted by the Führer the honor of having the supreme authorities of the Reich staying within its walls." (Schindler Museum, 2019)

Labor

Poland was forced to contribute in two major ways to the German economy: providing labor and exporting farm products. Germany confiscated a large percentage of Polish food resources and sent these commodities to Germany. The result in parts of Poland was serious deprivation. Further, the Nazis arrested Polish civilians and sent them to work in Germany. The overriding fact was that Germany constantly needed more workers and as a result the General Government* of Hans Frank decreed that all Poles between ages sixteen and twenty-five were eligible for compulsory labor. As in Ukraine, if the Nazis did not fulfill their quota because young men and women ran away, the Wehrmacht* had no hesitation in burning houses or shooting locals at random.

The Germans took 400 men per day for slave labor, amounting to two million men by the end of the war. Categorizing these men as "inferior," they were overworked and underfed in factories or on farms. According to Nazi concepts of race, this power relationship was normal. In addition to arresting and sending workers to Germany, the Nazis kidnapped about 200,000 Polish children for relocation to Germany. The children who were taken were blond with blue eyes, thereby fitting the racial stereotype of the Nazi regime, and they were given to German families to make up for the shortage of men killed during the war.

After Russians, Polish workers were the second-largest group in Germany. In some ways this information is surprising due to Nazi mistreatment of Poland. Nevertheless, Polish agricultural workers found ready employment on German farms where German men had gone to war. In these cases, the possibility of sexual relations between Poles and German women created a problem for the race-conscious Nazi authorities. According to detailed German race laws on sexual relations, a German man could have a relationship with a Polish woman but a Polish man could be executed for relations with a German woman.

Housing in Kraków

As soon as the German authorities entered Kraków, the population of the city was subject to restrictions on every aspect of their daily lives. The residents of the city were viewed as a source of cheap labor and treated harshly, but Jews, Roma, professors, and intellectuals were considered expendable and were rounded up and sent to concentration camps and death. Everyone lived in fear of behavior that could lead to their arrest and possible torture. The Nazis hoped eventually to make Kraków a totally German city with only a few Poles left to carry out manual labor.

As Germans moved into Poland and especially Kraków, the new German capital of Poland, they established themselves as a privileged elite over both the Catholic and Jewish inhabitants. With their right to select their own housing, Germans could throw a family out of a house and take it for themselves, and of course they took the best houses and apartments. When a German occupied the house of a Polish Catholic, that person had twenty-four hours to collect personal items and move. Polish Jews were given about one hour to clear out of their own apartments. The nicest furnishings had to be left for the new German tenants, with many household goods shipped to Germany for civilians there.

The new Nazi capital in Kraków grew more crowded as Polish refugees and German officials arrived in the city. Some Polish residents returned after the fighting stopped while others fled to the Soviet occupation zone. At the same time the German population grew quickly, as officials, bureaucrats, and businessmen moved there with their families.

Population figures indicate this trend toward Germanization. Before the war the city of almost 260,000 people included 190,000 Catholic Poles, 68,000 Jewish Poles, and only a few hundred Germans. These numbers changed as Poles were killed and replaced by Germans. The Nazi authorities were actually proud of the elimination of the Polish population. Governor-General Hans Frank bragged early in 1940: "If I had to put up a poster for every time we shot seven Poles, we'd have to cut down all the Polish forests, and we still wouldn't be able to produce enough paper for all the posters I'd need" (Sontheimer, 2011). By 1943 the city had 150,000 Polish Catholics (down 40,000), 8,000 Polish Jews (down 60,000), and over 21,000 Germans (up 20,000).

The situation was similar in Warsaw, where Germans took the best houses in the rich neighborhoods. Polish Catholics were given a short time to relocate, whereas Polish Jews were simply ordered to leave almost immediately. Despite the efforts of the Nazis, however, Warsaw remained a hotbed of anti-German sentiment.

FRANCE

Agriculture

The German occupation exploited French agriculture for the benefit of Germany, and this action led to difficult times for the French population. As the wealthiest country under German occupation, France was expected to supply Germany with a surplus of food and industrial output. While France did provide the largest amount of goods of any occupied nation, it could not deliver the agricultural abundance that Germany anticipated. There were many reasons why none of the occupied countries met German expectations.

Following the German invasion, French production in several important agricultural areas dropped. This economic decline in rural areas was predictable, not only because many French farmers were drafted and had to leave their farms but also because the invasion that started in May 1940 disrupted farming. In the northeastern part of the country, where World War I had been fought, farms and villages were again destroyed. As the Wehrmacht poured into France, many animals were killed and others died from neglect when farmers fled the battle zones. Animal flocks and herds could not recover overnight, as breeding demands sufficient time to replace lost animals. German soldiers added to the problem by killing and eating livestock as they crossed France. Some animals were exported to Germany for breeding or food for the German population. Horses were also in short supply. The Germans confiscated half a million horses for military use, and since French agriculture mostly used horses to pull plows, farm production suffered.

Agricultural recovery had to wait for French soldiers to be released so they could return to their farms and begin the rebuilding process, but the thousands of skilled farmhands with knowledge of animals and crops were not easily replaced. Supplies that might be used for reconstruction were often taken by the military for other purposes, making repair of a bombed or ruined farm far from simple. Similarly, animal feed was used by occupation forces for German farms, leaving the attempt to breed animals in France exceedingly difficult. Grains such as wheat and oats, also confiscated by the occupiers, were scarce. The French population, subject to rationing and an unhealthy diet that was low in protein, had less energy for work.

Birth Rate

The birth rate in France dropped dramatically during World War I. It recovered in the 1920s and early 1930s, but by the second half of the 1930s it was dropping again. It fell during World War II, but there is controversy about the rates that show declines of 4.4 percent in 1940, almost 4 percent in 1941, 2 percent in 1942, 0.3 percent in 1943, 1 percent in 1944. By 1945 there was a very small increase, but the rate rose sharply in 1946. Why is there a controversy and, if the figures are accurate, how can we make sense of them? First, it is easy to see that in the first years of the war in 1940 and 1941, with mobilization and then imprisonment in Germany taking husbands away from the home front, the population was bound to drop. The Germans kept about two million French POWs, perhaps partly to force the French birth rate down. Subsequently, many French POWs were released, leading in 1943 and 1944 to a birth rate only marginally lower than normal. The return of all soldiers and a rising marriage rate in 1945 easily explains the large increase in births in 1946. The controversy is about the numbers themselves, as statistics are not considered totally reliable from the war years. Nevertheless, the trend is probably correct: a decline while the French army was being held in Germany and a general return to normal after the men were released.

Clothes

The occupation served as a social class equalizer for much of Europe since everyone was dependent on rations and faced many of the same shortages. Most people in France, in the city or in towns and villages, worried about survival, about German patrols, about their son who might be in German custody, about staying out of trouble, or about news on Allied progress.

In larger cities such as Paris, finding adequate food remained the main priority, but dealing with clothing shortages was also important. Nothing was thrown away or wasted; everyone sewed and fixed dresses or coats and saved cloth scraps to make children's clothes. Despite the scarcity of material, some in the upper class or among those collaborators* who frequented nightclubs tried to look as elegant as possible. To appear fashionable, women painted a thin vertical line on the back of their legs to give the impression of wearing stockings; they made their own high heels by using wood to build up the back of a shoe. For these women, decorative hats became a way to make a fashion statement, but again the shortage of material meant that some of them were made from paper or wood or almost any scrap material available.

Housing

In occupied France, the Germans took the best housing for themselves. The forced evacuation of French families was not as harsh as in Poland, but owners were never given any choice if a Wehrmacht officer wanted their residence. The high command occupied hotels, manor houses, and castles. Other buildings such as schools and factories were taken to serve as barracks. More ominously, the Germans requisitioned the land along the coast and forced French workers to begin building the fortifications that became the Atlantic Wall.

Occupation Costs

France was considered the most important nation for German exploitation. As a result, the Germans imposed high occupation fees on France in order to extract wealth from the country. France was forced to pay for the cost of the occupation army of 300,000 German troops stationed throughout the country. The cost of paying the German soldiers was established at twenty million Reichsmarks per day (German currency), with the value of the Franc (French currency) set at an artificial exchange rate of twenty Marks to one Franc. In other words, it cost France 400 million Francs per day to pay for the occupation. Some economists estimate that the Reichsmark was overvalued by 50 percent. As Germany collected more than the real cost of maintaining its army in France, the difference was profit for the German government. Germany paid its soldiers in France with French money taken from the local population, and German soldiers often assumed the right to enter restaurants and shops and help themselves without paying. If they did pay, and there was no way to predict if they would, they used an inflated German mark that was equal to twenty francs. German soldiers were by definition rich under the system that they imposed.

In addition to the humiliation of being occupied, the French had to pay for it; this form of Nazi exploitation added to the hatred that many in France felt toward the Germans.

Rationing

In Western Europe under German occupation from 1940 on, the system was intended to prevent starvation, but it clearly worked better in some countries than others. At war since the fall of 1939, France introduced rationing of some items to assure more food for the army. Even before the occupation, cities dealt with shortages by limiting the availability of some products to a few days a week. For example, in cities such as Cherbourg or Caen in Normandy, meat was available only Wednesday through Saturday, and alcohol could be purchased on Monday, Wednesday, or Friday. Then on May 10, 1940 Germany attacked, and everything changed. German bombing of Cherbourg was not extensive but nevertheless led to the closing of the fish market and the dairy cooperative. In June, France surrendered, and soon thereafter the Germans arrived. Ration coupons were necessary to buy food or drink, but in rural areas farmers tried to hide some of their own harvest for private consumption. Because Normandy was a rich farming province known for its dairy products, it became a supplier to the Germans of meat, milk, butter, cheese, and some vegetables.

How much actual food was included in a ration? The answer again depended on the country as well as the year since rations tended to decrease everywhere as the war went on. In France, an adult received 350 grams (12 ounces) of bread per day, but

300 grams of meat and 50 grams of cheese per week. In Belgium the numbers were 225 grams of bread per day and about 900 grams (2 pounds) of meat per month. For all foodstuffs, the ration also depended on one's job: military personnel had the highest ration, followed by factory workers, and trailed by seniors and children. Ration allocations dropped everywhere as the war continued, and resources became scarcer. With the decrease in quantity came a drop in quality as well. For example, as the ingredients for bread became hard to find, bakers substituted a variety of grains and vegetables. Coffee was diluted with water but also with seeds, plants, leaves, chicory, and other items.

Trade and Labor

In addition to occupation costs, Germany imposed a trade agreement that listed the costs of occupation as a credit against purchases of French goods. That meant that Germany could requisition any item from France, send it to Germany, and charge it against occupation expenses. During the four years of occupation, the cost to France was enormous. Germany's extraction of French wealth was not the same in all parts of France, and it was higher where useful military goods were produced. Germany demanded 75 percent of France's iron ore, more than 50 percent of its bauxite, and 15 percent of the coal in order to contribute to the German military. French workers, miners, or manufacturers were not compensated fairly for their labor.

At first, as long as Germany anticipated a short war, the occupation exploited the French economy in a direct, if somewhat unorganized, way. Specific items were taken to help sustain the war but without a long-term plan. Individual plants or materials would be seized to satisfy a pressing military need. As the war drained Germany's economy, the Nazis squeezed France for more resources. By the end of the war, France had been forced to provide a large economic surplus to the Nazis, both in terms of workers and in terms of raw materials.

France was a source of workers for German industry and agriculture. In addition to the two million French soldiers who had been captured, the French provided about 200,000 voluntary workers, all of whom had been promised good wages and extra food. The Vichy* government also established a forced labor system called STO (Service du travail obligatoire)* or Compulsory Work Service.

STO was basically a draft of French males over twenty years old—not for the army but rather for German factories. The new regulation meant that anyone born in the early 1920s would be available for German industry. This plan was one part of the economic exploitation of France by Germany, but it was so unpopular that it added to the slow but steady disenchantment with Pétain and contributed to the rise of the resistance.

Women

When France declared war on Germany in September 1939, the government encouraged French women to take factory jobs left vacant by men serving in the military. The French Ministry of Defense promised priority and good-paying jobs for women whose husbands were in the army. As the nation prepared for the battles ahead, armaments factories increased production and women filled the vacancies. The government also needed replacement workers and accepted women to work in the male-only post office.

After June 1940, the division of the country between the Vichy regime in the south and direct German occupation in the north complicated the situation for workers. Although France was officially at peace with Germany and did not need to produce armaments for itself, plants in the occupation zone continued to turn out weapons for the Wehrmacht. Some workers were also forced to assist in building fortifications along the Atlantic Ocean and English Channel for the Todt construction company.

In the south, the Vichy regime encouraged conservative values under the slogan "Work, Family, Nation." Women were expected to stay home, cook, raise children, and have more children. To a certain extent, women were blamed for France's defeat because they had allowed the population to decrease while they were pursuing, according to this allegation, frivolous life styles of work, parties, and fashion. Now women were to become traditional mothers, with new laws enshrining the role of stay-at-home moms. A 1940 decree made it illegal for married women to work outside the home if their husband made a certain salary considered sufficient to support a family. Another law in 1942 created a Mother's Day holiday. The government launched a poster campaign to praise mothers who cooked, smiled, and had many children. Eventually, Vichy abandoned this ideal "mother" and family, not in theory but in practice, due to increased labor shortages that necessitated allowing women back into the factories and even on the police force.

Some French women were able to find jobs working for Germans, but this form of employment was controversial. In reality, Germans had more money and privileges, and a job for a German official tended to bring a higher wage and sometimes more benefits. Jobs such as house cleaner, cook, secretary, phone operator, and translator were all in high demand. These positions often brought access to better food, but a woman with one of these jobs might be accused of collaboration or sleeping with the enemy.

Given the other shortages and limitations on making a sufficient living, it followed that prostitution increased during the war. There were official brothels in both parts of France, with rules that mandated the use of condoms to prevent disease. It is impossible to state with precision how many prostitutes were working at this time, but estimates put the number at 80,000–100,000 in Paris alone. Probably a minority of prostitutes worked in official brothels; more worked on the streets where they had control over when and how long they wanted to be available. Some of the prostitutes were wives or mothers who had to supplement the family income or food ration.

VARIOUS COUNTRIES

Agriculture Throughout Europe

Throughout Europe, war meant economic dislocation on the farm and in the factory. Wherever the German army moved, fields were ruined, as local farms were burned, bombed, and destroyed. At the same time animals were killed in the crossfire of battle or eaten by the invaders or by desperate civilians. Either way it was clear that farming would need a long recovery period after an invasion. To make the situation worse, farmers were drafted into the army, removing the skilled farm workers needed to recover from the destruction.

Western Europe had an easier time than Eastern Europe. The reason was fairly simple—while war continued to rage in the east, Western Europe was relatively quiet under occupation from 1940 to 1944. Of course, there were bombings and resistance actions, but in general France, Belgium, and the Netherlands settled down under German control.

Medicine

The field of medicine had a hard time keeping pace with the growing lethality of weapons used in World War II. Nevertheless, there were several significant innovations that saved lives, and sometimes limbs, in the fight against wounds, infections, gangrene, and disease.

Penicillin was discovered in the 1920s but was not mass produced until after D-Day in 1944. Despite its limited availability early in the war, it proved to be successful in fighting infections and disease. Sulfa drugs, first developed in Germany in the 1930s, also saved lives that would have been lost in previous wars due to wounds and infection. Morphine served as a quick response to pain while a wounded soldier awaited further medical treatment (often delayed until a battle had concluded).

In addition to pain and infection, wounded soldiers had to worry about bleeding to death. New and improved blood transfusion techniques, including the storing and delivery of blood plasma to the battlefield as well as field hospitals, saved many lives. Unfortunately, the American army continued to segregate blood along racial lines and refused to allow white and black soldiers to receive blood from each other.

Besides licensed doctors who generally worked in field hospitals, every military trained soldiers to serve as medics. In addition to their regular gear, these men carried medical equipment and often exposed themselves to danger by running through a battle zone to administer first aid to a wounded comrade. While the rules of war prohibited the targeting of medics if they wore identifying helmets or insignia, in reality enemy soldiers did shoot at medics to prevent them from saving the wounded. Medics in all armies (corpsmen in the United States navy) are among the unsung heroes of the war.

Burial in War

As discussed previously, the 900-day siege of Leningrad created a level of suffering that is hard to imagine. Because of the extremely low temperatures during the winter, frozen ground made burial difficult. With the infrastructure of the city largely destroyed, many buildings did not have heat. Corpses could remain on the ice-covered street or even in a cold apartment for days or longer, and in the worst case until the spring thaw softened the earth and made digging possible. The accumulation of bodies posed health threats as well as the sad necessity to step over or around the dead, who were often left where they fell. Today in St. Petersburg's Piskaryovskoye Memorial Cemetery (Merchant Yard named after its old area), a visitor can see grassy mounds that cover mass graves of approximately 500,000 people who were victims of the siege.

Throughout Europe, burial of the dead was delayed, often due to ongoing battles that made it impossible to stop the action for a funeral. Some battles lasted for day, weeks, or months, and there was no possibility of calling an intermission to deal with the situation. Nevertheless, it was important to bury the fallen quickly if possible before decay and disease became a problem. As a result, dead soldiers were often buried close to where they fell or in a nearby field as soon as the firing stopped. Most soldiers carried two identifications (dog tags in American army) so one could remain with the temporary grave while the other could be used by an officer to keep track of the causality and inform the family.

After the war, different countries dealt with the situation in a variety of ways, but in most cases the soldiers had to be reburied in official cemeteries. For example, French dead were returned to their families for burial in their home towns. British and American dead were either sent home or buried in France on land donated by the French government in gratitude for the sacrifices made. The American cemetery at Colleville-sur-Mer just above Omaha Beach has over 9,000 graves, all in neat rows but not according to rank. The concept is a democratic one—all sacrificed for their nation and are considered equal in death.

After the war and during the planning of the cemeteries, about half of the American families asked to have their soldier sent home, but the other half wanted their husband or son to remain where he died with his comrades. The American Battle Monuments Commission takes care of all the American cemeteries from both world wars.

Labor

Germany started the war with full employment, but the longer the war lasted, the more desperate Germany became for factory and farm workers to replace soldiers. The initial use of paid workers from occupied countries was slowly supplemented by forced labor from all over Europe. As the war progressed, the number of foreign workers increased each year: over three million in 1941, over five million in 1942, seven million in 1943, and eight million in 1944. The largest numbers were Russians and Poles, but they were mostly forced workers who were mistreated, received low rations, and responded with poor productivity. From Western Europe, the French, Dutch, and Belgians provided volunteers attracted by the promise of high salaries. Each national group seemed to have a slightly different reason for agreeing to work in Germany, but overall there was a pattern that brought them to Germany: first was high unemployment at home that made the promise of better-paying jobs in Germany seem attractive, and second was a tradition of cross-border work involving Danish, Dutch, and Belgian workers who had always lived close to Germany.

In Denmark, the Netherlands, and Belgium, close economic ties with Germany both predated and survived the Nazi takeover. Occupied Denmark was treated well by the Nazis, as Hitler viewed Danes as almost "Aryan"* in heritage. As a result, Denmark remained in a special category until 1943 when a Danish strike brought a Nazi crackdown. Until then, the Danes simply shifted their agricultural exports from Britain to Germany, supplying about 10 percent of goods such as butter, fish, and pork products to Germany. Danish unemployment encouraged voluntary enrollment in German factories. Denmark's reputation for resisting the occupation is generally based on the heroic actions to save Danish Jews in 1943, but until then Denmark collaborated quite closely with Germany. A large number of Danish factories opened branches in Germany, mostly employing Danish workers, and provided cement and other valuable commodities. The line of German fortifications, known as the Atlantic Wall that the Allies faced on D-Day in 1944, stretched much further than Normandy; the section along the coast in Denmark itself was built by 100,000 Danish workers.

As in Denmark, the situation in the Netherlands also changed in 1943 after Germany's defeat at the Battle of Stalingrad, where the Wehrmacht lost more than half a million soldiers. The German manpower shortage became more serious, and labor demands in every occupied country increased. At the end of April 1943, the Germans announced a massive program in the Netherlands, focusing on the 300,000 Dutch POWs who had been released after the Netherlands surrendered in 1940. Now the Germans wanted to call them back to Germany for employment in factories and on farms. Immediately, Dutch workers and farmers went on strike in protest. The large number of farmers who refused to bring their produce to the factories gave the strike its name: Milk Strike. The Nazis responded by shooting strikers—eighty at first and then another ninety-five to break up the strike. The repression was successful as the strike was called off after less than two weeks.

There was at least one innocent victim of the strike in the town of Hengelo. The Germans made all workers appear for roll call to find out who was on strike, and an engineer named Loep was not present when they called his name in a machine factory. He was arrested on the street a short time later. While he sympathized with the strikers, he truthfully reported to the Germans that it was his day off from work. He was executed despite his legitimate excuse. For many Dutch residents, this kind of German repression hardened local opposition to the occupation.

Once the strike had been suppressed, the Nazis again demanded more workers. The forced labor program called all men between eighteen and thirty-five for compulsory labor assignments. Wealthy men with the right connections could get an exemption from a doctor or government employee. While the Germans expected 170,000 Dutch men to report for work, only 50,000 showed up. As the German labor shortage continued, the Nazis expanded the age requirements and in 1944 ordered all men from sixteen to forty to report. Before the war was over, about half a million Dutch men spent time working in Germany.

To escape German labor demands, an estimated 300,000 Dutch citizens went into hiding. Some of those in hiding were Jewish, but soon joining them were members of the resistance and men who did not want to be sent to Germany for forced labor.

The Dutch economy suffered as the war continued into 1944. As an agricultural country, the Netherlands depended on trade before the war, but under the occupation the Dutch lost several trading partners and saw import and export markets disappear. In addition to reducing everyday food supplies, such as bread, the shortages blocked the import of high-demand items like coffee, tea, and tobacco. These goods became increasingly expensive and were available only on the black market.

In addition to the decrease in trade, the Netherlands endured an artificial food crisis due to a deliberate German policy. The crisis resulted from German military defeats, anti-Nazi action in the Netherlands, and a German decision to crack down and punish the people for daring to challenge German authority. After the D-Day landings in Normandy, Allied forces moved toward Germany. Some Allied generals and planners thought they could break through German lines, possibly in the Netherlands, and push into Germany before the end of the year (1944). As Allied troops approached the Netherlands, the Royal Dutch Government-in-Exile in London called for a railway strike to cripple German troop movements inside the country. Unfortunately, the Allied attempt at a breakthrough called Operation Market Garden failed (see Chapter 2), and the Nazi occupation of the Netherlands continued.

German troops sought revenge against the strikers. Although it was the beginning of a very cold winter, the Nazis blocked all coal and food supplies from entering the northern and western parts of the country. The result was called "Hunger Winter," when the Dutch experienced starvation. The situation was desperate: those with something left to trade resorted to the black market, but those who had little to offer were forced to eat tulip bulbs.

The situation for children became urgent, with thousands facing starvation and death. Many local organizations, including churches and businesses, organized a movement to send children to farms. Traveling by bike as well as truck or bus, more than 40,000 children were taken to the countryside and saved from likely death. The situation was tragic in the cities, with 22,000 deaths during that harsh winter, including 5,000 in Amsterdam. While the overall Dutch numbers may seem small in comparison with Leningrad or Warsaw, these deaths shocked a Dutch population that was not used to such treatment and suffering. Relief finally arrived in April 1945 when the Allies were able to airdrop food and other supplies. The worst aspect of the situation was that the famine was intentional, brought about because the Germans cut off supplies to punish the population.

Rationing

Despite the invasion and occupation of Poland in 1939, most of Europe remained temporarily at peace, but by the following spring much of the continent was at war. When countries mobilized, the military had a priority on whatever was grown or produced. That meant that civilians in all countries literally received the leftovers. In theory rationing was designed to equalize consumption in times of shortage, and the system worked as long as sufficient resources existed for distribution. When invasion destroyed farms and factories, food coupons became useless in empty stores. In other words, rationing made sense to help regulate the economies of wartime nations facing shortages of consumer items, but in practice it always faced difficulties in terms of implementation.

There were three problems with rationing: The first was the Germans, the second was the black market, and the third was the length of the war. In the first instance, if food production increased, in theory the citizens in an occupied country should have received an increase in the ration allocation. Instead, the Germans confiscated any surplus, either for the Wehrmacht or for German civilians, always leaving the local population suffering from shortages. That left little incentive for an increase in production unless the surplus could be hidden for personal use or sold illegally. Second, the black market made goods not found in stores available for a higher price, and this illegal activity is in practice the exact opposite of the concept of the rationing system. Rather than equalizing distribution and consumption, the black market rewards the rich at the expense of the average consumer. Black market sellers seek the highest price in money or barter, thereby removing certain food items from being equally divided among all ration coupon holders. The third problem was the length of the war. Germany planned for a series of short wars, each of which would economically sustain the next. This scenario did not work. The longer the war lasted, the more resources the Wehrmacht stole from European consumers. After 1943, the German army became increasingly desperate for food, labor, and other items, and shortages everywhere in Europe became more acute. Anti-Nazi sentiment also rose accordingly.

If we look at specific cases, we see variation in the amount of food available in different countries. Germany kept itself well fed by confiscating and stealing food and resources across Europe. The Nazi goal was to provide a steady food supply for their own population and army, and rations within Germany were maintained at close to 2,000 calories per person per day. In Western Europe, rations were lower than Germany but higher than Eastern Europe. For example, Belgium held steady at about 1,300 calories per day, while France started at 1,300 in 1941 but dropped to 1,100 after that. The Netherlands started rationing at about the German level in 1941 but dropped each year until 1,500 in 1944.

Sexual Relations

In this wartime situation, sexual abuse and rape were common problems, and there were several reasons why this particular crime was so prevalent. Traditionally, war was a masculine activity, combining aggression, testosterone, and the exercise of power. Millions of soldiers stationed throughout Europe, wielding total control, and brainwashed to believe that they were superior to the local population, led to exploitation of all kinds. In this case, hostility toward locals was often expressed at the expense of defenseless women. The rape of women of all ages was a way to establish power, destroy the dignity of the community, and humiliate opposing soldiers and psychologically take away their masculinity.

Since the Nazis held power in most of Europe, it was Germany that established the criteria for dating, marriage, or sexual relations with women in occupied countries. In general, the German government encouraged German men to marry German women, thereby preserving the purity of the "Aryan" race. With the large number of unmarried German women and young widows available at home, Wehrmacht soldiers were urged to seek a wife within Germany. In practice, however, German soldiers stationed abroad often looked for local female companionship.

For Germany, having millions of its young men deployed in all of these different countries created a serious ideological problem. Since race was at the basis of almost all German policies, it is not surprising that relationships between German men and Danish, Norwegian, or Swedish women were accepted far more readily than those involving Polish, Greek, Yugoslav, or Italian women. This last case was difficult since Italy was an ally of Germany, and Mussolini was insulted when he learned that the German military discouraged such relationships.

Moving further east, the German military banned any sexual contact with Slavs, not out of respect, but rather for racial reasons. In the Soviet Union, it was not uncommon for a woman in Russia or Ukraine to be sexually abused or raped by the Gestapo or SS, but also by regular Wehrmacht. Soldiers in the armies of Germany's allies, such as Hungary and Romania, were especially brutal in taking advantage of women in the Soviet Union. The widespread sexual abuse of women in the Soviet Union was repaid by the Red Army when it entered Germany at the end of the war.

Some historians raise additional issues related to sexual relations in occupied countries, questioning the motives of women who dated German soldiers. Were some of the women in love, seeking better rations and food, agents of the resistance seeking information, collaborators and supporters of the fascist message, or possibly prostitutes looking for money or food? There are historians who are uncomfortable with raising these issues because the motives of men are usually not questioned in this same way. In any case, the reality of sexual relations during the war also created a problem with venereal disease, which was fairly common among occupation troops; since the disease knocked men out of combat, officers had another reason to discourage sexual contact between their soldiers and local women. Officers preferred that their men avoid casual relationships and urged them to use official brothels that checked women for disease and where soldiers were encouraged to use protection.

The creation of official brothels was considered normal in most occupied countries, but it is a practice most associated with the war in the Pacific and the Japanese army. In that case, so-called comfort women were forced into prostitution by the Japanese army. In all occupied countries, the creation of sanctioned brothels was supposed to cut down on the incidence of rape, but it still raises questions about whether women who served or worked as prostitutes did so voluntarily or were coerced by circumstance. In a country under occupation, the Germans had the power, the money, the food, the access to social status, and everything else that made them "attractive" partners for single and vulnerable women. Finally, in every occupied country, there were children born from such relationships. The numbers remain controversial to this day, since acknowledging mixed nationality children is a recognition that women slept with or were taken advantage of by Nazis. No one wanted to admit that.

At the end of the war, resistance forces carried out a kind of popular revenge against women suspected of sexual relations with the enemy. The women were subject to public humiliation—their hair was shaved so they had to walk through the streets with a bald head. Sometimes they were also stripped naked or had swastikas painted on their heads. Some historians question the fairness of this form of justice since it blamed women but did not hold male collaborators accountable.

Nevertheless, recent research suggests that not all women condemned in this manner were guilty. Accusing a woman of sleeping with the enemy could not always be proven, but more importantly it could not be disproven—a woman accused was assumed to be guilty. Like accusations of "witchcraft" in previous centuries, charges of having sexual relations with a Nazi were impossible to deny. There might have been a variety of reasons for accusing a woman of collaboration that were not true, but nevertheless she would end up being publicly shamed.

The exact numbers of women who were intimate with German soldiers remain unknown. While some estimates suggest there were 20,000 French women whose hair was cut off at the end of the war, the number of women with German boyfriends is estimated to be higher than that. The same would be true for other countries in Western Europe where combat ended in 1940 and German soldiers served as occupiers, generally with time for leisure activities. In Norway, the estimates are between 30,000 and 50,000 German-Norwegian relationships, with similar numbers in Denmark.

Women and Men

The war left millions of women on their own, as men were in the military or prisoners, engaged in ongoing battles or already dead, subject to forced labor for the enemy, or in hiding with the resistance. All of Europe faced this problem. When the French army surrendered, Germany held over two million French soldiers; while the Soviet Union never surrendered, it lost millions of men in the first years of fighting and millions more as the war dragged on. In all countries men were absent from their families. The practical consequence was that women, children, and the old and weak were on their own for several years.

In addition to their traditional activities of cooking and raising children, women were forced to take over typical male roles such as providing food for the family, working in the factory, or taking care of the farm. In the countryside, women had always participated in farm work, but during the war they went from assisting with the chores to taking on primary responsibility for crops and animals. Without a male presence or protection, they operated in a potentially hostile environment, subject to mistreatment and sexual abuse by invading forces.

The existence of single-parent families applied to Germany as well as the occupied countries. German men were stationed all over Europe: France, Poland, Norway, Belgium, the Netherlands, Czechoslovakia, Yugoslavia, Greece, Denmark, and later in Italy and Hungary. In addition, there were millions of German soldiers caught in the continuing struggle in the Soviet Union. The success of the Wehrmacht, that is, its presence throughout Europe, stretched its resources and manpower, and left millions of German women without male partners.

THE SOVIET UNION

Collaborators

The Soviet Union was one of the few countries that did not engage in the head-shaving ritual. As indicated earlier, women in the Soviet Union were more likely to be victims of rape or abuse rather than girlfriends of Nazi occupiers. A woman who spent time with the Germans in occupied areas may have been a Soviet spy or agent and working for the Soviet government. Any genuine relationship between a Soviet woman and a German did not end with a bald head. If caught or seen during the war with a German soldier, a Soviet woman might be killed by partisans who had a good idea what was going on in occupied territories. If that woman survived the war, she was certainly turned over to the Red Army in 1945 and quickly executed.

Labor

The USSR and Poland supplied the largest number of workers to Germany. Germany controlled more than three million Soviet prisoners, and early in the war they were joined by volunteers from occupied Ukraine and other areas that were subjected to heavy propaganda campaigns promising a better life in Germany. As the mistreatment in Germany of "inferior" Slavs became better known in the Soviet Union, the supply of volunteers dried up and the Nazis resorted to "round-ups" of forced workers instead. The Nazis targeted entire villages and towns in Ukraine, but if a quota was not achieved, the local population was severely punished and brutalized. It was certainly not a surprise that workers in the Soviet Union not only stopped volunteering to go to Germany but also increasingly joined the resistance and partisan groups to oppose German occupation. It is worth recalling two other lessons from this experience: Nazis lost an opportunity to win friends and allies in Ukraine by mistreating the population, and the Red Army repaid German behavior in Ukraine and elsewhere when Soviet troops arrived in Germany in 1945.

Orphans

To deal with the high number of orphans in the Soviet Union, the government created medals and awards to encourage women to take care of homeless children. Various levels of "Mother Heroine" rewards, along with benefits such as increased food rations, were established in 1944 to reward women who "adopted" orphans from newly liberated territory. Mothers with between five and nine children were recognized with a "Maternity Medal"; women with ten children received the "Order of Maternal Glory" third class; twenty children earned second class; thirty children received a first class medal.

TESTIMONIES

Testimony from Various Countries

Oral history projects have recorded the personal experiences of survivors of the war, and some of these testimonies deal with the daily life issues addressed in this chapter. It is interesting to note that so many individuals, despite being from different countries, suffered similar ordeals during this time period.

Life, Death, Food, Women: Belgium

A survivor from a small town in Belgium recalled that as soon as German officials arrived, they took a census of every house and farm to determine what goods could be confiscated for the Wehrmacht. Ignoring the impact on ordinary families, the occupying army seized all the cheese, butter, and milk. Farm animals such as cattle, pigs, sheep, goats, and chicken disappeared to feed the foreign military. The local population was left with ration coupons, empty stores, and hungry children.

Bread was considered the main staple for survival, but as the war continued the taste of bread changed; shortages meant that ingredients other than wheat were added to the recipe. Despite its poor quality, people were desperate and stood in line for hours for their one loaf per family per week. Lucky families might own a hen that laid eggs, but many animals had to be protected at night from hungry neighbors. Unlucky families were forced to eat rats.

While German soldiers had been told to treat women in Western Europe with some respect, that rule was often violated. With men away at the front or working in factories, many households were inhabited only by women. At times, drunken soldiers took advantage of that situation.

Another experience shared by almost everyone on the continent was the sound of Allied bombers, air raid sirens, and time spent in the claustrophobic shelter. Inside the shelter there were two buckets—one for drinking water and the other for a communal and very public toilet. Many survivors remember the public toilet with great embarrassment.

Innovation: France

Some people adapted to the shortages by innovation. One oral testimony talked about the use of an old washing machine to grind wheat and how to make soap out of fat (lard), caustic soda (lye) and resin. Having soap was crucial since diseases of the skin were so common: fleas, lice, and scabies all thrived on weakened immune systems. Some doctors even used human fat to make soap. Occasionally when a patient went into the hospital for an operation, the patient would awaken with some fat scraped out by the medical team who saved it for personal use.

Without tobacco, cigarette smokers tried a variety of leaves and herbs but never discovered the same flavor as a real cigarette. Another commodity in demand was coffee, and like tobacco the substitutes such as barley or oats did not provide the taste of the real thing. In addition to cigarettes and coffee, every family needed a bicycle to get to a store or to a field to find alfalfa to feed rabbits, a source of food available without ration coupons. Rabbits, chickens, and pigs were prized possessions throughout Europe. Many pigs were nicknamed Adolf.

The Enemy and Innovation: France

Animosity to the Nazis could not be displayed openly, but in France many people referred to Germans as "Boches," a derogatory name used in World War I as well. The term was common in Paris, where Germans were seen everywhere. One testimony expressed disgust at seeing neatly dressed goose-stepping "Boches." The presence of Nazi flags and German soldiers in the theaters, cabarets, and opera house reminded the population of its humiliation.

City life created challenges for those who hated the occupation but whose jobs forced them to work with Germans. The owner of a small café in Paris who watched Nazi officers walk in to order coffee had a few options: greet the officers with a smile, a scowl, or a neutral face. The next choice was just as difficult—serve good coffee, spit in the coffee, spill it accidentally, or engage in another act of resistance. Each action had consequences: serving great coffee with a smile could mean more business and food for the owner's family, whereas an act of resistance could mean prison or worse. This dilemma impacted Europeans throughout the continent—everyone in an occupied country dealt with these choices nearly every day.

Toys, Life, Death: The Netherlands

Children often viewed war as exciting and played war games by putting their arms out to the side and pretending to be airplanes dropping bombs. They also used their free time to make weapons out of sticks for imaginary battle. As the war continued, air raid drills at school, announced by the principal cranking a large cylinder to sound the alarm, or at home with the entire family scrambling to run for the nearest shelter, diminished the enthusiasm for war games. The nature of Nazi occupation removed the romanticism surrounding war.

There is one overriding issue that resulted from the war: the psychological impact on children of death around them every day. In 1944 one child witnessed hundreds of Allied planes flying overhead, and he did not know that it was the beginning of a failed Allied attack known as Operation Market-Garden. He learned about the mission the next day when he went to church and saw bodies being buried in the graveyard. Hoping for imminent liberation by Americans or Canadians, the young boy was disappointed that the dead behind the church were Allied soldiers and not Germans.

Life and Death: The Netherlands

Oral testimonies indicate that some in the Netherlands ate tulip bulbs to fight off starvation. Even at a young age, they learned that right and wrong might depend on the circumstances; while killing was immoral, every dead German made victory more likely. Similarly, while stealing was wrong, taking goods from Germans was an act of resistance. Children in Europe grew up in a world of relative morality—killing and stealing might be acceptable under certain circumstances. Behavior that was clearly wrong in an ideal world might help shorten the war. Staying alive took precedence over normal morality, and many people committed acts they would never consider during peacetime.

Victim of Germany and Soviet Union: Poland

Caught between Hitler and Stalin, the population of Eastern Europe suffered terribly during the war. In a war full of horrific stories, many individuals spent time as prisoners of both the Nazis and the Soviet Union. Desperate for workers, the Nazis blocked streets in Polish cities and grabbed everyone caught in the middle. Despite their screams and cries, these Poles taken at random were thrown into the back of trucks and driven to German military headquarters for processing before being sent to work in a German factory. When the war ended, these same forced laborers were arrested by Russian soldiers for collaboration with the Nazis and sent to Siberia. They often spent ten years in the Gulag prison system, having lost the prime years of their lives to the regimes of Hitler and Stalin.

Seeking Shelter: Serbia

Yugoslavia was split into Serbia and Croatia by the Nazis in a brutal invasion in April 1941. When the Germans entered Belgrade, they announced that the killing of one German soldier by the resistance would lead to 100 Serbian deaths, and it was soon clear that this threat was a reality. A few people escaped into the woods to hide in caves, abandoned cabins, or any makeshift shelter they could find. City dwellers in the forest quickly adjusted and learned survival skills. They gathered straw, twigs, and leaves to make beds while they searched for a stream with clean water. If they were lucky, local farmers offered them food; if they were unlucky, the Nazis tracked them down.

CONCLUSION

While the specific circumstances of daily life under the occupation varied from country to country, the evidence indicates many similarities in the ways that the war impacted men, women, children, sexual relations, labor, housing, food, and other areas. Everyone lived with ration coupons, but some coupons became worthless due to shortages in shops. Some couples sold their wedding rings or other valuables in exchange for food, but if they ran out of items to trade, they were left desperate and confronting starvation and a slow death.

FURTHER READING

Barber, John and Mark Harrison. *The Soviet Home Front, 1941–1945: A Social and Economic History of the USSR in World War II*. London: Longman, 1991.

Collingham, Lizzie. *The Taste of War: World War Two and the Battle for Food*. New York: Penguin Books, 2011.

Dublin, Louis. "War and the Birth Rate—A Brief Historical Summary." *American Journal of Public Health*. Vol. 35, April 1945, 315–320.

German-Russian Museum Berlin-Karlshorst, Berlin. https://www.museum-karlshorst.de

Gildea, Robert, Olivier Wieviorka, and Anette Warring, eds. *Surviving Hitler and Mussolini: Daily Life in Occupied Europe*. Oxford: Berg, 2006.

Klemann, Hein and Sergei Kudryashov. *Occupied Economies: An Economic History of Nazi-Occupied Europe, 1939–1945*. Oxford: Berg, 2012.

Mazower, Mark. *Hitler's Empire: How the Nazis Ruled Europe*. New York: The Penguin Press, 2008.

Merridale, Catherine. *Ivan's War: Life and Death in the Red Army, 1939–1945*. New York: Picador, 2006.

Milward, Alan S. *War, Economy and Society, 1939–1945*. Berkeley: University of California, 1979.

Sontheimer, Michael. "Germany's WWII Occupation of Poland: When We Finish, Nobody Is Left Alive." *Spiegel Online*, May 27, 2011. https://www.spiegel.de/international/europe/germany-s-wwii-occupation-of-poland-when-we-finish-nobody-is-left-alive-a-759095.html. Accessed November 7, 2017.

Warsaw Uprising Museum, Warsaw. https://www.1944.pl/en/article/the-warsaw-rising-museum,4516.html

5

INTELLECTUAL LIFE

> Books cannot be killed by fire. People die, but books never die. No man and no force can abolish memory. No man and no force can put thought in a concentration camp forever.
> President Franklin D. Roosevelt, May 6, 1942

INTRODUCTION

Education has a major impact on how a person views life, and there are few better examples of that effect than students in France and Germany in the 1920s. For those born shortly after World War I in both countries, children came of age just in time to fight in World War II. There was a dramatic difference, however, in the upbringing of French children compared to German children and their subsequent attitudes toward war. While celebrating their victory, the French in the 1920s also heard about the horrors of the trenches, the loss of a generation of young men, and a lesson that warned that future wars should be avoided. Germans in the 1920s also learned of World War I, but they studied it as a national humiliation and defeat. For young Germans, only revenge for the Treaty of Versailles* could restore national pride. We do not know how many Germans, and perhaps even Hitler who lived in Munich after

World War I (as well as before 1914), visited the war memorial in the Hofgarten that features a statue of a fallen soldier on his back, with a rifle on his chest, and an inscription that reads: "he shall rise again." As a result of these differing educations, it is not surprising that the French population wanted peace at almost any price, while many Germans were not content with the status quo, making them susceptible to a charismatic leader who promised answers to all their problems.

GERMANY

Education

Nazi concepts of education were based on an ideology that proclaimed the German race, or "Aryans,"* as superior to all others. Hitler made this claim in *Mein Kampf:** "All the human culture, all the results of art, science, and technology that we see before us today, are almost exclusively the creative product of the Aryan." Other cultures were considered inferior and a threat to Aryan power, and therefore they were not respected and were subject to destruction. During World War II, the exact details of occupation varied from country to country, but the overall concept was the same everyplace: non-German populations were not worthy of education, and their cultures were decadent and dangerous.

Nazis believed that they had a monopoly on truth and that competing ideas had to be destroyed. They hated democracy because it is based on faith in average citizens, open access to conflicting ideas, and the protection of the rights of minorities; Nazis did not accept any of those principles and believed that only members of the Nazi Party should hold office and exercise power. The elimination of free speech and freedom of thought were major Nazi objectives, and any challenge to their control was likely to lead to arrest followed by prison or a concentration camp, without a trial and without appeal.

Book Burning

Dictatorships and dictators hate books because books are where ideas can be explored and made available to everyone. Books encourage people to think, sometimes about things they already know but also about new concepts that may be inspirational or that challenge the status quo. Since Nazis believed that they already had all the answers and knew the best way to run society, no free discussions needed to take place. In fact, they viewed other opinions as a threat, as possibly subversive, and as ideas that should be eliminated.

As soon as the Nazi government was in place, it moved to force its views and ideology on all Germans and eventually on other Europeans. One of the first steps taken in this direction was the book burning of May 1933, only four months after Hitler became chancellor. The Nazi racist and Minister of Propaganda Joseph Goebbels (1897–1945) joined with pro-Nazi student groups to organize the book burning at Berlin's prestigious Humboldt University. This location had two advantages for the Nazis: it would receive maximum publicity because it was in the middle of the capital city, and it would serve as a warning to all independent thinkers because it was on the campus of a famous center for intellectual learning and discussion.

Minister of Propaganda Goebbels launched the Nazi campaign against "subversive" books in 1933. Nazi zealots wanted to destroy books by pacifists, Marxists, Jewish writers, and others they considered threats to their ideological crusade. Students were enlisted to participate in the confiscation and burning of books. (Anthony Potter Collection/Getty Images)

Hitler's plan was to destroy books so that the German people would only read what the government wanted them to know, and he was convinced that they would accept and believe the government's official view. Despite his claim of superiority for the "Aryan" race, in reality he did not even respect Germans. He believed that all people could be easily controlled and manipulated by the use of propaganda, and the louder and more often repeated the propaganda, the more likely the population would accept it:

> The more modest its intellectual ballast, the more exclusively it takes into consideration the emotions of the masses, the more effective it will be. The receptivity of the great masses is very limited, their intelligence is small, but their power of forgetting is enormous. In consequence of these facts, all effective propaganda must be limited to a very few points and must harp on these in slogans until the last member of the public understands what you want him to understand by your slogan. (*Mein Kampf*)

In other words, once you destroyed the books, you could tell people whatever you wanted them to believe.

On May 10, 1933, more than 40,000 people heard Goebbels rant about subversive writers and the need to eliminate all Jewish thought from German life. Thousands of volumes were thrown onto a bonfire that consumed not only the physical books but also the thoughts of the authors considered too dangerous for Germans to read. Socialist thinkers such as Karl Marx as well as other German writers including Berthold Brecht, Thomas Mann, and Stefan Zweig were on the list for destruction. Erich Maria Remarque, a German veteran who wrote the famous antiwar novel, *All Quiet on the Western Front*, was another target of the book burners. The Nazis did not want Germans to read antiwar books, since war was necessary to destroy "inferior" races that supposedly threatened German control. Foreign authors were not neglected: the books of Americans Jack London, Ernest Hemingway, and Helen Keller were destroyed. The book burning spread to other universities in Germany, and more than thirty schools eventually took part in this anti-intellectual activity.

Art and Daily Life

One Nazi goal was the control of all artistic production, with only Nazis deciding what art anyone could see, read, or experience.

Nazi art included large sculptures of strong Aryans and landscape paintings of a romanticized German countryside populated by idealized families. Paintings by Van Gogh, Picasso, and other artists were banned.

Consistent with these beliefs, the Nazis removed from German museums any art that they considered "degenerate."* This category included modern art forms such as impressionism or cubism, but it also condemned specific artists. The policy of "cleansing" the country of these hated works extended to all cultural fields beyond books or painting; sculpture, music, and films were all judged according to the Nazi agenda. Of course, works by Jewish artists were removed and destroyed.

Several German artists whose paintings were not acceptable were considered traitors and their works were similarly targeted. One example was Ernst Ludwig Kirchner (1880–1938), who was attacked and labeled "degenerate" by Nazi critics for his paintings. In 1937 in Munich, as a form of ridicule, the Nazis put the "degenerate" art they had collected on display, including twenty-five of Kirchner's more than 600 paintings confiscated from museums. Facing humiliation and the prospect of his life's work ruined, Kirchner committed suicide.

FRANCE

Art

The Nazi occupation introduced a new crime to the war—the theft and looting of art from museums across the continent. Both Hitler and Hermann Göring (1893–1946) thought that they were brilliant art critics, and each one had plans for Europe's cultural artifacts. Hitler was planning to build a huge museum in Austria to house his collection after the war, while Göring was collecting for his private chateau in the Bavarian Alps. Once in control of art museums in other countries, they started the process of stealing and looting the most valuable items and shipping them to Germany. With the war still raging, they made plans to hide most of the art in mines and caves until it was safe to display their wares. As they combed through museums, they also imposed their racial and narrow-minded ideas about what they called "degenerate art," destroying works by Jewish artists or modernists. As a result of their actions, thousands of pieces of valuable art of all kinds were lost and never recovered.

One target of Nazi greed was France, home of the Louvre, one of the greatest art museums in the world. Göring visited Paris twelve times during the occupation, with many of those visits concerned with the confiscation of art that belonged either to French museums or private collectors, some of whom were Jewish. When the war started, several large collections belonging to Jewish art dealers were given to the French government for protection, but when the Germans found such items they seized them and shipped them to Germany. The Vichy* police helped the Nazis in this action.

Fortunately, even before hostilities started, the staff of the Louvre and other major museums in France understood that war was likely. Immediately after the Nazi-Soviet Nonaggression Pact* in August 1939, the *Mona Lisa* was packed and shipped away from Paris; it would be moved five times during the war. The museum staff decided to send many of their most valuable holdings to out-of-the-way spots in the countryside that were unlikely to be bombing targets. Sculptures like *Winged Victory of Samothrace* and *Venus de Milo* were packed in crates and loaded on trucks for the trip to various chateaux, abbeys, and farmhouses. When the Nazis occupied Paris, they found a largely empty Louvre, but they kept the museum open, with free admission for Germans and a fee for the French. They continued to plunder and steal from private collectors who had fled the country, and they used parts of the deserted museum and the nearby Jeu de Paume for storage and cataloging of items that would be sent to Germany. In 1943 outside the Louvre, the Nazis burned an unknown number of paintings they considered worthless.

Rose Valland (1898–1990), who worked in the Jeu de Paume situated next to the Louvre, quietly but bravely opposed this German greed. Valland continued to work in the Jeu de Paume without revealing that she understood German, and in this manner she was able to listen to conversations dealing with paintings and train schedules and keep notes about the destination of various art works. Her boss was Jacques Jaujard (1895–1967), who was the director of French National Museums and was also opposed to the German theft of art. Both Valland and Jaujard were members of the resistance, and they secretly passed on information about these art transfers so that British and American planes would not bomb those specific rail cars and destroy the valuable art on board. Sadly, however, they were unable to stop more than 20,000 art works from being sent to Germany and could not prevent the destruction of more than 500 paintings by modern artists whose works the Nazis considered to be "degenerate."

THE NETHERLANDS

Art

France was not the only country that took measures to protect its cultural heritage. Before the Netherlands was involved in the war, Willem Sandberg (1897–1984), the conservator at the Stedelijk Museum in Amsterdam, organized a committee to consider how they might protect their collection. He visited Spain to investigate what Madrid's Prado Museum had done during the civil war and discovered that the collection had been moved to caves for safekeeping. When he returned to the Netherlands, his committee consulted with experts on air pressure, humidity, fungi, and other matters related to protecting the paintings. Since the Netherlands has neither mountains nor natural caves, they decided to use sand dunes and built underground bunkers or vaults in the camouflaged dunes about twenty miles from Amsterdam. There was little time to lose, as trucks carried precious art works to the vaults even as German troops were driving into the country on May 10, 1940. Among many other works, *Night Watch* by Rembrandt and several paintings by Van Gogh were saved in this manner. The bunker was soon home to art collections from the Stedelijk and the Rijksmuseum as well as private collectors, some of whom were Jewish. After the war, many of the Jewish owners were dead, and there were many legal issues related to claims on those works. Nevertheless, the Netherlands had saved some of the world's greatest paintings from the viciousness of Nazi ideology.

In Belgium, the Nazis stole two great art works: Michelangelo's *Madonna and Child* and *The Adoration of the Lamb Altarpiece*. Both of these masterpieces were recovered at the end of the war by the Monuments Men* and returned to their home cities of Bruges and Ghent.

GREECE

Art

Classical Greek sculpture remains one of the most important cultural legacies of western civilization. The curators of the National Archeology Museum in Athens had the foresight to anticipate the tragedy that war would bring to their museum. As soon as Italy invaded Greece in the fall of 1940, the museum staff developed a plan to protect its collection, especially from air raids. The challenge was daunting since large sculptures are not as easily moved or hidden as paintings. The museum staff accomplished the difficult task of digging huge trenches under the basement of the museum. These ditches ran under the city streets of Athens, with citizens going about their daily activities without any idea of the massive project not far beneath their feet. After a statue was placed in a wooden case and covered with protective straw, it was lowered into its designated hole, reinforced with concrete, and covered with dirt and sand. When the Nazis arrived in April 1941, they entered an empty museum. Despite persistent questioning, the staff remained silent about the location of the art works, and the collection was preserved for the future.

POLAND

Art

It is astonishing to consider the extent of German cultural theft of art and monuments just in Poland. The Nazis stole around 13,000 paintings as well as sculptures, rare books and manuscripts, with an estimated total of more than half a million art objects of all types.

Among these was the world-famous altarpiece from St. Mary's Basilica in Kraków. Although the artist Wit Stwosz (German name Veit Stoss) was originally German, he lived in Kraków for twenty years around 1480 and the altarpiece was intended for that city. The Nazis also removed paintings from museums throughout Poland, including works by da Vinci, Rembrandt, and Raphael. As they did throughout Europe, they stole art from every museum or private collection under their control.

The Poles were able to hide a few items with deep national significance such as Jan Matejko's *The Battle of Grunwald* (1878) and *Prussian Homage Tribute* (1880–1882). Those works carried special patriotic meaning as they depicted Polish victories over Germany—the first work showed a Polish-Lithuanian defeat of the Teutonic Knights in 1410 and the second illustrated the Prussian king paying tribute to the Polish ruler in 1525. The Nazis were disturbed by these historical allusions to Polish victories, and while the Nazis could not find those two paintings, they did destroy the monument to the Battle of Grunwald in Kraków. In Warsaw the Germans removed the statue of Chopin from Lazienki Park and later claimed that the great composer had German ancestry (Warsaw Uprising Museum).

Unfortunately, the theft of Polish art and culture went even further and was intended not only to steal specific art works but also to destroy Polish culture entirely. Two months after Germany invaded Poland, Minister of Propaganda Joseph Goebbels told Hans Frank that Poles were not worthy of a nation or a culture. As in Germany when the Nazis organized book burnings to purge the country of unacceptable authors and titles, the Germans in Poland confiscated and destroyed books that did not support the German view of the world. The elimination of books was part of the plan to close all centers of learning, since Poles were considered not capable of higher intelligence.

SOVIET UNION

Amber Room

Built in Germany and given as a gift to Peter the Great of Russia, the amber room was part of the Catherine Palace outside of Leningrad. Nazi invaders dismantled it and shipped it to Germany. The room has been missing ever since, with a variety of rumors about its fate: it was destroyed in bombing raids as it left Russia, it was loaded on a ship and sunk, or it is hidden in an undiscovered mine or cave. The 180-square-foot room made of amber and gold has been valued at several hundred million dollars, and treasure hunters continue to search for it to this day.

MONUMENTS MEN

The Monuments Men was a special task force established by the Allies to find as much of the art as possible; by the end of the war they had recovered five million art works from various sites in Germany and Austria. The Nazis used old salt mines, including the famous Altaussee in Austria, because the mines had miles of tunnels and natural preservative conditions such as a steady temperature of 40–47 degrees and 65 percent humidity. In the Altaussee mine, the Monuments Men discovered 6,500 paintings, 2,300 drawings, 950 prints, 135 sculptures, and various pieces of armor, furniture, tapestries, and books. When these and other art works were recovered, the lists kept by Rose Valland in France and Willem Sandberg in the Netherlands proved invaluable in restoring them to their owners.

Lost Art

The story of lost masterpieces does not end there. When the Germans bombed Warsaw and Rotterdam, they hit museums and churches where precious art was destroyed, never to be recovered. When the Allies bombed German cities, they also damaged museums, churches, and other art treasures. The Allies believed they had good reasons to bomb the monastery at Monte Cassino in Italy, but in the process they destroyed one of the oldest abbeys in the western world.

Bombs could not be precisely targeted during World War II; in order to destroy an armaments factory in a city, bombers had to lay down a carpet of bombs* hoping that the factory would be hit in the process, while buildings nearby were considered "collateral damage."* In the midst of the carnage were ancient buildings, museums, churches and cathedrals, abbeys and monasteries, and thousands of places where important historical events had occurred in previous centuries. In the end, it was considered to be the price of war.

Recovered Art

In 1942, the Nazis completed a catalog of 16,000 so-called degenerate art works that were (or had been) in their possession. Some of the works had been destroyed by the Nazis, while others were sold to art dealers for cash or traded for other paintings that Göring wanted for his collection. Nevertheless, the fate of many such works remained unknown until 2012, when an apartment in Munich that belonged to the son of a German art dealer was found with more than a thousand paintings. These artistic treasures by what Nazis called "degenerate" artists are greatly admired—works by Chagall, Matisse, Monet, Renoir, and many other famous artists. The recovery of these paintings raises questions about undiscovered art that might still be hidden by present-day collectors or in unexplored caves and mines. Today much of the collection from the Munich apartment is in the Museum of Fine Arts in Bern, Switzerland.

ATOMIC BOMB

It was in the area of physics that the twentieth century produced new and innovative scientific advances that transformed our understanding of the fundamental principles of the universe. Scientists theorized about what was inside the atom, including questions about what might happen if the nucleus of an atom were to be smashed—how much energy would be released? It was a German Jewish scientist who came up with the now-famous formula to predict the outcome: the energy released would equal mass multiplied times the speed of light squared.

Before the Nazis came to power, German universities were considered among the best in the world, especially in science and physics. In the 1920s, the University of Göttingen in particular was famous as a leading center for scientific advances and research, and as a result Germany produced an extraordinary group of physicists and mathematicians. The Nazis in power considered ideology and race more important than science, and shortly after Hitler became chancellor universities fired non-Aryan professors; the sciences at Göttingen were immediately robbed of leading scholars. Some of the researchers were threatened with arrest and concentration camps, and many of them immediately made plans to leave Germany and emigrate to England or the United States, where western universities were anxious to hire the most famous among them. In the next few years, Germany lost 25 percent of its physicists, including eleven former and future Nobel Prize winners. As a result, the Allies obtained the benefit of a large number of talented European scientists, and some of their research was later applied to creating weapons systems designed to defeat the Nazis. Nazi racism was so deep and vicious that it was applied even when it destroyed Germany's fine university system and possibly sacrificed the development of an atomic bomb.

Some of the scientists who left Germany are not well known today outside the scientific community, but they were among the most talented physicists and mathematicians of the twentieth century. The most eminent scientist was, of course, Albert Einstein (1879–1955), a German Jew who recognized the threat of anti-Semitism even before the Nazis took power. Known for the theory of relativity, his fame and Nobel Prize (1921) gave him almost unlimited choice of university positions when he left Germany; he selected the Institute of Advanced Study at Princeton University. Einstein did not work on the Manhattan Project* to build an atomic bomb, but his theories were fundamental to its success. In addition, he cowrote a letter to President Roosevelt asking for funds to finance the project. Other scientists, less famous than Einstein, had been unable to convince the U.S. government of the urgency of this investment, but Einstein's reputation captured the attention of the American president and military. Einstein and other scientists who had worked in Germany testified to the importance of developing a bomb before German scientists were able to do so. The project was expensive, and its success was not guaranteed. President Roosevelt decided to trust the scientific argument that theoretical physics could produce a practical weapon. Shortly after FDRs death, an atomic bomb was tested; the Manhattan Project was a success. The new president, Harry Truman (1884–1972), decided to use the weapon against Japan, and two Japanese cities were targeted in August 1945. While many cities in Europe and Asia had been destroyed by bombing raids during the war, never before had an entire city been devastated by a single bomb. The use of the atomic bombs, one in Hiroshima and the other in Nagasaki, introduced a new era in warfare—the atomic age.

Physics

Not all of the scientists who fled to the United States were German by birth, but the reputation of universities in Germany had brought scholars from all over Europe to study there. As a result, many of the physicists who worked on the atomic bomb project in the United States during World War II already knew each other. This remarkable group included Hans Bethe, Niels Bohr, Max Born, George de Hevesy, Enrico Fermi, James Franck, John von Neumann, Rudolf Peierls, Leo Szilard, Edward Teller, and Eugene Wigner. This list of scientists who fled Germany is an illustration of how narrow Nazi ideology was, even when the result was detrimental to their own cause.

Hans Bethe (1906–2005) was born in Strasbourg, which was under German control from the Franco-Prussian War in 1870 through the end of World War I. Although his father was not Jewish, his mother was, and therefore according to Nazi racial categories he was Jewish as well. He held posts at several physics laboratories before taking a position at the University of Tübingen in 1932. The following year he was dismissed for religious reasons; he left Germany first for England but then accepted a post at Cornell University. He contributed to the Manhattan Project during the war and won a Nobel Prize in 1967.

Niels Bohr (1885–1962) was Danish; his mother was Jewish. He won the Nobel Prize for Physics in 1922, one year after Einstein. He was a brilliant physicist who considered himself safe in Denmark until the Germans occupied the country. In 1943 he was warned that he would be arrested as a Jew, and he escaped to Sweden where he used his fame to help other Jews find refuge. He was then invited to work in England where he participated in the Manhattan Project.

Max Born (1882–1970) was a leading physicist at the University of Göttingen, the famous center of German science. The Nazis dismissed him because he was from a Jewish family. After leaving Germany, he held several positions before moving to the University of Edinburgh. His Nobel Prize in 1954 cited his work in quantum mechanics.

Niels Bohr (1885–1962) was a brilliant Danish scientist and recipient of the Nobel Prize in Physics in 1922. In 1943, the Nazi occupiers of Denmark moved to arrest the nation's Jewish population, producing a list that included Bohr because his mother was Jewish. Bohr escaped to Sweden, encouraged the government there to provide refuge for Denmark's Jewish population, and then flew to Britain where he participated in the Manhattan Project that created the atomic bomb. (Library of Congress)

George de Hevesy (1885–1966) was from a Hungarian Jewish family that converted to Catholicism. A renowned chemist, he was working in Denmark when the Nazis occupied the country. Considered Jewish by the Nazis, he left Denmark for Sweden where he received the Nobel Prize in Chemistry in 1943.

Enrico Fermi (1901–1954) was an Italian scientist who received the Nobel Prize in Physics in 1938. After picking up his prize in Stockholm, Fermi and his Jewish wife went to the United States rather than return to Mussolini's fascist state. He worked at Columbia University and the University of Chicago and made important contributions to the Manhattan Project.

James Franck (1882–1964) won a Nobel Prize in Physics in 1925. He worked with Max Born at the University of Göttingen but left Germany in 1934, first for Denmark and then for the United States. He became the head of the Chemistry Division for the Manhattan Project.

John von Neumann (1903–1953) was born to a Hungarian Jewish family, but he later converted to Catholicism. An exceptional mathematician, he moved to the United States in the early 1930s and worked at the Institute for Advanced Study at Princeton University. He contributed to the Manhattan Project, especially on the concept of implosion.

Rudolf Peierls (1907–1995) was a physicist born in Germany. He was in England when Hitler came to power and, being Jewish, decided not to return to Germany. He remained in England where he played an important role in the Manhattan Project.

Leo Szilard (1898–1964) was born to Hungarian Jewish parents. He lived in Germany before moving to the United States where he worked with Fermi on creating a nuclear reactor. His letter to President Roosevelt, warning that Germany was working on a super bomb, was co-signed by Einstein and helped to persuade FDR to approve the Manhattan Project.

Edward Teller (1908–2003) was from a Hungarian Jewish family. A gifted physicist, he worked at the University of Göttingen under Born and Franck but left Germany after Hitler's appointment. He continued his work in England and Denmark before moving to the United States, where he became an important contributor to the Manhattan Project.

Eugene Wigner (1902–1995) was also from a Hungarian Jewish family. He left Europe in the early 1930s and held positions at Princeton University and the University of Wisconsin. He worked with Szilard and others on the Manhattan Project and received the Nobel Prize in Physics in 1963.

One scientist who was not born in Germany or Hungary was J. Robert Oppenheimer (1904–1967). He was a precocious American who studied in Germany at the University of Göttingen under Born and Franck and received a PhD at age twenty-three. During World War II, he was the head of the Los Alamos Lab in New Mexico, with the mission to build the first atomic bomb.

These accomplished scientists, many German or Hungarian by birth, were forced to leave Europe by Nazi racist policies. Germany devastated its educational system at the highest university and research levels and lost some of the world's best scientists.

FRANCE

Intellectual Life

From the 1890s through the 1920s, Paris was considered the cultural center of Europe and the world. The city was known for its openness, liberal values, and tolerance of new and experimental ideas. A variety of music, literary, and artistic forms flourished, and many African Americans escaped homegrown racism to contribute to the cultural flowering in the French capital.

France in the 1930s was a divided nation politically. The governments of the Third Republic were unstable and weak, and some citizens looked to the rise of a self-assured and strong Germany as a possible model for a new social order. Other French citizens remained loyal to the values of the democratic tradition, with the result that France was unsure of its own identity and political leanings. The French military defeat in 1940, followed by the occupation, added to the crisis by splitting the country between supporters of Pétain and followers of de Gaulle. The occupation reflected the divisions already present in France, especially among intellectuals.

Intellectuals, Collaboration, and Resistance

Any discussion of collaboration and resistance necessitates a good deal of explanation when applied to artists. During the war, some cultural figures left France for the safety of England or the United States, but many others stayed and continued with their careers despite the occupation. For those people who remained in France, critics often apply a few general categories: pro-Nazi, supporters of Vichy but not necessarily pro-Nazi, and opposed to both the occupation and to Vichy. Realistically, these descriptions do not adequately describe the vast areas of nuance and ambiguity in the behavior of many writers, artists, composers, actors, and others. For example, it remains impossible to label an artist who had German friends or acquaintances but also tried to help Jewish friends.

For reasons such as these, many artists cannot be classified—some revised their view as they acquired more information about the Nazis and others changed positions along with the fortunes of war.

Many writers compromised in order to keep their books and articles in print. Some writers found a positive message in Pétain's call for rejuvenation of the nation, ignoring the implicit racism and authoritarian content of the general's speeches. Still other intellectuals who were not pro-Pétain allowed their articles to appear in journals or newspapers that had been purged of Jewish editors, or "Aryanized" according to German propaganda. Among these writers were a few racists who openly welcomed the right-wing message, but there was also a group who later claimed surprise that the regime embraced such far-right ideas. As a result, some historians oppose using the labels of "collaborator"* or "resistor," while others find those categories to be useful in establishing general concepts.

This chapter will use the terms with the cautionary note mentioned earlier. The intellectuals, writers, and artists included here were well known before and during the war, but there were other intellectuals equally important. The selection that follows represents various responses to the occupation but is not comprehensive.

Collaborators

One of the most notorious pro-Nazi publications was *Je suis partout* (*I Am Everywhere*). The paper was ultra-nationalist and anti-Semitic, supporting the racist views of the Nazis. Edited by Robert Brasillach (1909–1945), the weekly was so extreme that it revealed hiding places of Jews and resistors to help the Gestapo. The publication of a safe house address, if it led to an arrest by the German police, meant death for those who were captured. After the war, Brasillach was put on trial for collaboration, convicted, and executed by firing squad.

Louis-Ferdinand Céline (1894–1961) was infamous for his extremist political and racist views. His best-known novel was *Voyage au bout de la nuit* (*Journey to the End of the Night*), celebrated as an innovative and modernist work. Even before the war, his anti-Semitic writings placed him on the far-right wing of French politics. During the war he continued to champion an especially virulent and violent racism in a series of pamphlets and essays. As the war was ending, he fled to Denmark to escape prosecution as a collaborator.

He was nearly successful in this endeavor; the French put him on trial, but he was given only one year in prison. By 1951 he was back in France, where he continued to support the far right and became a Holocaust* denier.

Writers Opposed to Nazis

Strong opponents of the occupation included several well-known writers of that time: Louis Aragon (1897–1982), Jean Bruller (1902–1991), Albert Camus (1913–1960), Marguerite Duras (1914–1996), Paul Éluard (1895–1952), and André Malraux (1901–1976).

Aragon was a novelist and poet, a founder of the surrealist movement, and a member of the Communist Party. Despite being over forty years old, he fought in the French army in 1940, and after the armistice he moved to the southern part of the country with his wife Elsa Triolet (1896–1970), also an important writer. Together they worked for the resistance throughout the war.

Jean Bruller, using the pseudonym Vercors, was a founder of "Les Éditions de Minuit," an underground publisher for members of the resistance. Despite the great risk, these courageous writers and printers were able to distribute several works that violated Nazi restrictions.

Born in Algeria, the celebrated author of *L'Étranger* (*The Stranger*) Albert Camus was increasingly involved with the French resistance. He became the editor of the resistance magazine *Combat* during the war. He received the Nobel Prize for Literature in 1957 but was killed in a car crash only three years later at the age of forty-six.

Marguerite Duras was born in French Indochina and moved to France in the 1930s. During the war she held a job for the Vichy regime but simultaneously joined the resistance. Her husband, Robert Antelme was arrested for resistance activity in 1944 and spent a year in the camps. Duras worked with future president of France François Mitterrand in the resistance.

Paul Éluard was an important French poet and a close friend of Picasso and Louis Aragon. During the war he wrote the inspirational poem "Liberté" (Liberty), and it was so popular in France that copies were dropped from British planes flying over France. Along with other poets, he helped put together an anthology by resistance poets in 1943, *L'Honneur des Poètes* (*The Honor of Poets*), that was published in England with the goal of raising money for the resistance.

André Malraux, who wrote *La Condition Humaine* (*Man's Fate*) in 1933 about events in China in the 1920s, joined the army when the war broke out but was captured with thousands of other French soldiers. He escaped from German captivity and supported the resistance; in 1944 he was part of the tank force that helped to liberate the province of Alsace. After the war, Malraux supported de Gaulle's return to power and then served as his minister of culture for ten years (1959–1969).

Ambiguous and Nonpolitical Writers

The well-known writer Colette (1873–1954) lived in Paris with her Jewish husband at the beginning of the occupation. He was arrested in 1941, but with the help of influential friends she obtained his release. Worried that any political involvement might lead to his arrest again, she avoided direct action and focused on her memoirs.

The position of Jean Cocteau (1889–1963) was even more ambiguous. An important novelist (*Les Enfants Terribles*), playwright, and film director, he was friendly with many Germans, such as Arno Breker (1900–1991), Hitler's favorite sculptor. Despite being homosexual, Cocteau remained on good terms with the German authorities, who allowed his plays to be produced during the war. At the same time, he had friends who were not collaborators throughout the broader artistic community; he seemed to know everyone on both sides of the political divide. After the war, Cocteau was charged with collaboration but not convicted. His career continued for almost two decades after 1945.

The writer and diplomat Paul Claudel was famous for writing using a verse style. He was conservative and deeply religious, and he welcomed the end of the Third Republic and the restoration of a pro-Catholic government in 1940. Nevertheless, his politics was more complicated than pro-Nazi or resistant. He hoped that Pétain's regime might lead a regeneration of traditional French values, but he rejected the extremism of the Nazi agenda. He opposed the racism of the Nazis, and by 1944 he welcomed de Gaulle's return to France. He is a good example of the difficulty of labeling each person as a collaborator or resistor.

Antoine de Saint-Exupéry (1900–1944), an enthusiastic aviator and author of *Le Petit Prince* (*The Little Prince*), spent a few years in the United States and Canada, and his friendship with the pro-German Charles Lindbergh (1902–1974) made the resistance suspicious of him. Nevertheless, he eventually opposed the Nazis and in 1943 went to North Africa to join the resistance; he died in a plane crash over the Mediterranean the following year.

In an essay written after the war, "Paris sous l'occupation" ("Paris Under the Occupation"), Jean-Paul Sartre (1905–1980) tried to explain the difficulty of remaining innocent during the war. He described moments when anyone might be considered a collaborator, such as responding to a polite German soldier speaking excellent French who asks for directions, and the subsequent feelings of ambiguity and unease for helping that German find his destination. Sartre's writings emphasize that life under the occupation always involved complicated moral choices. Perhaps Sartre was talking about himself as well as other Parisians.

His philosophy of existentialism focused on freedom and decisions, an interesting juxtaposition of concepts when living under Nazi occupation. One of Sartre's decisions was to accept a teaching position as professor of philosophy made vacant when Vichy fired the Jewish teacher who held that post. Sartre published two works in 1943: *L'Être et le néant* (*Being and Nothingness*) and *Les Mouches* (*The Flies*). Some French critics wondered why Sartre's works were passed by the German censors when other writers did not receive permission to publish.

Foreigners

Paris was always a gathering spot for foreign artists, so it is not a surprise that several famous writers lived there at the time of the invasion. Perhaps more interesting is the varied responses and fates of some of the well-known artists who were in France when the Germans arrived. James Joyce (1882–1941), author of *Ulysses* and *Finnegans Wake*, was ill and played no role in the war. As the Germans approached Paris in 1940, he left and made his way to Switzerland. Already frail and almost blind, Joyce arrived in Zurich but died soon thereafter in 1941.

Samuel Beckett (1906–1989) was born in Ireland and became famous after the war for his play *Waiting for Godot*. From the first day of the occupation, he opposed the Nazis, and in 1942 he left Paris with false papers for Lyon. Realizing that cities were not safe because of the large Nazi and Gestapo presence, he went into the countryside and resumed his resistance activities, keeping guns and ammunition on his property for local resistance fighters to use.

Gertrude Stein (1874–1946) and Alice B. Toklas (1877–1967) were Americans who stayed in France during the war and somehow avoided any repercussions from the Nazis. They were both from Jewish families, met each other in Paris early in the century, and became lifelong companions. The story of how they avoided arrest remains unclear but has intrigued historians and biographers ever since. Stein and Toklas spent the war years in the eastern part of France in a country house, where Bernard Faÿ, a collaborator with friends in the Gestapo and German administration, may have safeguarded them. The controversy about whether they were profascist or just trying to protect themselves remains subject to debate. Stein died of cancer a year after the end of the war, but Toklas lived another twenty years and struggled financially.

The Spanish artist Pablo Picasso (1881–1973) moved to France early in the twentieth century. A prolific painter, Picasso is known for his famous "periods": blue, rose, cubist, and others. One of his best-known works is the mural *Guernica*, completed in 1937 and named for the town in northern Spain (Basques region) that was destroyed by German bombing during the Spanish Civil War. Although the Germans considered Picasso's style decadent, he continued to live in Paris. He had friends in the resistance who brought him food and even art supplies, but he was not particularly involved in political activities.

Education under Vichy

The Vichy regime and its supporters believed that France under the Third Republic had been weakened due to liberal values, social experimentation, and the freedom allowed to women. Marshal Pétain promised to reverse those trends by using Germany as a model. His program, called the National Revolution, would regenerate French society through the motto "Work, Family, Homeland"—a slogan borrowed from right wing and anti-Semitic parties in the 1930s.

To motivate the population, the Vichy government started a propaganda campaign to create a cult of personality around Pétain, a technique the Vichy government learned from German and Soviet actions in support of Hitler and Stalin. Those rulers were praised excessively, and their pictures were hung in every building throughout their countries.

As part of the French version of the cult, Pétain ordered a tapestry from the world-famous Gobelin factory portraying the general in his military uniform and riding a majestic white stallion. This image was reminiscent of a famous painting of Napoleon. Pétain's picture soon appeared everywhere, and his words were constantly on the radio or reprinted in newspapers and magazines. According to this new image and message, France was to follow Pétain's lead without hesitation and demonstrate its love for him through hard work.

Pétain's cult of personality and conservative ideology had an immediate impact on French education. After the armistice, the new curriculum emphasized the traditionalist views of the regime, including Catholicism, visits to French historical sites with a nationalistic message, and physical exercise. Study of the liberal arts was discouraged, and school teachers were punished for discussing current events or politics in the classroom. In addition, because the right wing blamed women for the weakness of France, gender roles in the schools were imposed. Boys learned to make, build, and repair things, while girls were expected to master cooking, sewing, cleaning, and meal planning. Girls were allowed to pursue a career as a nurse but not as a doctor.

In addition to Catholicism, primary schools focused on the image of Pétain. Children listened to messages from the leader, such as "you must know that I count on you to rebuild France," and students were encouraged to follow his example to restore the "glory" of France. Music became part of the campaign to create a cult focused on Pétain. A new anthem and the traditional anthem were played one after the other. The new anthem, "Maréchal, nous voilà," praised the general as a religious savior who was responsible for the rebirth of the nation.

Every morning school children under the Vichy regime stood and sang the new national anthem in tribute to Pétain: "Maréchal, nous voilà!" (Marshal, we are here). This song portrayed Pétain using religious images and language; words such as savior, reborn, immortal, and heaven reminded children to honor the "supreme call."

Some members of the public who did not support the Vichy regime refused to recognize the new anthem. They understood the message of the pro-Pétain music to be one of exclusion, praising a France where liberals, socialists, democrats, foreigners, dissenters, and Jews were not welcome. In response to growing opposition, in 1941 the government passed laws requiring public displays of respect for both the anthem and the French flag.

In the northern or occupied zone in France, the Nazis banned *La Marseillaise*, the French National Anthem, fearing that it might arouse the emotions of the French population. Written during the French Revolution in the 1790s, the anthem calls on the citizens of the nation to arise against tyranny, an appeal that the Nazis clearly could not tolerate.

Youth Organizations

In Germany all young people were required to join Hitler Youth groups that indoctrinated them with Nazi propaganda. The Vichy government was not as well organized, but it did offer voluntary membership for young people in its youth organizations such as Chantiers de Jeunesse (Youth Work Camps). Emulating Nazi practice, the official goal was to engage young people in so-called healthy work that emphasized exercise, gymnastics, fresh air, class visits to museums and historical sites, and practical education on agriculture and science. These French groups were never as successful as their German models. In 1943 the Nazis demanded that many of the French volunteers be sent to Germany, and 15,000 were transferred to work in Germany. In order to avoid that fate, some ran away and joined the French resistance.

Nazi propaganda often depicted Hitler surrounded by smiling and adoring children or receiving flowers from young girls with blond hair. German children were required to join the Hitler Youth, where extensive Nazi propaganda was emphasized. This photo was taken at Obersalzberg in Bavaria, Germany, where Hitler's Berghof retreat was located. (Library of Congress)

POLAND

Nazi Control

Education as a normal part of daily life changed under Nazi control. As they did in all occupied countries, the Germans singled out intellectuals for special punishment. Universities were closed, and faculty and professors were arrested and sometimes executed along with writers and political leaders. As the Nazi goal was the destruction of intellectual life, all aspects of culture—writing, art, and music—had to go underground to avoid the censors.

Many of the writers who died in the Warsaw Uprising in 1944 knew each other from their resistance activities. They lived in a world of Nazi control—of the publishing houses, of paper, of writing supplies, and of the bookstores. They also lived in a world of fear. One wrong word or misstep on the sidewalk could send anyone to a concentration camp. With little to lose, many of them risked their lives in the 1944 Uprising (see Chapter 8).

Universities

German racial policy viewed Poles as inferior and not worthy of education. According to Himmler, Poles were to be limited to an elementary school education, sufficient only to prepare them to serve as agricultural workers for their future German-Aryan overlords: "The ability to do simple sums no higher than 500, write their names, and understand that it is their divine duty to obey Germans, be honest, diligent and well-behaved." The country was to become a permanent German colony; German became the official language, and Poles could be punished for speaking their native language. German teachers replaced Polish faculty and taught German culture; the teaching of Polish history or literature was outlawed.

Hans Frank, in charge of the General Government,* announced the closing of universities when he visited Lodz at the end of October 1939: "The Poles are to be allowed to educate only to the extent that will make them realize that they have no prospects whatsoever as a nation. The universities are practically all closed down now. The seminaries will unconditionally be closed down as well, since they are nothing but the mines of hatred towards the Germans" (Schindler Museum).

This announcement was followed by an attack on the one of Poland's best universities. German authorities invited the faculty of Jagiellonian University in Kraków to a general meeting. The faculty believed that they were going to discuss a new curriculum and the rules they would have to follow under the Nazis, but rather than a discussion, the professors walked into a trap. First the room was locked and then Bruno Müller (1905–1960) who was an officer (*Sturmbannführer*) in the feared SS, made an announcement to the assembled professors:

Ladies and Gentlemen! You have tried to resume work in your research units and organize exams without asking our permission. By doing so, you have indeed proved that you have no idea about the real situation in which the University has recently found itself, and which shall continue at least until the end of the war. Your attempts to carry out examinations and to resume the University's normal operation are an act of malice and hostility towards the Third Reich. Besides that, the Jagiellonian University has always been a center of anti-German propaganda. Consider yourselves arrested. You shall be taken to a POW camp where you shall be properly informed of your real situation. No questions should be asked. I will now ask the ladies to leave. And you (gentlemen) shall be taken away immediately. I think that Mr. Rector will deign to go first. (Schindler Museum)

Immediately 150 faculty members were arrested and sent to concentration camps. Part of a plan to remove the intellectual leadership and elite from Poland, this action on November 6, 1939, just two months after the invasion, signaled the end of Polish educational independence. By arresting all the male professors, the Germans sent a message of threat and fear throughout Poland.

In order to fight these restrictions on education, the Polish resistance ran their own schools. Former teachers removed by the Nazis taught classes at great risk, but despite the hardships involved, the "Secret Teaching Organization" was able to educate more than a million elementary school students, 100,000 high school students, and 10,000 university students. After the war, the Polish government accepted these wartime diplomas in honor of the resistance to the Nazis.

For Polish Jews, the Nazi assault on education was more direct and brutal. Quickly after the invasion, schools were closed and Yiddish books destroyed, teachers fired, students ordered to wear a star on their clothes so they could be identified, and families forced out of apartments to allow German officers to move in. Rabbis were regularly abused or treated with disrespect, stopped on the street and made to cut off their beard or publicly deface their own holy books or religious objects. Soon all Jews were confined in a ghetto;* shortly thereafter they were sent to a concentration camp.

News and Censorship

The Nazis insisted that Polish access to news be restricted to the German version. According to Propaganda Minister Goebbels at the end of October 1939:

> The entire Polish information system must be liquidated. The people should not possess radio sets; they must be left with newspapers only; opinion press must not be allowed. (Schindler Museum).

In Poland as well as all occupied countries, books by national and international authors were censored, removed from libraries and private homes, and destroyed. Movies made during the occupation had to present a German perspective on events and avoid Polish history or nationalism. The Germans closed Polish newspapers and replaced them with German propaganda papers written in Polish.

As Goebbels had promised, radios were confiscated; trying to hide one meant death. The Germans put up loudspeakers in the city that broadcast German propaganda during the day. In order to frighten the population, the loudspeakers also announced executions of resistors by firing squad. These names were also published on walls in what the Poles called "the death poster."

CONCLUSION

The examination of intellectual life in three countries—Germany, France, and Poland—demonstrates that the Nazis were fundamentally anti-intellectual. They hated any ideas that conflicted with their own ideology, and they did not hesitate to burn books or kill the thinkers who disagreed with their beliefs. German policies imposed on France or Poland were indicative of the occupation throughout Europe. University professors were harassed or killed, the school curriculum was rewritten to promote Nazi propaganda, local leaders either collaborated or faced punishment and prison, Jewish teachers were sent to concentration camps, and Gestapo headquarters took care of troublemakers through the use of torture.

The autumn of 1939 was the beginning of six years of war. Anyone born in 1926 spent all of his teenage years, from age thirteen to nineteen, seeing his country at war. Every teenager faced the psychological challenge of witnessing sacrifice, struggle, and death.

A generation of young people in Europe missed crucial years of education, and for some of them there was no opportunity to make up that loss after the war. Europe lived through an intellectual nightmare, but unfortunately the Nazis were not just a bad dream.

FURTHER READING

Naliwajek-Mazurek, Katarzyna. "The Use of Polish Musical Tradition in the Nazi Propaganda." *Musicology Today*, 2010, 243–259.

Nicholas, Lynn H. *The Rape of Europa: The Fate of Europe's Treasures in the Third Reich and Second World War.* New York: Vintage Books, 1994.

Rhodes, Richard. *The Making of the Atomic Bomb.* New York: Simon and Schuster, 1987.

Riding, Alan. *And the Show Went On: Cultural Life in Nazi-Occupied Paris.* New York: Vintage, 2010.

Schindler Museum, Kraków. https://www.muzeumkrakowa.pl/branches/oskar-schindlers-factory

Sontheimer, Michael. "Germany's WWII Occupation of Poland: When We Finish, Nobody Is Left Alive." *Spiegel Online International*, May 27, 2011. https://www.spiegel.de/international/europe/germany-s-wwii-occupation-of-poland-when-we-finish-nobody-is-left-alive-a-759095.html. Accessed November 7, 2017.

6

RECREATIONAL LIFE

> The enjoyment of the rights and freedoms set forth in this Olympic Charter shall be secured without discrimination of any kind, such as race, color, sex, sexual orientation, language, religion, political or other opinion, national or social origin, property, birth or other status.
>
> The Olympic Charter

INTRODUCTION

How can one understand the concept of recreation and leisure in the midst of war? Normally leisure involves time spent pursuing favorite activities. One person might prefer to read a book, another might want to go to the beach, take a walk, or see a movie. People in World War II had little free time, as their activities were limited by the circumstances of their immediate vicinity: was there a battle nearby, was their town being shelled by artillery, was there likely to be a bombing raid, were there enemy soldiers patrolling, was there a curfew or blackout in force, and many other issues such as these that prevented time from being free, leisurely, or recreational while the war continued.

During the occupation, necessity replaced freedom. What might have been a leisurely stroll in the woods picking mushrooms and berries before the war became a desperate search in the forest for edible mushrooms and berries to supplement a meager ration during the war. If a civilian lived in a city before the war and wanted to see a film, he or she might have a variety of choices in terms of what theater to go to as well as what type of film to enjoy. During the war, there would be only a limited number of theaters open and they would all be showing the same propaganda and approved films selected by the occupiers. While all wars limit freedom, the Nazis were oppressors as well as occupiers, and they intentionally destroyed free choice throughout Europe.

THE POLITICS OF SPORTS

Olympics

Many people across Europe looked forward to the modern Olympic Games that had been held every four years since 1896, except in 1916 when, ironically, they were scheduled for Berlin and cancelled due to war. In 1932, the Olympics were awarded to the Weimar Republic* to celebrate Germany's new democracy, but in 1933 the Weimar Republic gave way to Nazi dictatorship. Just as the war they started in 1939 destroyed so many cities, towns, villages, and people, the Nazis also ruined the Olympics held in Berlin in 1936.

The philosophy of the Olympics seeks to transcend politics and nationalism, as the world comes together to admire pure athletic skill, without concern for race, religion, or national origin. In fact, the games have frequently failed to live up to their ideals, including 1940 and 1944 (no games), 1968 (track and field protests), 1972 (massacre of Israeli athletes), 1980 (U.S. boycott), and 1984 (Soviet boycott). Among all of these flawed contests, the 1936 Olympics are still considered the most notorious for violating the spirit of the games.

Visitors to Germany after Hitler consolidated power could not fail to see Berlin bedecked with swastika flags or hear the constant drone of Nazi propaganda on the radio. The Nazi racist agenda was clear, leading Olympic officials to debate a change of venue to another country. The fear was that the games would be spoiled by a Nazi ban on Jewish athletes and a simultaneous propaganda barrage glorifying the Nazi Party. Representatives of the IOC (International Olympic Committee) visited Germany to seek assurances that Nazi propaganda would not dominate the city and that German racial policy would not prevent athletes regardless of religion from participating. IOC officials were greeted by Minister of Propaganda Goebbels, who saw the games as a propaganda bonanza for the Nazis and had no scruples about lying and affirming that the games would be open to all. The IOC believed Goebbels and allowed the games to proceed in Berlin.

The result was exactly what people had feared. Nazi officials broke their pledge and refused to allow Jewish athletes to participate. Already in 1933, the German Boxing Association had expelled Erich Seelig, their light heavyweight champion, due to Jewish heritage. For the same reason, Germany's number-one tennis player was cut from its Davis Cup team, and Gretel Bergmann, a strong contender for a medal in the high jump, was put on the German team and then, with less than two weeks to go, was not allowed to compete. The Nazis disguised this discrimination by waiting until the American team was already on its way to Germany before they dropped her because she was Jewish. As she was the favorite for a medal, this treatment indicated that initial fears of keeping the games in Berlin were justified.

Germany turned the games into a Nazi propaganda showcase, with the Nazi flag flying from every balcony in Berlin. Hitler himself

The XI Olympic Games opened on August 1, 1936, in Berlin. As intended by Minister of Propaganda Goebbels, the sporting event was used to glorify the Nazi regime. Opening ceremonies focused on the well-staged arrival of Hitler and his acceptance of flowers from a young girl, the singing of the German national anthem (Deutschland Über Alles) followed by the Nazi anthem (Horst Wessel song), and the parade of athletes in front of the German Führer. (The Illustrated London News Picture Library)

opened the games in the new Olympic Stadium on August 1, to the sound of 100,000 spectators shouting "Sieg Heil"* (Hail Victory) as they gave the Nazi salute. A record-setting forty-nine teams paraded into the stadium; Germany had the most athletes in the stadium, with the United States bringing the second-largest team to Berlin. Interestingly, the medal count finished in that order as well: Germany won the most gold medals and the most overall medals, and the United States finished second in both medal categories. To complete the spectacle, the last of over 3,000 runners who carried an Olympic flame from Greece arrived to light the torch in Berlin. This Nazi innovation of having the last runner light the flame was intended to link ancient Greece with the present "Aryan"* athlete.

The American team experienced both triumph and self-embarrassment. Jesse Owens, the star of the American track and field team, had already won three gold medals when the coaches called a meeting just before the relay. Owens was not scheduled to participate in that event, but two Jewish Americans had qualified and were anxious to go. One of them, Marty Glickman, described what happened at the team meeting:

> The event I was supposed to run, the 400-meter relay, was one of the last events in the track and field program. The morning of the day we were supposed to run in the trial heats, we were called into a meeting, the 7 sprinters were, along with Dean Cromwell, the assistant track coach, and Lawson Robertson, the head track coach. Robertson announced to the 7 of us that he had heard very strong rumors that the Germans were saving their best sprinters, hiding them, to upset the American team in the 400-meter relay. Consequently, Sam Stoller and I were to be replaced by Jesse Owens and Ralph Metcalfe. We were shocked. Sam was completely stunned. He didn't say a word in the meeting. I was a brash 18-year-old kid and I said "Coach, you can't hide world-class sprinters." At which point, Jesse spoke up and said "Coach, I've won my 3 gold medals [the 100, the 200, and the long jump]. I'm tired. I've had it. Let Marty and Sam run, they deserve it," said Jesse. And Cromwell pointed his finger at him and said "You'll do as you're told." (U.S. Holocaust Memorial Museum: Nazi Olympics Berlin 1936)

American coaches had caved in to the Nazi agenda. There were never any secret German runners, and moreover the American coaches had decided that winning with Jewish runners would upset the Nazis more than winning another race with Jesse Owens.

Owens went home with four gold medals, while Marty Glickman never got to participate in another Olympics due to the coming war. The United States celebrated the medal victories of Owens, but this great track and field star returned to a segregated America where he could not freely choose a restaurant or hotel for his post-Olympic celebration.

Despite the mixed legacy of these games, the IOC was optimistic that 1940 would see an improvement. The games were planned for Tokyo, but Japan withdrew from hosting because of its military activity in China. Immediately the 1940 Olympics were rescheduled for Helsinki, Finland, but again the games were cancelled when war started in nearby Poland in 1939. With the war still in progress, there was no possibility of holding the games in 1944, so the next Olympics were finally staged in London in 1948.

During the war, the Nazis killed more than forty Jewish Olympic athletes in occupied European countries.

Boxing

One of the greatest American boxers of all time was Joe Louis (1914–1981), and he became part of the story of the intersection of politics and sports in the immediate prewar period.

Like Jesse Owens, Louis was born in Alabama, but his family moved to Detroit when he was twelve years old. In the early 1930s he started boxing in amateur bouts and soon turned professional. In the summer of 1936, his managers scheduled a bout for him against a former heavyweight champion, Max Schmeling of Germany.

The boxing match was held at Yankee Stadium in New York, where Louis suffered his first professional defeat when he was knocked out in the twelfth round. One year later, however, Louis defeated the reigning heavyweight champ, Jim Braddock, with an eighth round knockout and took the crown.

Following Schmeling's 1936 victory over Joe Louis, German propaganda outlets praised his win as proof of "Aryan" superiority. Both sides wanted a rematch, and it was scheduled at Yankee Stadium again two years after Schmeling's initial victory. The Schmeling and Louis supporters were both confident of victory and treated the fight as a political contest. The bout itself ended in the first round. Schmeling went down twice but resumed the fight; on the third knockdown, his handlers climbed into the ring. The match was over.

Schmeling was not a Nazi and even had a Jewish manager, but the bout had been presented and sold as a struggle between dictatorship and democracy. In November 1938, during the Nazi rampage against Jewish shops and religious places called Kristallnacht,* Schmeling protected two Jewish boys from the crowds. After the war, Max Schmeling and Joe Louis became friends, with the financially secure German assisting the bankrupt American by paying some of his debts.

The Schmeling–Louis rivalry was part of the political hype of the 1930s, and it was certainly unfair to the German boxer. The United States took pride in the second bout and the knockout of the German representative by an African American. Joe Louis went on to become a great heavyweight champion at a time when African Americans did not have full rights in the United States.

Football (Soccer)

Football was extremely popular in Europe before the war but, like other sporting events, took on political meaning. The World Cup tournaments in 1934 and 1938 were both won by Italy, victories that Mussolini celebrated in terms of nationalism and fascism. When the Italian team arrived in Marseille for the 1938 games, 3,000 anti-fascist protestors jeered the Italians. Nevertheless, the Italian team gave a fascist salute before their match and proceeded to win again, the first consecutive tournament victories by one country. Due to the war, the 1942 and 1946 matches did not take place, with the first postwar tournament in Brazil in 1950.

In Poland soccer players organized secret leagues and held games far away from occupation troops in order to avoid attention. Because it would have been impossible to keep matches in the vicinity of major cities secret, teams often played away from bigger cities; nevertheless, they still attracted large crowds. Sometimes German soldiers quietly watched, but other times they broke up the games and carried out mass arrests.

A famous match took place in Ukraine during the occupation in August 1942. The members of a prewar Kiev team were challenged to a match by a team composed of some professional players serving in the German military. Of course, the match took on political meaning, as everyone was supposed to know that "inferior" Ukrainian Slavs could not defeat a group of "superior Aryans." Shortly before the match started, an SS officer warned the Ukrainians against winning. The first indication that the Ukrainians might not cooperate came during the opening ceremony when German players and their fans shouted "Heil, Hitler" while the Ukrainians refused to do so. The Ukrainians were again warned at intermission but went on to win 5–3 or 5–2. Most of the Ukrainian players were subsequently arrested, and one was tortured to death; the others went to labor camps, where some were killed the following year.

Despite this heroic struggle, the Ukrainian team did not receive recognition for its achievement for many years. Although they had embarrassed the Nazis, the Ukrainians had also violated Soviet policy by playing a match with Germans. Some Soviet officials suspected collaboration, but it was clear from the way the players were treated that cooperation had not taken place. Today Ukrainians proudly view the match as an act of patriotism.

Soccer remained popular during the war, and recreational matches continued to be organized by civilians to relax. Players were limited by their food rations as they could not risk burning too many calories if they were already losing body mass.

Tennis

The French Open was officially halted with the outbreak of war, but once the occupation was in place, the Vichy* regime sponsored the continuation of the tournament as a way to encourage exercise and physical health. Because of the war, it was not possible to invite players from other countries; all of the participants were French. In London, the Wimbledon tournament was suspended for the entire war; the decision was justified when Germany bombed the tennis court in 1940.

Chess

"It seems unbelievable that people were playing chess in besieged Leningrad and in the course of fierce bloody battles near Stalingrad,* and tournament score sheets were drawn up. Even during the horrible winter of 1941–1942, newspapers wrote about the results of tournaments, and qualification passes were issued" (Kublashvili, 2015).

As a form of recreation, chess had international appeal. Photos from the war show people playing chess everywhere: in hospitals, in darkened bomb shelters, and in cities under siege or bombardment. After the war, handmade chess sets were found in POW camps and even in concentration camps. In Poland and the Soviet

Union, hundreds of professional chess masters were killed, some as combatants in the army and some shot by the Nazis if they were Jewish.

How could a game like chess take on a political meaning? The French chess champion (born in Russia and emigrated to France) was captured by Germany in 1940 and collaborated by writing articles for German chess magazines claiming that Jewish chess players were cowardly and cheated while "Aryan" players were aggressive and the best masters in the world. The French champion survived the war but was banned from international competition due to his collaboration. He was found dead in 1946 under mysterious circumstances.

ENTERTAINMENT IN GERMANY

Strength Through Joy

The "Strength Through Joy" movement in Germany in the 1930s was a form of propaganda combined with a means to provide healthy exercise and diversions for all Germans. The program was subsidized by the German government and quickly became popular by offering leisure activities for the middle and lower classes, that is, people who could not previously afford a vacation. Millions took advantage of the opportunity to go to sporting events, the movies, hiking and other excursions, and on cruises, all at a subsidized price sponsored by the national labor board. It was made clear to participants that they were receiving a benefit from the Nazi Party, and police spies sometimes participated to make sure that everyone understood that they owed thanks and loyalty to the government.

Films

The German film industry was active under the Nazis, making movies for entertainment as well as for propaganda purposes. One of the best-known Nazi-era directors was Leni Riefenstahl (1902–2003), who made *The Victory of Faith*, a propaganda documentary showing a Nazi Party rally in Nuremberg in 1933. The film was a prelude to her more famous propaganda film *Triumph of the Will*, depicting the events at the Nuremberg Nazi Party rally of 1934. Critics still consider *Triumph of the Will* to be a masterwork of political propaganda, loaded with religious symbolism and a flattering portrayal of Hitler. The central focus of the film is clearly Hitler, who is treated as a god descending to save his enthusiastic followers. The "documentary" includes Nazi speeches, thousands of cheering party members, and nighttime parades and celebrations. Riefenstahl was a favorite Nazi director who also filmed the 1936 Olympics, in which she used close-up camera shots to show off the bodies of the "Aryan" athletes. After the war, Riefenstahl was put on trial as a Nazi sympathizer, but she always claimed she was only a filmmaker with no political views. Many critics considered her to be a Nazi who was also a talented director. She escaped any punishment for her actions and lived beyond the age of one hundred.

Kristina Söderbaum was born in Sweden but made films in Germany, and she was considered the epitome of the "Aryan" woman during the war. She appeared in several famous productions, including the notorious anti-Semitic film *Jud Suss* (meaning the "Jew named Suss") in 1940. It included all of the stereotypes: the evil Jew who cares only about money, then disguises himself in order to assimilate and trick the rest of the population, and finally forces himself on the innocent and attractive German girl, played by Söderbaum. This movie was made with the encouragement of Propaganda Minister Goebbels, and its portrayal of the leading Jewish character was so negative that Himmler ordered members of the SS and concentration camp guards to view it for anti-Jewish motivation. The film was financially successful in Germany, but after the war most of the actors who appeared in it claimed that they had been forced to participate.

In the same year, 1940, Goebbels ordered the making of *The Eternal Jew*, depicting Jews as filthy, wearing rags, and the source of disease. Part of the movie was filmed in the Warsaw Ghetto* and other ghettos in Poland, showing a Jewish population that had already been confined, starved, and abused. In this case, they were not shown as sympathetic victims but as less than human, a major rationale of the Holocaust* itself. The population was explicitly compared to rats, and the conclusion of the film included a speech by Hitler warning that war would lead to the destruction of the Jews. Goebbels was the moving force behind the making of both *Jud Suss* and *The Eternal Jew*.

Music

"Lili Marlene" was a song that became popular on both sides of the battlefield. It was taken from a poem written during World War I by a German soldier. Like "Wait for Me" in Russia, this was a poem about hope and a promise to meet again. Published in 1937, the poem was set to music just before World War II. Lale Andersen recorded it in Germany, but Nazi officials found the love story too emotional and not warlike, and they ordered it off the radio. It had already been broadcast to soldiers in North Africa; it was so popular that demands forced the Nazis to play it again. Allied troops also heard it and liked it and requested an English version. The song is closely identified with Marlene Dietrich (1901–1992), an anti-Nazi German émigré who sang it in German and in English. The English singer Vera Lynn (1917–) also made it part of her repertoire when performing before troops. With these different recordings, the message evolved from the original male perspective to a female point of view—the song became a woman faithfully waiting for her soldier.

FRANCE

Entertainment

In almost every French town and city where there were German troops, the Nazis established entertainment clubs called Soldiers' Clubs (*Soldatenheim*) that only admitted Germans. Since most German soldiers did not speak French, these gathering spots for off-duty soldiers gave them a place to relax together and avoid some of the temptations of a French city. In every sense, Germans were a privileged social group in France; Nazis had their own restaurants, theaters, movies, cafes, seating on public transportation, and special food rations so they never went hungry. They even had half the sidewalk reserved for "Germans only."

German policy in the west was based on incentives and repression. In other words, if the French, Dutch, and other western countries behaved, they might receive rewards, allowing entertainment venues in the form of cafes or music clubs to open. In larger cities in Western Europe, the Nazis pursued this policy as if they were Roman emperors with a show in the Coliseum to distract the population from the real issues of the day. Paris was one example of this policy and was even used as a reward and rest area for Wehrmacht* soldiers who earned a commendation.

Paris

Paris has always been considered one of the most culturally exciting cities in the world; it attracted entertainers, performers, and artists from every country. Anyone who knew Paris before the war would find it almost unrecognizable under the occupation. During the invasion of France, thousands of Parisians fled south, and while some drifted back after the armistice, the city had a deserted feel after 1940. The Nazis restricted the use of cars and also imposed curfews to control who was on the streets at any time; what had been busy boulevards were mostly empty except for the official autos of German officers driving past French residents on bicycles or walking. The swastika flying over the Eiffel Tower and other important monuments was a reminder of foreign control. A row of Nazi flags replaced the French tricolor on top of stores and hotels along the fashionable rue de Rivoli from Place de la Concorde to the Hotel de Ville. Bookstores became Nazi propaganda shops, and the Hotel Meurice served as the headquarters of top Nazi generals.

Propaganda

German authorities hoped to give Paris the appearance of normal life. It was in the German interest to distract the French and to take their minds off of politics by allowing the population to enjoy nightlife, including movies, shows, music, and cabarets. An average French worker was unlikely to socialize or have much contact with a German, partly because they could not afford to frequent the higher-priced clubs and also because they had little desire to be reminded of their defeat when they were out to relax. The French usually preferred their own nightspots or local bars.

All live theater performances were censored in advance by the Nazis to make sure that no anti-German comments were made. The censors were required to eliminate political jokes, allusions, or insults. While most performers were happy to have work and acted as if everything was normal, a few actors attempted to use French slang or words that could be understood several ways in order to sneak a political joke into the show. One major change from the prewar days was the absence of French Jewish performers who were forbidden to act on stage or in films. As of October 1940, in a decree that applied to all of France, French Jews were banned from the movie industry as well as from teaching, journalism, or the military.

The Nazis set up a Propaganda Department in Paris, and as its name implied its job was spreading a positive German image as well as controlling any negative publicity. The Propaganda Department was also in charge of articles in newspapers, programs on the radio, movies, theater, music, and literature. Newspapers and radio were the most important media for information, and censors had total control over everything in print or on the air. Furthering the role of the Propaganda Department was the official German embassy in Paris under Otto Abetz (1903–1958); it too launched a culture war to bring Germanic cinema, painting, music, and performances to Paris, hoping that exposure to "Aryan" civilization would convince the French that they had been wrong about the superiority of their own artistic achievements for centuries. Concert-goers in Paris were likely to hear German or Austrian composers like Ludwig van Beethoven (1770–1827), Richard Wagner (1818–1883), and Anton Bruckner (1824–1896) rather than French composers like Georges Bizet (1838–1875) or Claude Debussy (1862–1918). The Paris Opera featured Wagner's works fifty-four times, followed by thirty-five productions by Mozart.

The city was divided by class and nationality; *The German Guide to Paris*, published shortly after the armistice, informed German officers which clubs would welcome them. Due to the cost, the more famous nightclubs or cabarets such as the Moulin Rouge, Folies Bergère, and Folies Belleville played to a primarily German clientele. French patrons of these expensive venues were male and female, seeking contacts to promote their businesses and products, to seek protection, and to have access to the rich and powerful. To encourage collaboration and to give the impression that Germans were welcome visitors in occupied countries, propaganda films and photos showed soldiers laughing with French women. Nevertheless, the Nazis were resented and disliked throughout the country.

Radio

Starting in the 1920s, the radio provided a new form of information and entertainment. In Europe, most governments ran their own state stations that broadcast news and so-called high culture such as classical music. By the 1930s, authoritarian governments saw the potential of using the radio to spread official propaganda, and for this reason both Nazi Germany and Soviet Russia maintained control over radio programing. During the occupation, the Nazis banned the private ownership of radios, fearing that resistance movements might communicate by radio or listen to the BBC from London. Indeed, possessing a transmitter could be punished with death.

Resistance fighters did use radio transmitters to plan clandestine actions, and spies sent information to their home government through transmitters. In June 1940, de Gaulle's famous speech calling on France to continue to resist German occupation was broadcast on radio from London. He famously told the French people that they had only lost a battle but not the entire war (see Chapter 8). His call for the fight to go on led the Vichy government to declare him a traitor and sentence him to death.

Entertainment and Postwar Evaluation

In Paris, there were many recreational opportunities in theaters, concert halls, and night clubs, but after the war performers were evaluated according to how they had made their living during the war. There were several actions that definitely led to charges of collaboration: singing for a German audience, sleeping with a German officer, appearing in films during the occupation, or escorting a German officer at a nightclub—all of these behaviors created the suspicion of collaboration.

In fact, there were actors and actresses who worked with the occupation forces, some out of genuine support for the fascist program and others for selfish reasons such as a desire to live and eat well. Most of them, male and female, had influential friends who helped them escape punishment after the war. Nevertheless, their reputations are always associated with their choices during the occupation. This chapter will examine a few of the more famous celebrities of that time.

Arletty (1898–1992), who professionally only used one name, was one of France's most famous theater and film stars in the 1930s. During the war she had a Nazi officer as a lover, and his connections allowed her to live far better than Parisians who depended on ration coupons. At the end of the war, she was tried for collaboration but received a light sentence that she served in a chateau. She resumed her film career as early as 1945 and continued to appear in films in the 1950s.

Coco Chanel (1883–1971) had become famous and wealthy due to a perfume line called No. 5. She shared the political views of the Nazis, including strong anti-Semitism, and she had no trouble adapting to the German message of racism. Her lover during the war was a German officer and probable spy for Germany, and Chanel was able to live a life of luxury in the Ritz Hotel in Paris. After the war she moved to Switzerland to escape prosecution in France and, like other collaborators,* resumed her life of wealth and glamor as quickly as France put the war experience in the past.

The famous singer Edith Piaf (1915–1963) lived a more ambiguous life during the occupation. In some of the most exclusive neighborhoods in Paris, expensive brothels existed for Germans and rich French collaborators. Piaf lived above one of those brothels, sang in those establishments, and became financially well-off during the war, actions that raised suspicions about her political views. To demonstrate the complexity of assigning labels to all performers, resistance fighters also hid in some of the brothels. Nevertheless, Piaf remained on good terms with German officials who allowed her to perform in French POW camps, where prisoners wanted their pictures taken with the famous singer. The photos could then be used to identify prisoners and let families know that they were alive. Neither a full-time member of the resistance nor a dedicated collaborator, Piaf took advantage of opportunities that came along.

Maurice Chevalier (1888–1972) was a popular French cabaret entertainer in the 1930s. He stayed in the south of France immediately after the occupation, where his public statements at the time supported Pétain. In 1941, he performed in Paris and then sang for French POWs being held in German camps. The resistance labeled Chevalier a collaborator after he traveled to Berlin and sang for prisoners there, and at one point he was even sentenced to death for friendship with Germans. Fearing for his life, he spent some time in hiding before the Allies liberated France in 1944. As soon as the liberation took place, he sang a song of welcome for General de Gaulle that he called "Fleur de Paris," a song about a flower that is the color of the French flag: La fleur du retour, Du retour des beaux jours (The returning flower is the return of the good old days). Chevalier was fortunate—he had influential friends who helped him escape prosecution after the war, and he quickly resumed his career.

POLAND

Entertainment

If German policy in the west can be described as "carrot and stick," then Nazi action in the east was based only on the "stick," or a plan of total repression with no reward system in the present or future. People in Eastern Europe were not considered worthy of any cultural activities, and what they produced throughout their own histories was also viewed as having little value.

In Eastern Europe, there was little recreation or leisure in a traditional sense. In Poland there were few entertainment venues for Poles—all cultural areas were censored. There were clubs for German soldiers, and a Polish entertainer who worked there would be considered a collaborator and might also become a target for the Polish resistance.

Chopin

Even though Frédéric Chopin (1810–1849) lived one hundred years before World War II, the Nazis wanted to control his legacy. At first they banned the playing of any Polish music, including Chopin's, but since he was so popular even in Germany, state officials looked for a way to claim him as their own. By 1941–1942, Nazi officials allowed classical concerts to be held in Poland with Chopin's music included in the program. To receive full credit and propaganda value with the population, the authorities asserted that these performances were a gift to the Polish people that would not have been possible if Jews or Soviets ruled Poland. The following year (1943), Hans Frank supported a display of Chopin artifacts, ironically held in the library of what had been *Jagiellonian University* and was now renamed the Institute for German Work in the East. Finally, they announced that Chopin had German ancestry and German music teachers, or in other words, Chopin was "Aryanized."

Just before Chopin died in 1849 in Paris, he had requested that his heart be returned to Poland. It was kept in Warsaw in the Church of the Holy Cross, until threatened by the heavy fighting in that area in 1944. The Germans, who were responsible for the battle to begin with, claimed credit for saving and returning the heart to the church; they also lied and denied their role in destroying most of Warsaw.

Songs

Poles took pleasure in averting Nazi efforts to crush their culture. Music was one of the few recreational outlets for Poles during the war. Nazi censorship could not stop Polish composers from using patriotic expressions to create politically powerful musical compositions that combined nationalism with anti-German sentiment. Polish writers affiliated with the Polish Underground Army wrote extensively, and their songs became instant hits and inspired the Poles preparing for battle against Germans in the uprising of 1944.

Polish Song: "Song in Camp"

One of the first musical responses to the German invasion combined themes of nationalism and religion. The anti-German message in "Song in Camp" was clear, calling on the Lord to help them crush the oppressors and restore a free Poland. Another song by the same writer continued this theme by proclaiming that Poles would fight for a month, a year, or more until they were free from "the scoundrel."

Polish Song: "Axe, Hoe"

Probably the most popular song of the Polish resistance was "Axe, Hoe," an older song reworked to apply to the occupation. Although the Nazis decreed the song to be illegal, it remained popular, possibly due to its criticism of the random roundups of workers for forced labor. When German soldiers surrounded a crowd of civilians, they would grab anyone who was in decent physical condition for factory or farm work. Many of those taken never saw their families again. Popular parts of the song referred to Hitler as the stupid painter who lost the war: "Mr. Painter is kaput."

Polish Song: "Red Poppies on Monte Cassino"

Another well-known song resulted from the Allied invasion of Italy. The battle was difficult and involved American, British, and Polish forces trying to break through the strong defensive line of the German army. One of the most important battles of this campaign was the assault on the monastery at Monte Cassino in January 1944. This action remains controversial to this day because of the bombing of the historic building, but nevertheless, Polish troops played a major role in this attack. Their job was to move up a hill covered with red poppies, and this song composed on the eve of battle was dedicated to the more than one thousand Polish soldiers who were killed.

Polish Song: "The Willows Are Weeping and Rustling"

There is a famous statue of Chopin under a willow tree in Lazienski Park in Warsaw, and the resistance adopted this song because of the symbolism of the tree. "O, willows, don't sigh for us ... Even though the life of a guerrilla fighter is hard, we sing as we march. We are calm and without fear. The soldier does not know how his life will end but we are confident in our victory."

Polish Song: "Fix the Bayonets, Boys"

One of the best-known Polish heroes of the war was Krystyna Krahelska (1914–1944), better known as Danuta. She was a poet and a member of the Polish Underground Home Army. She wrote her famous song in 1943, but she was killed while serving as a medic in the Warsaw Uprising. After the war, her poetry collections were published, and she received the Cross of Valor posthumously.

Polish Song: "Warsaw Children"

The Polish Home Army facilitated the creation of the song "Warsaw Children" by bringing a composer and a poet together in a safe house in Warsaw. They agreed to write a song for the resistance, and the new composition was published using underground printing presses and distributed to soldiers. Other songs written in this manner included "Let the People Rise," "Soldiers' Song," and "Farewell!" "Warsaw Children" was completed in 1944 just before the Uprising.

SOVIET UNION

The Soviet Union was a country that was attacked and then subjected to a level of brutality seldom seen in history. The Nazi agenda brought to Russia hangings, rapes, murders, mass killings, starvation, and ultimately the highest death toll of any country in the war. The Soviet Union defended itself on two levels: one was militarily, and the other was creatively. Poetry, songs, and films all played an important role in boosting the morale of the population and providing comfort to families waiting for information about their soldiers at the front lines. In the midst of the horror of war, these artistic endeavors became an essential part of recreational life with a new definition: rather than leisure time to kill, the culture of war focused on an enemy to kill. There was only one overriding obsession in the Soviet Union—hatred for the Nazis and the occupation.

Socialism and Culture

In the 1930s, Stalin's control over the government and economy also extended to the arts and culture. The government owned all the publishing houses, museums, and concert halls, making it impossible for any writer or artist to be recognized without official approval. The films, art, and music that Russians saw and heard in the 1930s were all censored and supported state-approved ideology.

During this time period, the Soviet state was worried about the rise and strengthening of the German state. Many prewar songs praised military readiness and imagined a potential victory in case of war. Several of these songs were written for films: the song "Seagull" was from the film *Sailors* and "Beloved City" was in the film *Fighter Planes*. The song "If There Is War Tomorrow" in the film of the same name focused on the desire for peace as well as preparedness. Many of these popular songs had a single theme: while we are a peaceful country we must be ready for any eventuality.

Official Songs

Immediately after the invasion, songs that appealed directly to Soviet ideology and the leadership of Stalin were written. Such titles as "Song of the Brave," "For the Honor and Glory of the Soviet People," "We Will Destroy the Fascists," "The Enemy Will Go to the Bottom of the Sea," "Battle Volunteer Corps," and "For the Great Soviet Land" are a few examples of songs with an obvious theme but little originality. These songs were intended to inspire opposition toward the Nazis and loyalty to the USSR. In reality, it was not necessary to create an artificial attitude of anger and patriotism for the homeland. Such sentiments were genuine. Soon these feelings were expressed spontaneously in new songs and poems that reflected the emotions of the people and helped inspire soldiers as well as civilians.

Destruction

At first the German invasion moved so quickly that art galleries and museums, concert halls and music clubs, drama and movie theaters were widely destroyed. While the terrible devastation created immense obstacles to artistic production, there was also a tremendous creative response in the area of music during the country's four-year struggle. The state, concerned with boosting morale among a population facing serious deprivation, encouraged artistic responses to Nazi propaganda and allowed limited free expression within prescribed limits. Rather than insisting that all published works or songs praise the Communist Party, its leaders, and the future of socialism, wartime culture allowed art to express the concerns of real people who were fighting for their lives. The regime loosened rules on artistic freedom but also encouraged nationalistic themes that played on venerable Russian customs. Rather than fighting for communism, the population was encouraged to defend traditional Russia. While state ideology did not disappear, songs and music also expressed a love of home and the Motherland, a devotion to family, and even religious or spiritual sentiments.

Talented writers, composers, journalists, and filmmakers in the Soviet Union were imaginative and prolific in the creation of works devoted to raising morale for both soldiers and civilians. Singing songs, reciting poems, and viewing films became important recreational activities that Soviet citizens engaged in during the ongoing brutality. In this wartime situation, it was not surprising that songs about home, women, and love became the natural expression of the population.

Some of the new songs were composed by professional writers, but others were written by regular soldiers whose compositions became popular locally and were then spread by reporters at the front lines. The most popular simply put into words or music the widespread feelings of civilians and military personnel. As a result, songs and poems became part of the daily life of Russians, who despite their toughness and fighting spirit also responded emotionally to compositions that focused on love and loss.

Katyusha

Written in 1938 before the war, the song "Katyusha" was one of the best-known and popular songs of that era. The original song is a love lament about a heroine who gazes at a river and thinks about her love for a soldier. While he protects the Motherland, she will keep their love and home safe as well. During the war, the song took on new lyrics that focused on love of country as well as the bond between lovers. The heroine also gave her name to the Red Army's terrifying weapon that first appeared at the Battle of Smolensk in July 1941 (see Chapter 2), a mobile mortar rocket fired from the back of a truck. The Soviet army loved the Katyusha fire power as much as the Wehrmacht feared it. The song simply merged prewar words with new verses that reflected the military meaning, and some sources claim that eventually there were 300 or so versions depending on where and when it was sung.

"Holy War"

Within one week of the invasion, the prolific and well-known composer Lebedev-Kumach wrote "Holy War" (or "Sacred War"). The song was performed for troops leaving for the front lines, and it quickly became an unofficial anthem for the war. In addition to its strong appeal to patriotism, the song used religious imagery and language. Most surprisingly, the song passed the official censors and indicated that traditional Russian values were acceptable themes for this struggle—the Great Patriotic War.

The song repeated certain key words such as "arise," "holy," and "sacred." The message dealt with love of the Motherland that was threatened by dark forces that had to be saved by the light. "We fight for the light and peace; they fight for the kingdom of darkness." The author, who later wrote "A Song about Stalingrad,"* used historical allusions in "Holy War" that Russians understood: his reference to "damn horde" meant the Mongols and the "people's war" suggested the fight against Napoleon. Germans were portrayed as evil, rapists, and torturers, representatives of a "fascist dark force" that had to be battled to the death (Great Patriotic War Museum).

Battle Songs

Sometimes specific events led to songs, such as "My Moscow," written by a soldier during that battle in December 1941. The line "My dear capitol, my golden Moscow" became popular throughout the country. Similarly, "In the Dugout" was also inspired by the Battle of Moscow. Written as a poem by a war correspondent, it had music added the next year and became popular with soldiers.

Another poem turned into a song was "Dancing Until the Morning," about a pilot on leave near the front lines who heard music playing. He found young people dancing and was going to ask a girl named Zina to dance when he was called to report for duty. When Zina tried to find the pilot, she learned that he had been shot down over German lines but refused to use his parachute so he could crash his plane into the enemy. The poem was renamed "Accidental Waltz" when it was turned into a song in 1943.

Leonid Lukov's film in 1943 told the story of average soldiers who shared a trench near Leningrad. "Two Soldiers" (Two Fighters) became popular because of the natural friendship that developed out of the situation—the soldiers go into battle together, relax together, and exchange memories while the war rages. As they sit in the trench, one of the soldiers uses the song "Dark Night" to express his feelings about his wife and baby waiting for him to return. The well-known Soviet singer Mark Bernes (1911–1969), who played one of the soldiers in the film, was known thereafter for this song. "The dark night, only bullets whistle by in the steppe. . . . In the dark night, I know that you, my love, are not sleeping, and are wiping a tear by the cradle."

Leningrad Symphony

Popular songs were joined by a triumphant moment in August 1942 in the besieged city of Leningrad. Officially this was the performance of the Seventh Symphony by Dmitri Shostakovich (1906–1975), who was one of the most famous Soviet composers of the twentieth century. Unofficially it was simply the victory of human will over bombs and artillery.

Of course, there was no orchestra left in Leningrad in 1942, as everyone was either at the front or engaged in civil defense or factory work. Most people in the city were already starving, including musicians who were trying to stay alive with the rest of the population. Nevertheless, when word went out that they were needed for a special performance, they gathered whenever possible in various abandoned spaces to practice.

Slightly more than one hundred musicians worked to master the difficult score by Shostakovich that ran 250 pages. Finally, the starving musicians played to a full house of famished listeners, as well as an audience around the city who heard the music over loud speakers. The conclusion of the performance was celebrated with a standing ovation. Later, the conductor summed up the experience: "And in that moment we triumphed over the soulless Nazi war machine" (Jones, 2008).

Writers and Journalists

More than one thousand artists and writers were involved in the war effort. Artistic production of all kinds was impressive, but journalism was popular due to its direct style and immediacy as it reported on life at the front. Many journalists became famous and trusted for their commentary. Readers were anxious to learn about conditions faced by their fathers, sons, brothers, husbands, and even sisters. Approximately 400 of these writers died during the war.

Ehrenburg

Ilya Ehrenburg (1891–1967) was one of Soviet Russia's most prolific journalists. He turned out thousands of articles during the war, and he was known for his strong patriotism and hatred of the Nazis. Immediately after the invasion, he wrote "Freedom or Death," a strongly worded attack on the German barbarians. "They are coming for us, the barbarian SS. . . . They want to Germanize us." He predicted that the Nazis intended to take over the land, wipe out Russian traditions, and spread destruction and death, and he bluntly called for killing the Nazis before they could kill. Perhaps ironically for someone living under Stalinism, Ehrenburg urged Soviet citizens to fight for their freedom as opposed to Nazi slavery. Ehrenburg continued to write articles for the army paper *Red Star* and other journals throughout war.

Fadeev

Despite the siege, Aleksandr Fadeev (1901–1956) traveled to Leningrad and reported on the impact of the blockade and the dedication of workers in the Putilov armaments factory (renamed in honor of Kirov). His stories about men and women who refused to quit or surrender inspired citizens in other parts of the country. Fadeev described the battle all around Leningrad and wrote openly about the starvation in the city. Toward the end of the war he also produced a novel, *The Young Guard*, which was made into a film of the same name in 1947. The plot involved an underground communist youth organization in Ukraine that struggled against the occupation. The members took great risks but continued their anti-Nazi activities until they were caught, tortured, and killed. The novel was especially popular because it was based on a true story. Fadeev was a dedicated communist and Stalinist, but in the 1950s he became disillusioned with the system and committed suicide.

Grossman

Another important journalist was Vasili Grossman (1905–1964), who also wrote for the newspaper *Red Star* (*Krasnaia Zvezda*). In November 1942 Grossman reported from Stalingrad, where one of the most important battles of the war was raging. "In the Main Line of Attack" he portrayed life of Russian soldiers who held out near the "dark, icy-cold Volga" against a large Nazi army with its artillery shells and dive bombers. Grossman focused on the dedication of men who were willing to die rather than surrender: "This battle, unequalled in its cruelty and ferocity, lasted for several days and nights uninterrupted. It was fought for every step of a staircase, for every corner in a dark passage, for every machine" (Sovlit.net).

Simonov

Within days of the invasion, Konstantin Simonov (1915–1979) was reporting from the front, where he saw chaos and panic among troops and civilians. When he returned to the same area several months later, he indicated that the situation had changed, with the Red Army beginning to wear down the Wehrmacht. According to Simonov, the arrogant German looked a bit more worried and the Soviet soldier seemed to have been psychologically strengthened by the slowing of the invasion force.

Simonov wrote three important poems during the war: "Kill Him," "Wait for Me," and "Smolensk Roads." His poem "Kill Him," like the song "Holy War," reminded the reader of the historical struggle against the Mongols. Like Ehrenburg and Grossman, Simonov established a sharp contrast between good and evil, and he made it clear that only one side could win.

Simonov wrote the celebrated poem "Wait for Me," dedicated to his wife, the famous actress Valentina Serova. The poem appeared in *Pravda* in 1942 and became popular due to its emotional appeal related to loss, devotion, and waiting. Readers identified with Simonov leaving his wife to go to the front lines, an action that thousands of soldiers and their loved ones also experienced.

Simonov wrote another poem that reminded readers of Napoleon's invasion and the Battle of Smolensk. The situation also looked bleak in 1812 until the Russians reorganized and retook the offensive. In "Smolensk Roads," Simonov focused on a Russian soldier who received the blessings of the local population, and we again see the Soviet government relaxing its prohibition against religious allusions.

Surkov

Alexei Surkov (1899–1983) was a poet and wartime journalist whose work "A Soldier's Oath" in 1941 earned him the nickname "soldier's poet." Like Ehrenburg and Simonov, Surkov referred to "the black hordes of Hitler that have broken my country. . . . Hitler the murderer and his hordes shall pay for these tears . . . for the avenger's hatred knows no mercy."

As a journalist for *Komsomolskaya Pravda,* Surkov was sent to report on a rifle division. When the unit came under fire, Surkov and others took cover in a trench. He wrote a poem about this experience, and it was quickly turned into the popular song "In the Dugout." Surkov continued to be an important literary figure after the war; he served as head of the Soviet Writer's Union in the 1950s.

Tvardovsky

One of the most famous Soviet poets was Aleksandr Tvardovsky (1910–1971) who wrote the poem "Vasili Tyorkin." Published in installments between 1942 and 1945, the poem portrayed an idealized soldier who faced every combat challenge imaginable. Tyorkin was fearless and selfless, and he knew instinctively how to use his intelligence and common sense to succeed. He was the model soldier, and his portrayal won a Stalin Prize for Tvardovsky.

Films

Before the war, going to the cinema was a popular form of entertainment in the Soviet Union. As in literature and painting and all cultural areas, the state controlled what films could be produced and shown. Among the variety of films made in the 1930s, some included a story line that revolved around the threat of war. The films that used war as part of their plot shared a message for the viewers. In all of the war movies, the Soviet army was ready and invincible, and Soviet citizens were united and prepared to fight heroically for the

Motherland. Several of the films made before the war were reshown after 1941 and provided inspiration for a nation at war.

The Soviet film industry was unique compared to other countries on the continent. In Eastern Europe in general, the domestic film industry was destroyed except for whatever pro-German movies were allowed by the occupiers. The situation was similar in Western Europe, where the Nazis permitted nonpolitical or pro-German movies to be shown. The Soviet Union was at war, but much of the country was safely removed from enemy lines. As a result, the Soviet film industry moved to Tashkent and produced films that were anti-German and pro-Russian as well as some purely entertaining films.

Alexander Nevsky

One of the most famous prewar films was *Alexander Nevsky*, which dealt with an invasion by Teutonic Knights in 1242. *Alexander*

The 1938 Soviet film *Alexander Nevsky* depicted Teutonic Knights committing atrocities during their invasion of northwestern Russia. Prince Alexander Nevsky of Novgorod swore that the enemy would not occupy Russian lands, and his army of patriotic warriors met the invaders on frozen Lake Chud (Peipus). The ice cracked under the weight of the heavily armored knights, who were swallowed by the waters and thus defeated. (Bettmann/Getty Images)

Nevsky had all of the star power that a Soviet film could muster. It was made by the legendary director Sergei Eisenstein (1898–1948), with music by the famed composer Sergei Prokoviev (1891–1953), and starred Nikolai Cherkasov (1903–1966) as Prince Alexander. The story picks up after the Teutonic Knights have taken the city of Pskov and shows the Knights burning the brave defenders of the conquered city. The Teutonic Knights, whose armor resembled Nazi uniforms, did not hesitate to drop babies into the flames. Roman Catholic priests blessed the massacre. Russian patriots escaped to inform Alexander, who was peacefully fishing and reluctant to go to war. Nevertheless, Alexander responded to the call of the people, who volunteered in the thousands. The final scene depicted the famous battle on the ice of Lake Peipus as the Teutonic Knights on their heavy horses crashed through the ice and drowned in a scene reminiscent of Pharaoh's chariots being engulfed by the Red Sea. Russia's invincibility demonstrated by Alexander's refusal to allow the enemy to step onto Russian soil was intended to warn adversaries to remain at a distance.

Other Films

While *Alexander Nevsky* used an historical episode to warn foreign enemies about invading Russia, two other films made in this time period focused on modern war. They imagined German invasions, but in both films the Soviet people rose up to drive the enemy out of the country.

If War Comes Tomorrow was another film of 1938 that contrasted a peaceful Russia with a warlike Germany. When German soldiers attacked without warning, the local population held off the invasion until the Soviet army arrived. The Red Army supported by volunteers from all over the country drove the Germans back to Berlin. Another film that predicted Soviet victory was *The Tank Men*. Once again the Red Army, led by its tank divisions, pushed through German lines all the way to Berlin. In this film, unlike real life, a Soviet soldier arrived at the Reichstag* building and arrested Hitler.

In addition to these prewar films that were reshown after 1941, the Soviet film industry produced several new films during the war. The two Soviet cities that suffered from German aggression were Stalingrad and Leningrad, and they both inspired films in 1942. *The Defense of Tsaritsyn* (the former name of Stalingrad) was made to encourage support for the Battle of Stalingrad then under way. In 1918 during the Civil War, Stalin was in charge of the defense of that city. When the enemy took over the city, Stalin refused to give up; he recaptured Tsaritsyn and in 1925 the city was named Stalingrad in his honor. The other inspirational film made at that time was *Invincible* about the city of Leningrad under siege. Filmed in Leningrad during the siege, the movie portrayed both the destruction and the sacrifice of the local population.

The most popular film of 1943 was Simonov's *Wait for Me*, written as a poem, turned into a play, and finally made into a screenplay. The story shows two wives waiting for their husbands who are at the front. While one wife gives up on her husband with tragic results, the other one is faithful and waits. Although her husband's plane was shot down, she never lost hope, and he eventually returned.

Two other films focused on the theme of resistance. One was *Kutuzov*, the story of the Russian general who fought Napoleon in 1812. Despite early retreats and heavy losses, the Russian army refused to quit and eventually prevailed. *She Defends Her Motherland* told the story of a mother who watched as Nazi villains killed her son and husband. She joined a partisan band and continued the struggle against the Germans. The theme of never surrendering was important and popular during the war.

An inspirational film that originally was a poem told the story of Zoya Kosmodemyanskaya (1923–1941), a teenage girl who sacrificed herself to fight the invaders. Margarita Aliger (1915–1992) wrote the poem about this school girl who joined a partisan unit and went behind enemy lines to sabotage their communications. Captured and tortured, Zoya refused to inform on her comrades. Before she was hanged, Zoya encouraged others to keep fighting and to avenge her death. The poem won the Stalin Prize and was made into a play and a film (Zoya), with world-famous composer Dmitri Shostakovich writing the music for the film version.

International Acclaim

It was rare for Soviet films to achieve international attention. *Alexander Nevsky* from 1938 was one such film, and *The Rainbow* made in 1944 was another. The film deals with an occupied village in Ukraine suffering from Nazi atrocities. Even children were brutalized, as they had been by the Teutonic Knights in *Alexander*

Nevsky. When the inhabitants finally took their village back from German control, they placed the occupiers on trial for their crimes. *The Rainbow* was also released in the United States and was given a positive review by the *New York Times*. According to the reviewer, the film "indelibly conveys the titanic burden of horror which the Russians were compelled to endure" (Crowther, 1944).

Two other Soviet films achieved international acclaim. In *Six O'clock in the Evening After the War*, a teacher and an artillery officer promise to meet in Moscow after the war. The film chronicles the many obstacles that conspire to keep them apart, but they keep their promise and find each other on a bridge as fireworks go off in the background. *The Great Turningpoint*, made in 1945, also received awards abroad. It returned to the beginning of the war and focused on attempts by Soviet forces to prevent the invasion. This film won a Grand Prize in Cannes, France, in 1946 and Stalin Prizes for many of the cast members.

CONCLUSION

Prior to the war, Europeans enjoyed many forms of recreation: competing in a soccer match, hiking in the forest, playing a game of chess, attending a concert, seeing a film, reading poetry, or singing along with a radio show. Between 1939 and 1945, everything changed, including the concept of what constituted recreation and leisure. In a world where families were divided, with fathers and sons in the military, wives and daughters working in factories, and everyone worried about survival and ration coupons, traditional leisure activities were not part of daily life.

In occupied countries, censorship was imposed not only on news but also on entertainment. To perform, write, publish, or appear in a film under the Nazis led to artistic compromise if not surrender. For some entertainers, the line between performance and collaboration was not always clear.

In both Poland and the Soviet Union, singing resistance songs and reading poetry were among the few recreational activities beyond the reach of the Nazis. In the Soviet Union, because only part of the country was occupied, the government was able to sponsor and encourage not only songs and poetry but also films that articulated a strong anti-fascist message. While traditional leisure activities were no longer possible, these forms of entertainment and recreational expression boosted morale and provided hope for a population facing death and destruction.

FURTHER READING

Ament, Suzanne. *Sing to Victory: The Role of Popular Song in the Soviet Union During World War II*. Ann Arbor: University of Michigan Press, 1996.

Crowther, Bosley. "Terror Reign by Nazis." *New York Times*, October 23, 1944. https://www.nytimes.com/1944/10/23/archives/teror-reign-by-nazis.html

Jones, Michael. *Leningrad State of Siege*. New York: Basic Books, 2008, 256.

Kublashvili, Eteri. "Chess During War—An Exhibition in Moscow." Chessbase.com, May 21, 2015.

Liebreich, Karen. "The Nazi Marilyn Monroe: Goebbels Had Very Nice Eyes—But He Was a Devil." *The Guardian*, April 3, 2017. https://www.theguardian.com/film/2017/apr/03/the-nazi-marilyn-monroe-goebbels-had-very-nice-eyes-but-he-was-a-devil?CMP=share_btn_link

Longman, Jeré and Andrew W. Lehren. "World War II Soccer Match Echoes Through Time." *New York Times*, June 23, 2012.

Merridale, Catherine. *Ivan's War: Life and Death in the Red Army, 1939–1945*. New York: Picador, 2006.

"Nazi Olympics Berlin 1936." U.S. Holocaust Memorial Museum. https://www.ushmm.org/exhibition/olympics/?content=jewish_athletes_more.

Polyudova, Elena. *Soviet War Songs in the Context of Russian Culture*. Cambridge, UK: Cambridge Scholars, 2016.

Sovlit.net., an online information source on Soviet literature. www.sovlit.net

Stites, Richard. *Soviet Popular Culture: Entertainment and Society Since 1900*. Cambridge, UK: Cambridge University Press, 1992.

Stites, Richard, ed. *Culture and Entertainment in Wartime Russia*. Bloomington: Indiana University Press, 1995.

Taylor, Richard. *Film Propaganda: Soviet Russia and Nazi Germany*. London: Croom Helm, 1979.

Werth, Alexander. *Russia at War 1941–1945*. New York: Carroll & Graf Publishers, 1964.

7

RELIGIOUS LIFE

First they came for the Socialists, and I did not speak out—Because I was not a Socialist.

Then they came for the Trade Unionists, and I did not speak out—Because I was not a Trade Unionist.

Then they came for the Jews, and I did not speak out—Because I was not a Jew.

Then they came for me—and there was no one left to speak for me.
Martin Niemöller

INTRODUCTION

The role of churches in World War II remains controversial, as historians and theologians debate the obligations of religious leaders and the teachings of Christianity. During the war, some clergy took heroic positions despite the danger of doing so, while others pretended that they did not see the evil or actually encouraged it by endorsing killings and executions. Should priests and ministers risk their own lives for a moral cause? Should Christian clergy care about people who are not Christians? Does becoming a member of the clergy, of any denomination, bring with it a mandate to set a higher example and defend a code of morality? Do church teachings require believers to take a stand against evil?

While these philosophical questions may not have seemed crucial before 1933, they became essential when Nazi atrocities confronted every religious institution in Europe with moral challenges. Theoretical issues became practical and immediate. The response to the Nazi threat, confronted by a few, ignored by others, and helped by some, continues to haunt the study of religion and war. Like the regular population, churches, clergy, members of different religions, sects, and denominations sometimes resisted and sometimes collaborated.

Religions of Europe

Most of Western Europe considered itself to be Roman Catholic until the sixteenth century. At that time, Martin Luther objected to certain practices of the Catholic Church and called for changes, igniting a movement that is called the Reformation. Since then, most of Europe has been divided religiously between Catholic and Protestant. Germany, where Luther lived, split into a Lutheran north and a Catholic south. Most of Scandinavia became Lutheran, and about 80 percent of Estonia and a slight majority of Latvia also became Protestant. The third Baltic State, Lithuania, remained Roman Catholic. Poland was overwhelmingly Catholic, and the church there was powerful both religiously and politically. Belgium, France, Spain, and Italy remained Catholic, as did Croatia, Hungary, and Czechoslovakia, but the Netherlands was split between Protestant and Catholic. In the Balkans, Greek Orthodoxy and Serbian Orthodoxy prevailed in Greece and Serbia. The result was that Europe, while overwhelmingly Christian, was divided by different sects of Christianity. Almost every European country also included a minority Jewish population and other small religious or ethnic groups.

GERMANY

Nazis and Religion

There is often some confusion about what religion the Nazis followed. Nazi Party members were born Christian but mostly did not practice it. They opposed Christianity in part due to their understanding of the German philosopher Nietzsche (1844–1900). Writing at about the time Hitler was born at the end of the nineteenth century, Nietzsche criticized Christianity for being a religion of the weak and meek. Hitler and his followers adopted Nietzsche's philosophy for their own purposes. Nazis perverted the theory of evolution of Charles Darwin (1809–1882). Darwin explained the adaptation of animals to their environments through a process called "natural selection." He did not use the expression "survival of the fittest," an idea that was added to his theory by subsequent writers in order to justify European domination (imperialism) over other parts of the world. The attempt to make the theory of evolution apply to conflicts in human society is called "Social Darwinism,"* and its claim that only the "fittest" societies and "races" survive was included in Nazi ideology.

Combining German romanticism with Nietzsche and Darwin led to Nazi racist rantings that claimed descent from a race of warriors called "Aryans,"* who would prove their superiority by eliminating all rival ethnic or religious groups. The Nazis believed that other ethnic and religious groups were trying to destroy the so-called purity and power of the Germanic people and that in an inevitable struggle only the strongest would survive.

Hitler was born and raised Catholic, but he was not religious. His lack of commitment to the Catholic Church did not stop him from using Christian symbolism in his political campaigns, speeches, and propaganda. Almost all leading Nazis were raised Catholic or Lutheran, and like their leader they embraced Christian imagery and language when it was convenient for them to do so. The Nazi Party cared only about the exercise of power, and top officials of the party would adopt any method to be able to dominate and control others. Sometimes that lust for power meant that the Nazis did not have any hesitation about exploiting Christianity if necessary, and when that was the case the Nazis would manipulate the churches through religious symbolism. The Nazis therefore made agreements with the churches in Germany, allowing churches to continue to function as long as they did not criticize the Nazi government. Churches in other countries were not protected by these agreements, and Christian leaders in occupied nations were sometimes persecuted by the German military and police. Even within Germany, the Nazis would break their agreements if it suited their purpose.

The Nazis understood that church support would help them to manipulate priests and ministers who would preach the Nazi message for them. For example, shortly after Hitler was appointed chancellor in 1933, the Nazi Party opened the Reichstag* (parliament) in a Protestant church with Hitler speaking from the church pulpit. This was an example of the exploitation of church symbolism for political reasons, and it was successful in convincing some church leaders that they could work with the Nazis.

Catholic Church

There was historical precedent for animosity between the German government and the Catholic Church. The German chancellor in the nineteenth century, Otto von Bismarck (1815–1898), feared the power of the Vatican to attract the loyalty of southern Germans, and he implemented measures to control the Catholic Church. His attempt backfired and created sympathy for the church and for the new Catholic Center Party. The Catholic Center Party remained an important political force in Germany until the Nazis came to power, when they acquiesced in supporting Nazi power.

The turning point came in 1933 after Hitler was appointed chancellor. The parliament building (Reichstag) burned down, and the Nazis blamed the communists for an act of arson. The Catholic Center Party feared communists more than Nazis and voted to support the Enabling Act that gave Hitler emergency powers. In reality, the Catholic Center Party was voting to abolish democracy in Germany and replace it with a dictatorship of the Nazis. The Catholic Center Party dissolved itself and contributed to the Nazi plan of making Germany a one-party regime. In the summer of the same year (1933), the Vatican and the Nazi Party signed an agreement (Concordat) that protected the church from interference as long as priests did not criticize the government or engage in politics.

Despite the Concordat, the Nazi regime did not trust the institution of the Catholic Church due to its allegiance to Rome. The Nazis wanted to control all the young people of Germany and, as a result, closed many Catholic organizations and enlisted all children and teenagers in various Hitler Youth organizations, where they would be indoctrinated according to the Nazi view of the world.

Overall, more than 2,500 Catholic clergy, most of whom were from Poland where opposition to the Nazis was strong, were sent to Dachau.* A smaller number of Catholic clerical prisoners came from Germany, France, or other European countries.

Pope Pius XII

Perhaps the greatest controversy related to the church and the war revolves around the figure of Pope Pius XII (1876–1958). He became pope in March 1939, just before war started. Prior to his election, he had served as cardinal secretary of state for Pope

The controversy about the relationship between the Nazi regime and the Catholic Church largely started with the signing of the Concordat or understanding of 1933. The Church pledged not to criticize the government in exchange for the protection of church property and privileges. Cardinal Eugenio Pacelli, who later became Pope Pius XII, signed the Concordat, and his political sympathies and actions during the war have remained controversial ever since. (Ullstein bild via Getty Images)

Pius XI. In this capacity he signed the controversial *Reichskonkordat* (State Concordat) between the Vatican and Nazi Germany in the summer of 1933.

Soon after Hitler came to power, the Vatican opened talks with the Nazi government on the terms of an agreement for the protection of the church. The Vatican accepted the Nazis as a strong deterrent to a possible communist government. The Concordat signed in 1933 guaranteed the existence of the Catholic Church in Germany in exchange for a pledge of loyalty by priests to the state. In effect, the agreement stopped priests from political action or from taking an anti-Nazi stand and in return promised that Catholic Churches and educational institutions would remain open. Church property was also guaranteed.

When convenient for them to do so, the Nazis violated the agreement, and some historians question why the Vatican did not immediately protest Nazi mistreatment of priests and nuns, the closing of church schools, the killing of disabled children, or other violations of the Concordat. On a few of these occasions in the 1930s, Pope

Pius XI considered a protest to Hitler but his secretary of state, the future Pius XII, urged moderation and generally talked him out of these actions.

Pius XII remains a controversial figure. His defenders say that he worked behind the scenes against the Nazis, but his critics argue that he did not do enough either secretly or publicly to try to stop Nazi atrocities. For example, while he criticized the T4 euthanasia program in 1943 (see Chapter 9), the program had already been in effect for several years and murdered thousands of children. The pope's defenders point out that he did object to the Nazi policy of killing children with disabilities, but his critics suggest such a position is not really courageous—the issue is whether his protest was strong enough and fast enough to make a difference.

A similar debate continues about the role of Pius XII in regard to the Holocaust.* Critics again argue that Pius XII, who was aware of what was taking place in ghettos* and concentration camps, refused to criticize the Nazis or to defend Jews who were facing persecution and death; his supporters suggest that his method was to work quietly behind the scenes, worried that a public protest would only encourage Nazi revenge.

The debate is centered around a fundamental issue—could or should Pope Pius XII have done more to help those in trouble? One argument in the pope's defense states that it would not have mattered anyway since the Nazis would not have listened to him or anyone else. Another argument claims that the pope would have been put in prison or harmed in some way. Some observers have said that these objections do not matter. They claim that the church has a moral responsibility to take a stand against evil regardless of the consequences, and these voices insist that setting a high moral example is the only issue. To this day, some of the Vatican archives dealing with Pope Pius XII during the war remain closed to scholars.

Bishop Alois Hudal

While the disagreement about the role of Pope Pius XII continues, there is little doubt that there were several Nazi sympathizers in the Catholic Church. Bishop Alois Hudal (1885–1963) was a Nazi supporter who helped known war criminals escape justice.

Born in Austria, Hudal was always pro-German, and he supported the annexation (Anschluss)* of Austria in 1938. His reputation as a collaborator* and Nazi sympathizer comes from his role in what was called the "ratline," a system of Catholic safe houses that aided Nazi war criminals to escape from Europe after the war. Taking advantage of the chaos in Germany in 1945, Nazi officials often disguised themselves and contacted influential friends to help them start the process of getting to South America. The road took those Nazis through Italy, where Hudal ran a seminary that gave them refuge. Hudal wrote letters of recommendation for them and helped them obtain Red Cross documents to facilitate travel. Hudal assisted some of the worst war criminals in world history.

Franz Stangl (1908–1971) was an Austrian-born Nazi who was part of the T4 euthanasia program that killed children with disabilities, and he subsequently ran the Treblinka concentration camp from 1942 to 1943. In 1945 he was arrested by the Allies but escaped to Italy where Hudal helped him go to Syria on a fake Red Cross passport. From there he and his family traveled to Brazil where they lived for twenty years before being extradited back to West Germany. He was convicted of the murder of 400,000 Jews. After a few years in prison, Stangl died of a heart attack in his cell.

Otto Wächter (1901–1949) was an Austrian lawyer, member of the SS, and governor of Kraków under Governor-General Hans Frank. In the latter capacity he ordered 50,000 Jews expelled from the city and then had the remaining 15,000 moved to the ghetto. In 1942, he was appointed governor of Galicia, whose capital was Lemberg (known today as Lviv), which had a large Jewish ghetto that was liquidated. At the end of the war, he was a wanted war criminal, but he escaped to Italy where Bishop Hudal protected him until his death in 1949.

Many other notorious Nazis escaped using the "ratline." Josef Mengele (1911–1979) was the doctor who often waited for the trains to arrive at Auschwitz.* When the cargo doors opened, he and others made the infamous "selection," deciding who would live and who would die. For this reason, he was ironically called the "Angel of Death." He is also known for his cruel medical experiments on inmates and prisoners. After the war, he lived for a few years in Germany and then went to South America. He moved a couple of times but finally settled in Brazil, where recent information suggests that he died in 1979.

Alois Brunner (1912–2001 or 2010) was an Austrian-born SS official who served as a chief aide to Adolf Eichmann. Brunner ran the Drancy* camp north of Paris for one year and also deported Jews to death camps from Vienna, Greece, and Slovakia. After the war, he escaped to Egypt using a false Red Cross passport and then to

Syria, where he became useful to the government there by teaching torture techniques to the local secret police. In interviews in the 1980s, he affirmed his pride in killing Jews and others.

Heinrich Müller (1900–1945?) was born in Munich and became chief of the Gestapo; he attended the Wannsee* Conference that helped to plan the Holocaust. His death date is usually listed as 1945, but there were rumors that he escaped to Panama after the war.

Klaus Barbie (1913–1991) was an SS official who ran the notorious Gestapo headquarters in Lyon, France, where he earned the title "Butcher of Lyon." Most famously, he tortured to death the leader of the French resistance, Jean Moulin. He escaped to Bolivia, where he helped local governments and possibly the CIA to develop torture techniques. Finally extradited to France in 1983, he died in prison in 1991 (see also Chapter 8).

Adolf Eichmann (1906–1962) was an SS official in charge of running the concentration camp system. He escaped to Argentina where he lived for fifteen years before being captured by Mossad, the Israeli intelligence agency, and taken to Israel for trial. During his trial, Eichmann did not deny his role in the Holocaust but claimed he was only following orders. He was convicted and hanged in 1962.

The evidence of a Catholic "ratline" network to assist these criminals is overwhelming, and the actions of Hudal and his helpers were a violation of the essence of religious belief. At the same time, it is important to remember the millions of Catholics from all nations who fought and died to destroy the Nazis, and these sacrifices need to be honored while those of Hudal need to be condemned.

Pastor Martin Niemöller

One of the best-known members of the Lutheran Church in World War II was Martin Niemöller (1892–1984). Born into a religious family, he was an officer on a German submarine in World War I, and between the wars, he followed his father's example and became a Lutheran minister. He disliked Germany's democratic government and at first supported Hitler as the strong leader that Germany needed. One year after Hitler came to power, he started to change his view, and then Niemöller became a founding member of the Confessing Church, led by ministers who split from the mainstream Lutheran churches that were supporting the Nazis. By the mid-1930s, he opposed the Nazi policy of Aryan superiority, although he also made some anti-Semitic statements. Nevertheless, his opposition to the Nazi program led to his arrest and incarceration in concentration camps from 1938 to 1945. After the war, he regretted that he had not opposed the Nazis sooner, and he dedicated his postwar life to world peace. He is best known for his poem written after the war that appears at the top of this chapter. Niemöller rewrote the poem many times and used different groups as examples.

Dietrich Bonhoeffer

Unlike Niemöller, Dietrich Bonhoeffer (1906–1945) was a consistent opponent of the Nazi program. In fact, he was one of the first critics of the Nazis in Germany; only two days after Hitler became chancellor, Bonhoeffer criticized the so-called *führerprinzip* (Führer principle or leadership principle of obedience to Hitler) on German radio. He was also active in the Confessing Church, formed to protect Christianity from Nazi control. Although he was visiting the United States in 1939 and might have remained to avoid arrest, he decided to return to Germany to share the fate of other German Christians who had to face the reality of Nazism and war. He worked with the small German resistance movement and was arrested in 1943. In 1945, only one month before the Nazi regime was destroyed, Hitler personally ordered that Bonhoeffer be killed; he was hanged on April 9, 1945. He remains one of the most admired church opponents of the Nazi regime.

POLAND

Catholic Church

The Nazis did not intend to occupy Poland; they intended to destroy it. Since Poles were on Hitler's list of expendable populations, their culture was also to be destroyed. Hitler was clear about his mission when he spoke to his army shortly before the invasion in 1939: "kill without pity or mercy men, women, and children of Polish descent or language."

The Catholic Church was an integral part of Polish life and culture, making the Nazis suspicious of the important role that it played. They viewed the Polish Catholic Church as a center of opposition to Germany and a supporter of Polish nationalism and independence. Actually, the Germans were correct in their assessment of the church in Poland, since the church opposed the Nazis, the Soviets, and any foreign control of Poland. At the same time, the church also opposed democracy; it supported the restoration of a conservative and Catholic Poland.

In the western part of Poland annexed by Germany, Nazi treatment of the Catholic Church was particularly harsh. Worried that Catholic clergy might organize opposition to their occupation, the Nazis used anti-Catholic propaganda to turn German Protestants against the church. Churches were closed, crucifixes and statues of the Virgin Mary smashed, and religious treasures and holy objects confiscated. Priests who would not accept German rule were arrested, sent to concentration camps, or executed.

Dachau, not far from Munich, was the main camp where priests were imprisoned. Several prison blocks were reserved for clergy, and Block 28 was used for Polish priests. To set an example and teach them a lesson about resistance, priests were subjected to terrible punishments—some were tortured, beaten to death, starved, used for medical experiments, guillotined, or sent to the gas chambers. In this process, more Polish priests were killed than clergy (except rabbis) from any other country.

The Nazis also tried to destroy the church in the area of the General Government under Hans Frank. After one year of Nazi rule in the cities of Poland, the Nazis had killed 50 percent of the clergy in Wroclaw, 48 percent of the clergy in Chelmno, 37 percent of the clergy in Lodz, and 31 percent in Poznan. Four bishops also died in concentration camps.

From the beginning of the war, the Vatican was aware of what was happening because the Catholic Church had a strong network of supporters in every part of Poland. In addition to the murder of priests and nuns, the Germans practiced harassment by limiting church hours, requiring sermons to be in German, and banning certain hymns. Catholic organizations like St. Vincent de Paul, Catholic Action, Pontifical Association for the Propagation of the Faith, the Association of Catholic Women, and Catholic youth groups were abolished. In some cities cathedrals and churches were closed, and Catholics were sometimes arrested just for going to Mass. In a report sent to the pope in 1942, Cardinal August Hlond (1881–1948) concluded that: "Hitlerism aims at the systematic and total destruction of the Catholic Church."

Catholics and Jews

The policy of the Catholic Church toward the Jewish population was inconsistent and for that reason remains controversial. While some Catholic leaders tried to assist Jews in escaping or hiding, others including Cardinal Hlond and Archbishop Adam Sapieha (1867–1951) of Kraków made ambiguous statements about Jews. Both church leaders criticized the Nazis for anti-Catholic actions, but they were not consistently critical regarding anti-Jewish measures.

The Franciscan friar Maximillian Kolbe (1894–1941) stayed in his monastery near Warsaw despite the occupation, but his anti-Nazi writings finally led to his arrest. Sent to Auschwitz, Kolbe was frequently beaten, but he continued to comfort others in his cell. After ten prisoners were sentenced to death by starvation, Kolbe offered to take the place of the prisoner who had a family. The Nazis were glad to dispose of Kolbe, so they granted his request and he died with the other inmates; he was canonized in 1982 by Pope John Paul II. Despite his brave action at Auschwitz, his writings connecting Jews with Freemasons and communists led to controversy at the time of his canonization.

There were Polish groups that did try to help Jews in Poland, but there were others that worked with the Nazis to eliminate them. On the positive side were the Franciscan Sisters of the Family of Mary, whose Mother Superior was Matylda Getter (1870–1968). She helped hide children in her convent and was later recognized as "Righteous Among the Nations."* Sister Anna Borkowska (also Borokowska 1900–1988) was a Dominican nun near Wilno, a city with a large Jewish population. She and the other nuns helped protect seventeen Jewish resistance fighters, and she was also honored as "Righteous Among the Nations" after the war.

The town of Nowogródek near Pinsk in Belarus had a population of 20,000 people, about 50 percent Jewish. The area became part of Poland after 1921, but then it fell within the Soviet occupation zone in September 1939. The German invasion of the USSR in 1941 brought the town back under Nazi control. The Germans moved quickly to destroy the Jewish community; in 1942 all 10,000 Jews were wiped out. The following year the Germans killed some Catholic priests and sentenced 120 more people to death. The Sisters of the Holy Family of Nazareth offered their own lives in exchange for the condemned. The Nazis accepted the offer and sent all the prisoners to labor camps and then arrested the eleven Sisters, drove them in a van to a spot in the woods, and machine-gunned them before dumping their bodies in a mass grave. The Sisters were declared "Blessed" by Pope John Paul II in 2000.

Pope John Paul II (1920–2005) had a personal connection to Catholics who resisted the Nazis. He was born Karol Józef Wojtyła in Wadowice, Poland, and attended university in Kraków. Following the German invasion, the university was closed and Karol worked at a variety of manual jobs for several years. Simultaneously he decided to become a priest, but he had to study secretly due to German restrictions. During these war years Karol knew, befriended, and helped several Polish Jews who were hiding from the Nazis. In 1978 Karol was elected Pope John Paul II. He beatified 108 Catholics who died at the hands of the Nazis, now known as the 108 Blessed Polish Martyrs. John Paul II was canonized in 2014.

Conclusion for Poland

The Catholic Church in Poland was a conservative and patriotic organization, and as such it opposed both Nazi and Soviet occupation. There were priests who collaborated with the Germans but none who supported the Soviet presence. In addition, there were priests who were anti-Semitic, but there were also some who offered assistance to Polish Jews. The Nazis ruled Poland by terror; they were brutal in their treatment of priests, nuns, intellectuals, political leaders, and the Jewish population.

FRANCE

Catholic Church

During World War II, the Catholic Church in France reflected French society and was split into different factions. At first, the prevailing sentiment in the occupied north as well as in the south was support for Pétain as someone who would revive French tradition. The Catholic hierarchy was pleased to find that religious instruction and education returned when the Vichy* regime overturned the law of 1904 that banned religious orders from the educational system. Fear of communist influence within the ranks of soldiers and workers further increased church support for Pétain. Cardinal Baudrillart (1859–1942) was the most vocal on this point. He supported the German invasion of the Soviet Union and applauded those French volunteers who joined the Wehrmacht* and even the SS.* Another French cardinal, Archbishop Emmanuel Suhard (1874–1949), was more liberal and supported the moderate wing of the resistance. He welcomed de Gaulle during the liberation in 1944. Overall, the French Catholic Church, like French society, was divided; some favored the conservative Vichy government, and some wanted the return of democracy. It is not possible to label the entire church as collaborators or resistors.

In the south of France, Jewish refugees found a protector in Father Pierre-Marie Benoît (1895–1990), a Capuchin-Franciscan friar in Marseille. He used his monastery to print false documents, baptismal certificates, and passports for those in danger. Working with the resistance, he was responsible for helping up to 4,000 Jews escape to Switzerland or Spain, in the latter case by printing fake Spanish ancestry documents. In 1966, he was named "Righteous Among the Nations."

Joan of Arc

As in other occupied countries, the French resistance invoked the memory of its heroes to inspire opposition to the Germans. Joan of Arc (1412–1431) was one of the most important French historical figures. A peasant girl who tried to liberate France from the English in the fifteenth century, Joan led French troops to victory, but she was captured and burned at the stake. By coincidence both she and General de Gaulle were born in Lorraine, and the Cross of Lorraine was adopted as the resistance symbol. Joan was canonized in 1920, partly to thank France for its sacrifices in World War I.

Le Chambon-sur-Lignon

In an overwhelmingly Catholic country, the residents of this small village fifty-five miles southwest of Lyon were French Protestants, or Huguenots, who themselves had a history of being persecuted for their beliefs. Led by several local pastors, the entire village participated in a program to give shelter to any refugee who needed help. More than 4,000 came to Chambon, the vast majority being Jewish refugees, seeking such assistance, and not one was ever turned in to the Nazis.

The most prominent pastor in Chambon was André Trocmé, who the day after France signed the armistice announced in his sermon: "The duty of Christians is to resist the violence brought on their consciences, through the weapons of the spirit. We will resist whenever our adversaries demand obedience contrary to the orders of the Gospel. We will do so without fear, without pride, and without hate" (*Christian Science Monitor*, May 15, 2008). This sermon set the tone for what became a united effort by the entire community. Occasionally Nazi patrols entered the area, but due to the town's location on a plateau, there was usually a warning that gave refugees time to hide. Some Jewish families were escorted to Switzerland, but most stayed in this town where no one asked why they were there or what their religion was. If they needed help, they received it with no questions asked. The entire village was declared "Righteous Among the Nations" in 1990.

Only one other village has been honored as "Righteous Among the Nations." Nieuwlande is 100 miles northeast of Amsterdam, and during the occupation a town meeting decided that each local family (just over 100) would take in one Jewish family. Like Le Chambon-sur-Lignon, Nieuwlande was inspired by local resistance leaders and its Dutch Reformed pastor.

NORWAY

Unlike the Lutheran Church in Germany where opposition to the Nazis was the exception, the church in Norway opposed anti-Semitism and the rest of the Nazi message. As in all European countries, there were pro-Nazi and anti-Semitic elements in Norway, but fascist views represented a minority opinion.

Germany invaded Norway on April 9, 1940, and fighting was intense for two months. Finally, King Haakon VII left for England and Bishop of Oslo and Primate of the Church of Norway Eivind Berggrav (1884–1959) agreed to participate in the administration to help to run the country. The Nazis did not accept this arrangement and instead placed the Norwegian collaborator Vidkun Quisling (1887–1945) in power. Quisling was not popular, and his name became synonymous with the word "traitor" (similar to "Benedict Arnold" in American history). When Quisling attempted to impose government control over the church, Lutheran bishops refused to cooperate and resigned from their posts. In 1942 Bishop Berggrav was arrested and isolated from the population. When the pro-Nazi puppet government called for the creation of a Hitler youth organization for Norwegian young people, many parents, teachers, and the Lutheran Church protested.

Theologically, the church in Norway used Martin Luther's teachings as justification for its opposition to the fascist state and its support of the resistance. It is perhaps ironic that in Germany most Lutheran Churches also used Martin Luther's teachings but for the opposite purpose—to justify their support for the state and Nazi policies. After the war Berggrav was recognized both in Norway and in other countries for his heroic stand against the Nazis.

SOVIET UNION

In the 1920s and 1930s, churches in the Soviet Union were persecuted—many were closed and their artworks and religious objects confiscated by the state. In addition, the Soviet government refused to allow a new patriarch to be elected and openly promoted anti-church propaganda. Government opposition to religion changed after the German invasion of June 1941, as the Soviet regime recognized the desperation of the situation and looked for support within the country. Stalin's first address to the Russian people about ten days after the invasion played down appeals to defend communism and instead emphasized the need to defend the Russian motherland. Stalin and his government broadened their patriotic call to all elements of the population, including the Orthodox.

The invasion led to a change in church–state relations and the way that the Soviet government treated the church. Stalin, who had encouraged anti-church actions before the war, reduced anti-religious propaganda and encouraged the church to support the war. He framed the war in nationalistic terms that included the defense of old Russian traditions and values. The Nazis were portrayed as anti-religion and specifically opposed to the Russian Orthodox Church. Both of those accusations were true, but the Soviet government's actual beliefs were not very different. Nevertheless, the Russian church supported the defense of old Russian ways and urged the entire population to join the war effort. Stalin agreed to return church property and to release some priests from prison.

In 1942, the nominal head of the church offered cash donations collected from the clergy to the government for the defense of the country. Stalin responded by allowing the election of a new patriarch. A church council elected Patriarch Sergei (1867–1944) in September 1943. He died in 1944 but Patriarch Alexei (1877–1970) replaced him and served beyond the war until 1970. Both Sergei and Alexei promised church allegiance to the state and the war effort. Of course, they were hoping that restrictions on the church would be lifted after the war.

The Great Patriotic War Museum in Moscow has many displays showing church support for the war. Clergy and church members made donations to the Red Army, including funds for tanks such as the Dmitri Donskoi (Russian military hero of 1380) tank battalion. As relations between church and state improved, clergy were pleased to note that a saint like Alexander Nevsky (Russian military hero of 1242) was treated as a hero and that the song

"Holy War" evoked strong emotions and became popular. At the end of the war several leading clerics in the church received awards and medals for their loyalty and contributions to victory, including the "Medal for the Victory over Germany."

Church and Nationalism

All Soviet soldiers under the age of twenty-five had been brought up in a country that professed atheism. While many in the younger generation considered religion to be a form of superstition, their grandparents had been raised in a religious country before the revolution, and many of them maintained a quiet faith in the Russian Orthodox Church. As a result, religious rituals persisted in the country as they were passed down through the generations. Despite official government opposition, Russian soldiers prayed, crossed themselves before battle, and carried a lucky charm such as a cross or a picture of a saint. One common item was a picture of someone at home wrapped in a copy of the poem "Wait for Me." In the Great Patriotic War Museum in Moscow, a display case includes an icon pendant of the Virgin of Smolensk that was carried by a soldier killed near Novgorod. Unless officers were members of special political units that reflected membership in the Communist Party, they usually ignored religious symbols carried by their soldiers. As the war continued, the Soviet government became tolerant of such behavior, but this type of religious practice was again discouraged when the war ended.

Saints and Heroes

Combined with more tolerance for the church, the Soviet government rehabilitated Russian heroes from previous centuries. All of them had fought against foreign enemies, and the first two had already been canonized by the Orthodox Church. Soviet officials created awards and medals named for Alexander Nevsky (1221–1263) who was famous for repelling the Teutonic Knights in 1242, Dmitri Donskoi (1350–1389) who defeated the Tatars in 1380, Minin and Pozharsky who fought foreign invasion to end the Time of Troubles in 1612, General Alexander Suvorov (1730–1800) who engaged in sixty battles with no losses in the late eighteenth century, and General Mikhail Kutuzov (1745–1813) who helped Russia drive Napoleon out of the country in 1812. The choices of Nevsky and Donskoi for medals added a religious dimension to the patriotic connotation for the population. To encourage sacrifice on the battlefield, soldiers received other incentives for heroic behavior; earning a medal might also include a leave or food for their family.

BELGIUM

Belgium is composed of two linguistic areas—the Flemish in the north who speak Dutch and Walloons in the south who speak French. The primary religion is Catholic for both groups, and the church during the war was led by the anti-fascist Cardinal Jozef-Ernst Cardinal van Roey (1874–1961). When a fascist political party gained support especially in the south (Walloon), Cardinal van Roey intervened and ordered Catholics not to vote for its candidates. During the war, he criticized the occupation regime for its treatment of Jews and urged Catholics to oppose anti-Semitism. Nevertheless, 30–40 percent (25,000) of Belgium's prewar Jewish population died in the camps.

Joseph André (1908–1973) was a Belgian priest who also worked to save Jewish children during the war. He established a youth center that provided refuge for Jewish children and teens who needed shelter. They stayed within his protective care until more permanent sanctuary on farms or other locations could be found. It is ironic that André's headquarters was next door to the Gestapo building in Namur, about forty-five miles from Brussels. In 1967, André was named "Righteous Among the Nations."

THE NETHERLANDS

The Netherlands was divided between Protestants in the north and Catholics in the south, but the majority of churches on both sides opposed fascism. During the occupation, church leaders sent letters to the Nazi ruler Seyss-Inquart protesting against German atrocities. Sermons encouraged parishioners to assist people who were hiding from the Nazis.

Shortly after the occupation started, Protestant church leaders sent representatives to consult with Karl Barth (1886–1968) in Switzerland. Barth was a famous and influential moral force in the Protestant Church. Barth told the delegates that resistance was not voluntary—it was necessary. Some parishioners took this advice seriously. For example, Hilde Dekker was interviewed after the war: "It gave me courage when a church minister openly called on people to resist." Hendrica de Visser added that being in church helped with a sense of togetherness and community. "That gave me strength to go on." She included the queen and people in need in her prayers at night (Verzetsmuseum Resistance Museum).

The Catholic Church was also strong in its opposition to the Nazis. After the invasion of the Netherlands in May 1940, the Church excommunicated Dutch Nazis and opposed the Nazi plan to take over education. Archbishop Johannes de Jong (1885–1955) was a leader in the anti-Nazi movement that condemned both the sending of workers to Germany and the deportation of Jews to concentration camps, and he provided funds for the "lifeline" program that helped downed Allied pilots get to safety. When a statement against racism was read in Dutch Catholic Churches in 1942, the regime of the Nazi ruler Seyss-Inquart retaliated by arresting 250 Jewish converts to Catholicism.

The most famous of those taken into custody was Edith Stein (1891–1942), who was born into a Jewish family in territory that was German at that time but is in Poland today. After World War I, Stein converted to Catholicism and entered a Carmelite monastery in Germany. After the Nazis came to power, Stein was transferred to a monastery in the Netherlands for safety, but when the Bishops Conference publicly opposed Nazi racism, Seyss-Inquart ordered the deportation of all of the converts. Stein was sent to Auschwitz where she was immediately killed in the gas chamber. She was canonized by Pope John Paul II in 1998.

Despite the position of most Dutch churches against the Nazi program, there were collaborators in the Protestant and Catholic communities. Members of the NSB (Dutch fascists) might go to church in the morning and participate in hate crimes in the afternoon. That situation was similar in every European country under occupation, where seemingly good Christians joined in military or police actions in conflict with church doctrine. At the same time, many other Europeans were motivated by faith to join the resistance.

CROATIA AND SLOVAKIA

The Catholic Church was completely allied with the Nazis in Croatia and Slovakia. Croatia was controlled by an extreme right-wing party called Ustashe* that established its own concentration camp to kill Serbs, Jews, Roma,* and others. A Franciscan priest, Miroslav Filipovic, ran the camp and supervised the killing of 30,000 people. He was hanged as a war criminal after the war, but many other

Catholic collaborators from Croatia used the "ratline" to escape to safety in South America.

Like Croatia, Slovakia was the result of the partition of a larger state. When Czechoslovakia was occupied in 1939, Slovakia separated and became an independent pro-Nazi state. Priests and the church hierarchy supported the anti-Semitic and ethnic cleansing policies of this fascist country.

Parishioners

What was it like to go to church during the war? In general, church attendance increased as families prayed for a loved one who might be in battle, wounded, or a prisoner. Even on a weekday, many individuals entered Catholic Churches to light a candle and pray for a soldier, or a Protestant church to say a silent prayer for the same reason. In small towns, assuming the church had not been bombed or destroyed, attendance increased but was not dramatically different from prewar days. Older women were in attendance, but men were generally at war and absent from services. It is not difficult to imagine an elderly woman with a scarf on her head and tied under her chin going to church on Sunday morning but walking straight home after Mass to avoid trouble with Nazi soldiers.

In larger cities, German troops generally stayed out of sight but watched suspicious clergy. Gestapo agents not in uniform infiltrated services, listened to sermons, or mingled with parishioners hoping to overhear information. The Nazis did not trust either the Catholic or Protestant church as institutions, but they were reluctant to close or interfere with specific churches unless they had evidence of resistance activity. For example, the mayor and the priest in Ste.-Mère-Église in Normandy were both members of the resistance; the small church in the center of town sometimes served as a meeting place, and a visitor even now can see the bullet holes from 1944 that remain in the stone walls.

In France, religious pilgrimage became more popular than before the war, with visits to Lourdes dramatically increased. As a form of religious devotion, a statue of the Virgin Mary called "Notre-Dame de Boulogne" was pulled by barefoot men through a variety of cities before its arrival at Lourdes.

In other parts of Europe, especially in the east, church attendance was more difficult. Many Polish churches had been closed, and in the Soviet Union Stalin did not encourage church-going despite better relations with the Orthodox clergy. While we know that no synagogues were left open in occupied Europe, we have testimony from survivors of the ghettos and the concentration camps of religious services and education continuing despite the war. According to Elie Wiesel in *Night*, there were arguments in the camps about fasting on Yom Kippur despite the fact that most inmates were starving to death.

CONCLUSION

There was no single church response across Europe—cooperation or opposition to Nazi occupation varied from country to country. Church hierarchies as well as individual priests and ministers responded in a variety of ways to the Nazi presence, some with passive compliance, others by collaboration, and still others with resistance. As we have seen, German churches used the words of Martin Luther to justify attacks on German Jews, while Norwegian churches also appealed to Martin Luther's writings to condemn attacks against Jews and others. Similarly, there were Catholic leaders who opposed anti-Semitism and tried to protect Jews, and there were also Catholic officials who accepted ethnic cleansing that included the killing of Jews, Roma, and others. The Catholic Churches in Belgium and the Netherlands opposed collaboration, while the church in France was as divided as the rest of French society. In Eastern Europe, the situation was quite different. In states like Slovakia and Croatia, the Catholic Church worked closely with regimes run by murderers, and when the war ended the "ratline" helped some brutal criminals escape justice. The Soviet Union, officially an atheist regime, turned to the Russian Orthodox Church for support during the fighting, but quickly brought the church back under control when victory was assured. Finally, Poland was caught between so many conflicting trends that it is difficult to categorize everything that transpired: the Church itself was a victim of both German and Soviet oppression, but within the Church there were elements who hoped for a Catholic-only Poland. The Church also produced priests and nuns who sacrificed their own lives to save others, and some have been recognized as martyrs of the church.

The Nazis were clearly an evil presence that carried out aggressive war and mass murder. Churches are moral institutions that must uphold ethical principles and provide leadership for parishioners. Many historians wonder why any church cooperated with the Nazis. Whatever reason or excuse a church had for cooperating, their response was hypocritical for an institution that teaches love, sharing, good works, and other ideals of how to live a proper life. While it remains important to criticize the churches that went along or collaborated with Nazi policies, it is also necessary to honor the individual members of the clergy who sacrificed their lives and stood up to Nazi tyranny.

Many parishioners found comfort in religion during the war, but Christians heard a variety of messages depending on where they lived and the view of their local church and clergy; some sermons were consistent with Christian ideals of love and mercy, and some encouraged hatred and vengeance. The concentration camps were physical threats to the Jewish population of Europe, but assisting or ignoring genocide was a spiritual threat to the intrinsic meaning and conscience of the theology of Christianity.

FURTHER READING

Bank, Jan with Lieve Gevers. *Churches and Religion in the Second World War*. Translated by Brian Doyle. London: Bloomsbury, 2016.

Hassing, Arne. *Church Resistance to Nazism in Norway, 1940–1945*. Seattle: University of Washington Press, 2014.

Kosmala, Beate and Georgi Verbeeck, eds. *Facing the Catastrophe: Jews and Non-Jews in Europe During World War II*. Oxford: Berg, 2011.

Madigan, Kevin J. "How the Catholic Church Sheltered Nazi War Criminals." *Commentary*, December 1, 2011.

Marquand, Robert. "A Protestant Town's 'Conspiracy of Good' in Vichy France." *Christian Science Monitor*, May 15, 2008.

Merridale, Catherine. *Ivan's War: Life and Death in the Red Army, 1939–1945*. New York: Picador, 2006.

Schnitker, Harry. "Catholic Church in WWII." *Catholic News Agency*, 2011.

Verzetsmuseum Resistance Museum, Amsterdam. https://www.verzets museum.org/museum/en/exhibitions/the-netherlands-in-ww2

Warsaw Uprising Museum, Warsaw. https://www.1944.pl/en/article/the-warsaw-rising-museum,4516.html

8

RESISTANCE LIFE

It would be impertinent for a country that did not suffer occupation to judge one that has.
Former British prime minister Anthony Eden,
interview in The Sorrow and the Pity, 1971

INTRODUCTION

Historians today challenge the categories of resistance and collaboration as too simplistic. Responses to the Nazis were more complicated and nuanced than either of those two positions. The majority of Europeans did not choose collaboration or resistance, but something in-between—not cooperating with the Nazis but also not going to the mountains and joining a military unit. Reactions to the occupation were varied, as people adjusted to the new reality, mostly without liking it, and in some cases waited for an opportunity to act against the oppressors. Like other aspects of daily lives, the more closely we examine this topic, the more likely we are to realize the difficulty of establishing a single standard or conclusion. Nevertheless, in this chapter we will use the terms "collaborator" and "resistance" when appropriate, but mindful of the restrictions and limitations that those labels entail.

GERMANY

Is it appropriate to include Germany in this section? "Collaborator" usually means someone in a foreign country who supports the occupiers, and therefore there is no perfect term for the millions of Germans who endorsed the Nazi program. Historians and psychologists have commented on the ecstatic faces that greeted Hitler, the cheers of "Sieg Heil"* (Hail Victory) wherever he went, the torchlight parades, and the participation of average Germans in brutal and horrific activities. After the war, many Germans claimed that they did not know what was happening, but historians have demonstrated that Nazi propaganda clearly stated the goals of the party for everyone. The speeches by Goebbels promising a Germany without Jews, the disappearance of neighbors, the train traffic to Poland, and the thousands of direct participants in the Einsatzgruppen* and concentration camps suggest support that contradicts most excuses.

We cannot say that every German knew everything, and we similarly cannot say that everyone in Germany agreed with all the details of the Nazi agenda. We can say, however, that the Nazi Party was German, millions of Germans voted for the Nazis, and millions more supported their activities. Germans were aware of Hitler's plans because *Mein Kampf** was widely distributed (free to soldiers and newlyweds in the 1930s), and Nazi propaganda was seen and heard constantly throughout the country. The German army fought to the last day, and their claim after the war that they were only afraid of Russians does not explain their tenacity on the western front from D-Day to the Battle of the Bulge* to Berlin.

Two Stories of Resistance

Other than the Confessing Church (see Chapter 7), there were two resistance events that were important. In 1942, a few university students led by brother and sister Hans Scholl (1918–1943) and Sophie Scholl (1921–1943) distributed mimeographed pamphlets denouncing the policies of the regime. This student-generated opposition was the most significant resistance movement in Germany during the war. Their protest documents condemned the genocide taking place for purely moral reasons, and this opposition took place while Germany was still winning and Hitler remained popular. Sophie Scholl's group, named for its symbol the White Rose, was centered at the University of Munich, where a janitor saw the students leaving pamphlets and reported them to the Gestapo. Each resistor was tortured and eventually confessed, but without informing on the others. They were all given an appearance, not a trial, in front of a Nazi judge who spent his time calling them traitors. Sentenced to death, they were killed almost immediately by guillotine; Sophie was twenty-one. Her brother was three years older.

In July 1944, a group of officers tried to assassinate Hitler, but the attempt failed. Colonel Claus von Stauffenberg (1907–1944) left a briefcase with a bomb next to the table where Hitler was holding a meeting, but when the bomb exploded, the heavy table leg protected Hitler and he received only minor injuries. The officers were arrested, brutally tortured, and killed. Stauffenberg, who had lost his right eye and part of his right arm in North Africa previously, was executed by firing squad. (Their attempt was made into a movie with Tom Cruise called *Operation Valkyrie*.)

Operation Valkyrie took place late in the war, after the successful D-Day landing of the western Allies, and while the Soviet army was pushing the Wehrmacht out of Russia. Some German officers wanted to kill Hitler so they could offer peace to the west and throw their strength against the Red Army. Unlike the White Rose, the officers in 1944 were not simply motivated by morality; rather they did not want to be defeated as in 1918. They were seeking to overthrow Hitler, take power, and position Germany for a way out of the war that preserved German military pride. During the Cold War, the United States promoted the action of these officers to prove to Americans and Europeans that the German military could be trusted to fight the Russians.

The White Rose, however, opposed the Nazis even when Germany was winning; White Rose was morally opposed to the Nazi and German agenda, and these young students died for their principles. They were genuine resistance heroes.

FRANCE

In World War I, France and its allies fought Germany to a stalemate for four years, and therefore many French citizens were shocked and confused by the collapse of Allied defenses in 1940. As German troops poured into the country, both the French military and the government were in disarray. With the chaos of defeat came economic collapse, as thousands of people became refugees and fled south in what the French call the "Exodus."* Soon, most of the French army was in captivity in Germany, and the nation was unsure what to do next. Desperate to reassure the people, the cabinet and parliament (Chamber of Deputies) gave control to a French general who established a new government with its capital in Vichy.* According to Marshal Philippe Pétain (1856–1951), the southern part of the country would be reborn in line with traditional principles, including love of country, hard work, and the Catholic religion; Pétain told everyone to resume a normal life. For French veterans of World War I, this advice was not immediately easy to accept.

Pétain and de Gaulle

At the same time that Pétain was reassuring the nation that Nazi occupation presented an opportunity to rebuild society, General Charles de Gaulle (1890–1970) broadcast from London on BBC radio on June 18, 1940, urging the formation of immediate resistance to German control. An officer in the French army, de Gaulle left France rather than serve the pro-German Vichy government, and his speech famously told the French people that while they had lost a battle they had not lost the war. He called on the population to continue the struggle. This speech helped create an organized resistance movement, known as the Free French, with de Gaulle as its leader and the Cross of Lorraine as its symbol (see Chapter 7). While he was not that well known in June 1940, eventually de Gaulle emerged as the most important and famous French leader of the war.

At first, many people felt that Pétain made a reasonable case for cooperation and de Gaulle's appeal for resistance appeared to be unrealistic. Certainly it appeared that Germany was on the verge of total victory after France surrendered. One year later everything started to change: England did not surrender, the Soviet Union was invaded but not defeated, the United States entered the war, and the true nature of German occupation was increasingly revealed.

Nevertheless, resistance in France was limited until 1941 because the neutral position of the Soviet Union was imposed on French communists who took their orders from Moscow. When Germany invaded the Soviet Union, communists across the continent were encouraged to rise up and fight the Nazis. French communists became an important part of the resistance.

In November 1942 after the Allies invaded North Africa (Operation Torch),* German troops occupied the southern half of France. Officially, the Vichy government continued to operate and control local affairs in France despite the presence of German troops, but in reality, the Germans increasingly ran the show. German repressive actions, now prevalent in the south as well as the north, led to greater anti-German feelings and strengthened the resistance forces. As the military landscape started to change in the Soviet Union during 1942–1943, and the possibility of German defeat seemed realistic for the first time, mental attitudes in France were transformed.

After the Battle of Stalingrad* in 1943, the supposedly invincible Wehrmacht retreated, and it never regained the initiative or its military reputation of superiority. Those two events—the German invasion of the Soviet Union and the subsequent Wehrmacht defeat at Stalingrad—energized communist resistors and anti-Nazi movements everywhere. Armed struggle and resistance became a realistic possibility; liberation seemed to be increasingly worth fighting for.

Daily Life in the Resistance

Every country in Europe produced a resistance movement, but only a few of them became famous due to size and effectiveness. One of the best-known resistance organizations operated in France, where it played a role in disrupting German military operations.

The life of a resistance fighter involved bravery and risk. That combination gave resistance a certain romantic allure, especially in the movies, but in real life there was little romanticism in running from the Gestapo. Resistance was perilous from morning to night, regardless of whether the fighter worked in Paris, in the countryside, in Vichy territory, or along the borders. Each venue demanded different sacrifices, but they were all dangerous due to constant German patrols looking for people who appeared suspicious or were traveling without proper identity papers.

In Paris, the resistance operated literally underground, sometimes using the sewer system or the catacombs. Each resistance cell was made up of only a few people, and each individual member knew only one or two other fighters. If arrested and tortured, resistance members would not be able to give up a whole list of names since they had only one contact. Women were always active and welcome in the resistance, often carrying messages; some German soldiers were reluctant to search women too closely. A woman on a bicycle with information hidden in a food basket or under the seat or inside her clothing might get through German lines more easily than a man would, but there were no guarantees for anyone. Women also engaged in combat, a practice they were not permitted in the regular military.

The resistance needed a variety of talents. Children could also pass through German lines with less scrutiny than a man might attract, whereas single French men walking alone or on a bicycle were always suspect and would be searched. Beyond messengers, the resistance needed many other specialists, including radio and broadcast technicians, weapons experts, forgers to make fake documents, providers of safe houses, medical technicians, and guides to lead downed pilots across country to the border. Each job was difficult, endangering the fighters and their families.

Individual Stories

A few resistance fighters became famous and have monuments in their name. Thousands more remain little known yet demonstrated amazing courage and died for their cause. Jacques Sabine joined the resistance when he was only sixteen years old. He performed several acts of sabotage against the Germans, including stealing fuel and ammunition. Arrested in 1943, Sabine was moved from prison to prison. After trying to escape, he was subjected to harsh treatment and died in 1944. He left a note for his brother asking forgiveness for any pain his death caused the family and especially imploring that the news of his own death be given carefully to their mother. "You may tell them that I die without regret. . . . Men are not just. At this moment I am not suffering although I spit up small amounts of my life blood that cannot be replaced. . . . Do not lament my death—I die with courage" (Memorial to French Civilians in the War, Falaise, France).

Unlike young Jacques Sabine, Jean Moulin (1899–1943) may be the most famous of all French resistance heroes. Arrested early in the war, Moulin slit his own throat rather than submit to Nazi torture, and the Nazis left him to die in a hospital. He recovered and escaped, but always wore a scarf to cover the scar; his scarf and a hat became his trademarks.

French resistance forces were split into several sections, but Moulin threw his support behind de Gaulle. In an attempt to unite the different resistance groups, Moulin called a meeting of all factions in the city of Lyon in 1943. It is still not known who betrayed Moulin to the Nazis, but the Gestapo raided the meeting and Moulin was arrested. He could not escape torture carried out by the sadistic Nazi Klaus Barbie (1913–1991). Known as the "Butcher of

Lyon," Barbie enjoyed supervising interrogations himself, and his questioning and torture of Moulin led to the death of the resistance leader.

Jean Moulin and Jacques Sabine both died bravely. Moulin became the symbol and martyr of the resistance, and he is currently buried in the Panthéon, the mausoleum for France's greatest heroes. Klaus Barbie escaped to South America, where he taught dictators in Bolivia how to use torture to elicit confessions. He lived in relative comfort for thirty-five years but was finally sent back to France in the 1980s. Barbie was sentenced to life in prison, where he died in 1991 (see Chapter 7).

D-Day and France 1944

Probably the most famous example of resistance came in 1944, when the Allies sent a signal to the French resistance that the invasion known as D-Day would begin soon. The coded message was broadcast over BBC radio as part of the poem "Chanson d'automne," by the nineteenth-century poet Paul Verlaine (1844–1896). The opening lines were sent on June 1 as a preliminary alert that the invasion would take place during the next two weeks, but on June 5 the next lines were broadcast to indicate that the invasion would begin within forty-eight hours. When the resistance heard "Blessent mon coeur, d'une langueur, monotone" (wound my heart with a monotonous languor), they understood that they were to blow up railway lines to prevent German reinforcements from rushing toward the beaches in the north.

Nazis in Paris monitored BBC radio and also heard the broadcast, but the Wehrmacht leadership could not agree on its meaning or its importance. Because the weather report called for storms over the English Channel, German officers did not expect imminent Allied action. Another factor working against the Germans was that General Erwin Rommel (1891–1944), in charge of the Normandy beaches, was in Germany to celebrate his wife's birthday. By the time Rommel returned to France, the massive invasion force had crossed the English Channel and landed on the Normandy beaches on June 6, 1944.

Liberation of Paris

General de Gaulle insisted that the Allies send forces to liberate Paris. General Eisenhower was reluctant to divert the Allied military toward Paris, arguing that it was not a strategic target and that moving directly east toward Germany was more important. General de Gaulle maintained that Paris was a symbol of freedom to people all over the world and had to be saved. In addition, de Gaulle pointed out that if he did not get to Paris quickly and take command, two serious problems would occur: Germans would destroy the beautiful capital and French communists in the resistance would grab control of Paris. Based on these arguments, Eisenhower agreed to provide support for the French Second Armored Division in its advance toward the city. In the disagreement between Eisenhower and de Gaulle, the French general was more perceptive, and when he arrived in Paris, he was able to prevent a communist takeover; in addition, the city was not destroyed.

The resistance in Paris played an important role in defeating the remaining Wehrmacht troops in the city, although not before the Nazis executed all of their French prisoners. According to some reports, the Nazis had several of the major monuments and buildings wired with explosives; Hitler wanted the city destroyed rather than surrendered. There are two versions of what happened next: either the German general in charge (Dietrich von Choltitz 1894–1966) planned to blow up the city but was arrested before he could give the order, or he never intended to use explosives and stalled until he was arrested. After being arrested, he asserted that the second version was correct and he had refused an order to use the explosives; some skeptics believe that it is likely that he was trying to save himself from prison with that claim. In any case, the resistance again played a crucial role in the liberation of France by rising up and helping to secure Paris for the Allies (the book *Is Paris Burning?* describes a phone call from Hitler who is screaming at the German general and demanding that he give the order to destroy the monuments of Paris).

Charles de Gaulle

General de Gaulle emerged as the leading French hero of the war. When most of the French military and political establishments had given up in 1940, de Gaulle went to London and called for resistance. Often using French colonies in North Africa as a base of operations, de Gaulle worked tirelessly for the liberation of his country. When he arrived in Paris in August 1944, de Gaulle walked from the Arc de Triomphe down the Champs-Élysées,* surrounded by thousands of jubilant Parisians and ignoring the threat of German snipers. He completed his victorious entry into the city at Notre-Dame Cathedral with a celebratory Mass. This euphoric moment in French history is commemorated in two places along the Champs-Élysées today: the words of de Gaulle's radio broadcast from London in June 1940 calling on the nation not to surrender are engraved on a plaque under the Arc de Triomphe; a statue of de Gaulle striding down the avenue can be found on the corner next to the Grand Palais.

Women in the Resistance

Recognized by burial in the Panthéon in Paris in 2014, Geneviève de Gaulle-Anthonioz (1920–2002) was a committed fighter for the resistance. She never wavered in her dislike of Pétain and

The invasion of southern France, code named Operation Dragon (originally Anvil), started in August 1944, two months after the landing in Normandy. With significant help from the French resistance, the allies took the important ports of Marseille and Toulon. These resistance fighters (women made up 15% of the resistance) emerged to celebrate the victory in Marseille. (Bettmann/Getty Images)

joined with other young Catholic resistors in the *Défense de la France* organization that printed its own newspapers. She distributed the papers personally and was caught with copies in the summer of 1943. After time in prison, she was sent to the concentration camp for women at Ravensbrück.* After the war she spent thirty years as president of a charity, Aide *Toute Detresse* that helped the poor.

Germaine Tillion (1907–2008) shared some attributes with Geneviève de Gaulle-Anthonioz. Tillion was a resistance member aligned with a group of intellectuals and scientists at the Museum of Man in Paris. Most of the members, including Tillion, were arrested in 1942; Tillion was sent to Ravensbrück concentration camp. She spent three years in the camp. After World War II she called for an end to the civil war in Algeria.

Josephine Baker (1906–1975) was a resistance fighter who came from the ranks of the entertainment world. Although not French, Baker began to work for French intelligence shortly after the start of the war. Her glamorous lifestyle gave her access to parties and receptions with diplomats from many countries, where she often overheard conversations that she passed on to her contacts. When the Germans occupied France, she moved south but continued to be an informant for the Allies, writing important information in invisible ink on her sheet music or pinning notes inside her clothes for transmission. In 1941, she moved to Morocco in North Africa where she performed for Allied soldiers. The French government recognized her after the war with several medals, including the "Croix de Guerre" and the "Chevalier of the Legion of Honor."

Collaboration

Certainly the most famous collaborator* in France was Marshal Pétain, who viewed Germany as a model for the regeneration of France. In 1940 he established his government in the resort town of Vichy in the Hotel du Parc, considered the best hotel in the city. The Vichy government's pretense of independence was shattered by Pétain's personal meeting with Hitler in October 1940 and his government's anti-Jewish actions. Pétain lost his fame and luster in French history by siding with the fascists in World War II. Nevertheless, due to his age and reputation, he was not executed after the war, as his prime minister Pierre Laval (1883–1945) and some other collaborators were. The French paid a high price for the collaboration of Vichy, transferring 400 million francs per day to Germany and supplying the Nazi war machine with weapons from French industry. In addition to economic subservience, Vichy collaborated by implementing anti-Semitic social laws that discriminated against Jews and sent them to concentration camps. The Vichy regime established a militia organization called the Milice,* a French version of the Gestapo that resorted to torture and assassination against the resistance.

Collaborators: Paul Touvier and Maurice Papon

Two notorious collaborators were Paul Touvier (1915–1996) and Maurice Papon (1910–2007). Touvier was in charge of the Milice, the French militia that used Gestapo methods in the city of Lyon, where Klaus Barbie ran the Gestapo that tortured Jean Moulin to death. At the end of the war, the government sentenced Touvier to death, but he escaped, went into hiding, and was protected by Catholic organizations. His pardon by French president Georges Pompidou in 1971 was so controversial that his case was reopened and he was arrested again and eventually died in prison.

Papon was a high-ranking Vichy official in charge of so-called Jewish Affairs in the Bordeaux area. In this capacity he oversaw the deportation of Jewish families to Drancy* in Paris and subsequently to Auschwitz.* Despite his record of complicity in genocide, he escaped punishment for several decades after the war and had a long career as police chief of Paris, government official, and recipient of many awards and honors. In the early 1980s his war record was revealed and after a long trial he was convicted. He spent only a short time in prison due to his age and health.

How did collaborators such as Touvier and Papon avoid punishment for so long? The postwar French government wanted to move the country toward normalcy as quickly as possible. They wanted to forget about the war as it inevitably raised memories of France's defeat and even humiliation. Ignoring history left the role of many citizens unexamined. If the government was not going to verify what people did during the war, then everyone could claim innocence or even a role in the resistance. By ending the search for collaborators, the Fourth and Fifth Republics allowed politicians, actors, and artists to resume their prewar lives as if the war had been a small obstacle in their careers.

French Gestapo or Carlingue (Reference to Part of an Airplane)

The French Gestapo was run by criminals, scoundrels, opportunists, and gangsters. They worked in collaboration with the German Gestapo and were valued by the Nazis for their contacts not available to Germans. Their address at 93, rue Lauriston became well known and feared in Paris. The leaders included Pierre Bonny, a former policeman known for corruption; Henri Lafont, a known criminal; and Pierre Loutrel, whose illegal exploits earned him the nickname of "mad" (crazy). They used extortion to accumulate wealth by arresting resistance fighters or Jews and then collecting ransom from their families. Then they killed the prisoner anyway. After the liberation of Paris some of these collaborators were arrested and shot for their crimes against the French nation, but it was probably impossible to find and execute all 30,000 members of this sadistic organization.

German Retaliation and Tulle Massacre

In the spring of 1944, German occupation forces began a campaign to eliminate the French resistance. On June 9, the notoriously cruel Second SS Panzer Division Das Reich moved against the territory near Tulle in south-central France. The SS arrested all men between 16 and 60, hanged 99 of them, and sent 149 to Dachau.*

German Retaliation and Oradour-sur-Glane*

Shortly after the Tulle Massacre, the same SS Division destroyed the town of Oradour-sur-Glane, killing almost 650 residents. Everyone in the village was ordered to appear in the square in front of the church for a check of documents. Women and children were locked in the church, and men were locked in barns. To start the massacre, German machine gunners shot into the barns and then set them on fire; the machine gunners waited outside for escapees who were killed as they ran. The church was treated differently; it was set on fire first, with the women and children inside, while machine gunners waited outside in case anyone tried to get out through a window. The village today is preserved as a war memorial, with burned-out shells of buildings visible as a reminder of the Nazi occupation.

German Retaliation and Vercors

The fight over Vercors (near Grenoble), a pro-resistance territory in southeastern France, culminated in a massacre in July 1944. In April, the Milice or pro-German Vichy police went on the offensive in this area, attacking the village of Vassieux. On the eve of D-Day in June, BBC radio called on resistance fighters of the Vercors region to support the invasion. In early July, Vercors declared its independence from German control, but the occupying forces were determined to destroy this insurrection before it spread. The Germans sent 10,000 pro-Nazi Russian and Ukrainian soldiers to suppress the movement, and hundreds of resistance fighters, as well as local villagers, were executed.

Anti-Vichy Music

Songs often boosted the morale of the resistance. The most famous music came from a Russian émigré who grew up in France. Anna Betulinskaia was born in Petrograd (St. Petersburg/Leningrad) in 1917 about the time when the Bolsheviks came to power. Her family left the country and she was raised in France, where she changed her surname to Marly. She lived as a songwriter, but she moved from France to London soon after the Nazis arrived. She associated herself with the French resistance overseas, and in 1941 was inspired by reports about Russian partisans who were fighting the Wehrmacht. As she stated after the war: "I had fled Paris when the Nazis occupied the city. In London, I was eagerly following the progress of the war by reading newspapers. One day I read about the partisans in the former Soviet Union where I was born. I was so impressed by how the Russians were defending their country against the onslaught of the German army" (Kirkup, 2006).

She wrote two songs that are easily confused with each other: one was called "The March of the Partisans," and the other was named "The Lament of the Partisan." The songs were played on BBC radio, and the French resistance adopted "The March of the Partisans" as its anthem but called it "The Song of the Partisans." The song warns of the dark flight of the crows (Luftwaffe)* flying over the country (France) that is in chains. It asks all citizens to rise up with guns, grenades, and other weapons and kill the invaders. With France still occupied and liberation only a dream for the future, it is not difficult to understand the popularity of this call for resistance. The lyrics were intended to rally the French people.

Marly's second song, "The Lament of the Partisan," imagines the thoughts of a solitary resistance fighter. In these lyrics, when the Nazis invade and demand surrender, the individual partisan must decide what sacrifices he is willing to make for the future and the potential liberation of France.

After the war, the French resistance anthem "The Song of the Partisans" was recorded by several well-known performers, and it was also played during a film made in 1997 about the resistance fighter Lucie Aubrac. "The Lament of the Partisan" gained international fame when it was recorded by both Leonard Cohen and Joan Baez as "The Partisan."

In June 2000, at the age of eighty-three, Marly was invited to Paris to sing "The Song of the Partisans" to mark the sixtieth anniversary of General de Gaulle's famous speech of 1940 calling on France to continue the struggle against Germany.

BELGIUM

It is difficult to imagine the daily danger and intrigue faced by Aline Micheline Dumon (sometimes spelled Dumont) (1921–2017). Born in Brussels in 1921, she devoted the war years to helping Allied pilots shot down over Belgium. She was part of an underground organization called the "Comet Line" that led 750 pilots through France to Spain and back to England, and she was personally responsible for saving 250 of them. In the process she was followed by Nazi agents, almost captured, and fought against double agents within her own group who were trying to destroy the entire operation.

Known as Michou or Lily, she was barely five feet tall and was mistaken for being younger than her real age. Nazis rarely stopped her because they did not think that someone who looked fifteen would be involved in such activities.

She started her resistance actions in 1942 after her parents and sister were arrested for their opposition to the Nazis. Working with many other women in the Comet Line, Lily soon became one of its leaders, and as a result she was constantly on the run from the Gestapo. Despite the dangers, she found sympathetic doctors who agreed to treat wounded pilots, and then she would lead the pilots to secure safe houses while forging identification papers for them; finally, she would guide them through the country crawling with German patrols toward the French border. In preparation for being stopped and questioned, she instructed the pilots, especially

Americans unfamiliar with European customs, how to behave. For example, the American flyers had to learn to eat without switching their fork to their right hand, how to hold a cigarette, how to wear a beret, and how to keep their hands on the table when eating and out of their pockets when walking.

Nazi spies were constantly after Lily and the Comet Line. Several of her agents were captured and shot, and some pilots were also caught. She had personal close calls as well, with her most dangerous encounter in Paris when she spotted a member of her own group who turned out to be a German spy. She closed in to keep an eye on him, but he saw her and came in her direction. As he ran toward her, she quickly ducked into a metro station and disappeared into a crowd on the train. She could see the spy looking for her, but as she was only five feet tall, she hid in the middle of a group of travelers and he never spotted her. Nevertheless, she knew that her identity had been discovered, and she had to follow her own escape route to Spain and safety in England. Her bravery and contributions were recognized with several awards after the war.

Train Attack

The Belgian resistance carried out a unique action in April 1943. A train known as the Twentieth Convoy was carrying over 1,600 Belgian Jews, Roma,* and other prisoners to Auschwitz when it was intercepted and stopped by a few resistance fighters. The lightly guarded train was held long enough to allow two hundred Jews and other prisoners to escape. After a short time, the train continued on its way to the camp, where one thousand Jews and several hundred Roma were killed. About half of those who had escaped the train survived the war, but some of the resistance heroes were captured and executed.

CZECHOSLOVAKIA

A brave act of resistance took place in Prague in 1942. The Allies planned to assassinate Reinhard Heydrich (1904–1942), one of the most notorious war criminals of the twentieth century. He was a cold-blooded killer who helped build the Gestapo into an organization that used torture. Among all of his evil acts, his supervision of the Wannsee Conference* in January 1942 might be the most heinous. In an attempt to organize the killing of all of Europe's Jewish population, and to do so "efficiently," Heydrich brought together the heads of various German departments that could contribute to this project. He wanted to coordinate the actions of these different agencies to streamline the process that the Nazis called the "final solution of the Jewish question."*

Subsequently, he was sent to establish tighter control over Bohemia and Moravia (Czechoslovakia); within three days of his arrival at least ninety Czechs were executed. By early 1942, he had arrested several thousand Czechs, most of whom perished in concentration camps; another 100,000 were sent as forced labor to Germany.

In London, Czech special agents were trained and then parachuted into Prague, the capital of Czechoslovakia. They waited for their target near a curve in the road that forced Heydrich's car to slow down, and then they attacked. Although one agent's gun jammed, the other threw a grenade that wounded Heydrich. He was not dead and shot back at the attackers, but when the firefight ended, the badly wounded Heydrich was taken to the hospital where he died a week later. The special agents took refuge in an Orthodox Church, but they were tracked down, surrounded by hundreds of Nazi troops, and killed.

German Retaliation and Lidice*

Not content with the deaths of the Czech agents and the bishop of the church where they were hiding, the Germans decided to eradicate nearby villages that they suspected of sympathy with the resistance. The villages of Lidice and Lezaky were destroyed, with all the men and many of the women killed, and the rest sent to concentration camps. A few "Aryan-looking"* children were given to German families to be raised. About eighty children were gassed to death, and four pregnant women were subjected to forced abortions before being sent to the camps where they died. In total, well over one thousand were killed immediately, but the Nazis took their memorial tribute to Heydrich even further. They built three new death camps and named their extermination plans in honor of the assassinated murderer—Operation Reinhard.*

THE NETHERLANDS

Compared to France, Poland, or Serbia, the Netherlands is not known for its armed resistance movement; Dutch resistance was more passive and individual, involving acts of conscience rather than military action. For example, the Dutch expressed their dislike of the Germans and support for the royal family by developing a code language that the Germans would not understand. The expression "so there" was "O zo" in Dutch and was understood to mean "Orange will triumph," since orange is the national color of the Netherlands. Another expression of Dutch support for the royal family occurred on June 29, 1940, the birthday of Prince Bernhard. Many people flew the national flag and wore carnations in honor of the royal prince. This "Carnation Day," like the expression "O zo," might have made the Dutch feel good about their secret signs to each other, but they did nothing to hurt or impede the German military. Later in the war, however, both sides escalated their actions.

Non-Cooperation

At first, Nazi racial policies considered the Dutch to be close to Germans in ethnicity, and therefore good relations were encouraged between German soldiers and local residents. Except for the oppression of Dutch Jews, most citizens were not treated harshly, but as the war continued, the true face of Nazi oppression revealed itself. One small example involved a newborn baby and a midwife who suggested a name in honor of the royal family. When Nazi censors noticed the newspaper announcement of the birth—Irene Beatrix Juliana Wilhelmina Niehot, they were not pleased. The midwife spent the rest of the war in the Ravensbrück concentration camp.

Individual Resistance

Wherever Nazis patrolled the streets, any act of resistance took great courage. In 1943, convinced that fascism had to be defeated, Hannie Schaft joined a resistance group. Hannie and another girl formed an assassination team, and they were given a list of Nazis to eliminate. To get close to their targets, one of the girls would dress like a boy, and they would pretend to be a romantic couple strolling in the neighborhood. They acknowledged the psychological difficulty of walking up and shooting someone, but they reminded each other of the evil they were trying to eliminate. Hannie's red hair was easy to identify, and the Nazis were soon looking for her. They caught up with Hannie in 1945, not long before the Germans retreated out of the Netherlands; Hannie was executed.

Semmy Woortman was one of those who tried to save Jewish children by visiting the nursery where they were held before deportation. To prevent German guards from seeing her carrying babies out of the nursery, she waited for a tram to arrive that blocked the view of the police across the street. Semmy then ran alongside the tram and used it as a shield until it was safe to get on and move the children to a safe house.

Hanna van der Voort was a maternity nurse in the Netherlands who emerged as a hero, risking her life to save children. She joined with others to organize a smuggling operation, moving Jewish children away from the transit points in Amsterdam to relative safety in Rotterdam. Taken first to Hanna's home, the children were taught two important survival skills: a general street map of Rotterdam and some basic information about the Catholic religion. Both of these concepts helped the children pretend to be locals, claiming that they were orphans from the bombing of Rotterdam in 1940. The children were given fake identity papers and then placed with sympathetic farmers who had access to additional food for the extra mouth they had to feed. Supporters in the resistance contributed toward expenses for clothing and other items. Of course, the Nazi police was always watching for these operations, and Hanna herself was arrested and withstood torture without revealing what she knew. Overall her organization was quite successful, as 123 Jewish children were saved in this manner. Hanna died in 1956, but she was not forgotten and was honored as "Righteous Among the Nations."*

Hiding and Escaping

Despite constant German military patrols, more than 9,000 people escaped from the Netherlands during the war. The goal was safety in England, but to get there was far from easy, especially since the Dutch coastline was patrolled by German troops and fortified with bunkers to prevent an Allied landing. As a result, guides had to cross Belgium, then France, and find the passes through the Pyrenees Mountains into Spain. Crossing Spain, which was officially neutral but pro-fascist, was not without its dangers, but arriving at the coast of Spain or Portugal meant that passage to England was finally within sight. This entire journey was dangerous. Was the person one hired reliable or an informer for the Germans? Would the border be clear when one crossed into Belgium or France or

Spain? Could one physically withstand the trek through the Pyrenees Mountains? Would one's health hold up for the long distances on foot? If one were stopped, could one talk or bribe one's way out of the situation?

Identity Cards

The Nazis introduced an identity card that had to be carried at all times, and these cards helped the police control the local population; the Gestapo knew everyone's name and address. The cards had a photo on one side and a fingerprint on the other, and the resistance tried to forge them to create fake identities for underground activities.

The Nazis kept the identity cards in the Amsterdam Registry Office, and members of the resistance decided to destroy the building; they dressed as police officers, tied up the guards, and set the identity cards on fire. The celebration was brief, as all the resistance fighters were soon arrested and executed.

The resistance retaliated by shooting a member of the Dutch fascist party, but the Nazis escalated the confrontation with a harsh crackdown. They drew up a list of Dutch anti-fascists and gave the assignment to local collaborators. The Nazi assassins would knock on the door and then shoot victims in their own homes; over the course of one year more than fifty resistance fighters were killed this way.

Putten Raid 1944

In 1944, the Dutch resistance attacked two Wehrmacht* officers and two corporals in a car near Putten, a town in central Netherlands. While the two corporals escaped the attack, one officer was killed and one wounded. One resistance fighter also died in the action.

The Wehrmacht and Gestapo immediately sought revenge. After taking over the town of Putten, the German army arrested and separated the men and the women and then burned down all the houses. More than 600 men were sent to a concentration camp, where 550 of them died.

The Nazis who carried out these crimes escaped punishment. The German commander in charge of the raid on Putten was put on trial after the war, but he was released from prison in 1948 and lived to the age of ninety-two.

Not all German commanders lived to ninety-two. Near the end of the war, another Dutch resistance attack took place near Arnhem. The resistance was hoping to steal a vehicle to use in another operation but by bad luck the car they stopped belonged to the head of the SS in the Netherlands. This led to a gun battle on the street, and two German officers in the car were killed; the SS chief (Hans Rauter) was only wounded. In order to punish the Dutch resistance, the Germans sent for an SS commander from Poland to lead the crackdown. The SS killed more than one hundred Dutch civilians chosen at random and then ordered additional prisoners executed in camps. Unlike those of the Putten raid, the SS officers involved in these events were executed for war crimes.

Collaborators

Perhaps the most notorious group of collaborators was led by Wim Henneicke and William Briedé, who served as bounty hunters, looking for Jews in hiding and turning them over to the Gestapo for a ransom of about 7.5 guilders (Dutch currency) or less than $50 per person. The so-called Henneicke Column had thirty-five members and was able to arrest between seven thousand and eight thousand Jews and send them to their deaths. Toward the end of the war, the Dutch resistance assassinated Henneicke in Amsterdam, but Briedé escaped to Germany where he died in 1962.

POLAND

Nazi rulers were determined to extinguish the peoples and cultures to the east of Germany. Nazi leadership arrived in Poland with a list of 60,000 Polish leaders and intellectuals who were to be eliminated. As previously discussed, Nazi plans called for wiping out the current and future leaders of the country and turning Poles into an impoverished working class that would provide cheap labor for German industry.

The German occupation of Poland was intentionally cruel and led to two of the most significant resistance uprisings of the war. These urban rebellions both took place in Warsaw, and both gave the German army a harder fight than either the Germans or the rebels themselves expected. Nevertheless, Polish Jews in 1943 and Polish Catholics in 1944 insisted on dying with dignity and on their own terms.

Warsaw Ghetto*

The largest ghetto in Poland was in Warsaw. The city of over one million inhabitants was about 30 percent Jewish before the war. The Germans occupied the city toward the end of September 1939 and immediately started to impose restrictions on the minority population. As in other parts of Europe, Jewish teachers were fired and Jews were ordered to wear white armbands with a blue Star of David. The plan, as in other countries, was to separate Jews from the rest of the population, make them feel alienated and dehumanized, and of course make it easy to identify them. Other restrictions followed, such as banning Jews from riding public transportation or sitting in public parks.

The following year, the ghetto was established. A ten-foot high wall was built around a 1.3 square mile area, and more than 400,000 Jews were ordered to move into this virtual prison. The intentional crowding squeezed more than seven people into a room. Hunger and starvation as well as diseases such as typhoid and tuberculosis were common. Starvation was intentional on the part of the German authorities, who provided less than 1,000 calories per person per day. In the first two years, about 85,000 Jews starved to death in the Warsaw Ghetto.

The Nazis preferred to have Jews in charge of regulating other Jews, partly to give the impression of self-governance and legitimacy to their operations. In Warsaw, the engineer Adam Czerniaków (1880–1942) was selected as the head of the Jewish Council, the group implementing German orders inside the ghetto. Czerniaków hoped that an orderly ghetto would save Jewish lives, especially children, but as a Jew himself he had no meaningful influence with the Nazis.

In 1942 the Nazis decided to liquidate all the Jewish residents of Warsaw, and as usual they did so in steps to avoid resistance. Nazi forces moved about 265,000 Jews to Treblinka concentration camp, where they were killed. The Nazis killed an additional 35,000 inside the ghetto, meaning that about 300,000 people from the Warsaw Ghetto were murdered in 1942.

In April 1943, the Wehrmacht returned to finish the job of liquidating the Warsaw Ghetto, but they did not know that two Jewish self-defense organizations were smuggling weapons to resist the German forces. From April 19 through May 16, 1943, the Jewish fighters, despite the limitations of being half-starved, using homemade weapons, and having no formal military training, held off the Wehrmacht for almost a month. Knowing that their resistance was a suicide mission, over one thousand starving Jews decided to fight, and with only 100 guns they defended themselves against more than 2,000 well-armed German troops. The Nazis had modern weapons and used flame throwers to force the Jews out of basements, attics, and sewers, and eventually the Warsaw Ghetto was literally burned to the ground. In the end the entire ghetto was liquidated—the last 40,000–50,000 people were killed in the Treblinka concentration camp.

One of the most heroic stories of the war involved Janusz Korczak (1878–1942), who ran an orphanage within the Warsaw Ghetto. He was well known in Poland as the author of children's books, so when the Nazis came to collect the almost 200 orphans under his care, he was given the opportunity for lenient treatment for himself. In other words, he had the chance to leave on his own, but he refused and insisted upon staying with his children. According to eyewitness accounts, he dressed them all in their best outfits and they walked together to the train that took them to death in Treblinka. This tragic scene is depicted in the 2017 film *The Zookeeper's Wife* as well as the Polish film *Korczak* from 1990. Shortly before this Nazi act of barbarism, Adam Czerniaków, the head of the Jewish Council, realized that he could not save the children or the rest of the ghetto; he committed suicide with a cyanide capsule.

Of course, it was inevitable that the Jewish fighters would lose, but some escaped and joined the larger Warsaw Uprising of 1944. It turned out to be another opportunity to die bravely, this time on the side of the Polish Home Army.

When it was over, Hitler was furious that supposedly "inferior" Jews could fight against his "superior Aryan" soldiers. In fact, the resistance in the Warsaw Ghetto was the largest urban uprising that German occupiers faced in any country and in any city in Europe up to that time. Only the Warsaw Uprising the following year was bigger.

The German general in charge of destroying the ghetto was Jürgen Stroop (1895–1952), who killed the defenders by burning the ghetto from one end to the other. When the revolt was over, Stroop announced that "the former Jewish residential district of Warsaw no longer exists," and then celebrated his victory by shouting "Heil Hitler" as he pressed a detonator button that blew up the Great Synagogue of Warsaw. When the war ended, he surrendered to the

Americans and was sentenced to death. Rather than execute him, the United States transferred him to Polish custody where he was retried. His death sentence was confirmed, and he was hanged in Warsaw in 1952.

Mizoch Ghetto

Despite being intentionally starved by the Nazis, ghetto residents in several cities rebelled against Nazi control. The Mizoch (Mizocz in Polish) ghetto was in Poland in 1941, but it is in Ukraine today. In October 1942 the ghetto was surrounded for liquidation, and the inhabitants resisted although they had no chance of success. After two days of brave but futile fighting, all the ghetto residents, including women and children, were taken to a ravine and shot one at a time. The standard practice was to have the prisoners dig a trench, undress, lay face down in the trench on top of the other dead bodies, and then receive a bullet in the back of the head. In this massacre, over 1,000 victims were executed in this manner. The Germans took photos of this action, as they expected to win the war and were proud of their activities. The pictures were eventually captured and used at war crime trials.

Bialystok Ghetto

When the Nazis announced plans to liquidate the Bialystok Ghetto, about 110 miles northeast of Warsaw, several hundred prisoners attacked the guards with homemade weapons, including Molotov Cocktails.* This short-lived uprising in August 1943 allowed perhaps one hundred prisoners to escape into nearby forest areas where some of them joined partisan units. Despite this effort, all the remaining ghetto inhabitants, about 10,000, were sent to Treblinka.

Sobibór* Uprising

Sobibór concentration camp was about 125 miles southeast of Warsaw and held 200,000 prisoners. In October 1943, a group of prisoners killed a few SS guards, while three hundred inmates made it out of the camp toward the woods; most were captured and killed but about fifty survived. The Sobibór camp was closed on Himmler's order shortly thereafter.

Like Sheep

Vilnius today is the capital of Lithuania, but when the war started it was called Wilno and was located in Poland with a population of 200,000. The majority of the population was Polish with about 60,000 Jews as the largest minority. When the partition of Poland took place in 1939, the Soviets gave the city to Lithuania, but two years later Germany invaded and took control of the city. German rule meant the establishment of a ghetto in the fall of 1941; it was liquidated two years later.

In the meantime, a group of activists in the ghetto insisted upon organizing a resistance organization to fight the Nazis. When some members of the Jewish Council argued that a fighting organization would provoke the Nazis, the young poet Abba Kovner (1918–1987) said, "We will not go like sheep to the slaughter." He kept his word, as he formed a militant group called the United Partisan Organization but later known as the "Avengers." When the liquidation of the ghetto took place, Kovner's group of 300 escaped into the forest. Kovner and his Avengers gave the Germans a hard time. In addition to killing 200 German soldiers and saving 70 Jews, they also destroyed 40 train cars, 180 miles of track, and 5 bridges.

After the war, Kovner's appeal to the ghetto elders was turned into an insult against Jews. It was incorrectly said that Jews went to death like sheep, while the record indicated just the opposite—that Jews fought harder and more effectively than any minority group in the war. Despite being starved and armed only with homemade weapons, Jewish prisoners inside ghettos rebelled and created problems for strong and well-armed German armies. Where Jews served in the military, such as the Soviet army, they received more medals for bravery than their percentage in the overall population.

Warsaw Uprising

Unlike several other occupied countries in Europe, Poland never had a collaborationist government. Instead, the Polish government went into exile in England, and inside Poland the underground Home Army (AK) waited for a chance to rise up against the occupiers. Warsaw was the center of the resistance movement.

The AK was composed of Polish nationalists who opposed both the Germans and the Soviets and wanted independence restored. By the summer of 1944, they had cause for optimism: Germany seemed to be losing, although no one could predict how long the war would last. The western Allies had landed successfully in France and were moving east toward Germany, and the Soviet army was pushing west toward Poland and Germany. Along with this positive news, however, there was also a problem: the AK was worried about the Soviet army and Stalin's intentions, and the closer the Red Army came toward Poland, the more pressing was the need for action within Poland itself.

The AK made two miscalculations as they moved toward a military uprising that they code named Operation Tempest:* the first mistake was the assumption that as the Red Army approached, the German army would retreat from Warsaw and the Poles would be able to seize control of the city; the second error was the belief that they could be anti-Soviet but still receive military aid and support from the Russians. Neither of those operating principles worked out, first because Hitler hated the Poles and ordered the German army to wipe them out, and second because Stalin was not about to help pro-western Poles take power in the capital city. The result was that the AK was attacked by the Wehrmacht while the Red Army stood by and offered no assistance.

As the Red Army approached Warsaw from the east, the AK commander General "Bor" Komorowski (1895–1966) gave the order to begin the uprising on August 1, 1944. The AK had almost 40,000 troops ready to go and expected to control the city in one week. On the first days they achieved significant victories by taking specific buildings and strong points, but they also lost 2,000 AK soldiers due to superior German fire power. That was not a good sign, nor was the fact that the Soviet army halted operations twelve miles east of the city. The level of casualties was not sustainable, and the AK would be in trouble if Stalin refused to provide assistance.

Further bad news for the AK arrived very quickly. Rather than retreating toward Germany, the Wehrmacht moved reinforcements in the direction of Warsaw. Hitler and Himmler both ordered that Warsaw be destroyed rather than abandoned by the Wehrmacht; the population was to be killed as well.

By the end of the first week, the Germans were back on the offensive, retaking areas of the city and systematically going house to house and executing all Polish residents whether they were involved in the uprising or not. In addition to the 65,000 killed in this manner, the Nazi forces executed doctors, nurses, and patients in a couple of Warsaw hospitals. Besides the outright murder of civilians, the German forces used Polish women as human shields in front of their tanks as they approached the AK.

Despite these setbacks, many Poles saw positive signs as an administration began to function in Polish-controlled areas. The first Polish newspaper since 1939 was published, young boy and girl scouts started mail service, and a Polish radio station called Lightning began to broadcast. In order to avoid the fighting in the streets, the brave scouts used the sewer system to deliver messages around the city.

On the German side, the Wehrmacht did not give up and reinforced its troops already in operation. Several areas of the city were subjected to steady bombardment without regard to distinctions between civilians and the military. The AK forces did not have enough fighters or heavy weapons to withstand German determination to wipe them out. When the AK retreated from what is called Old Town and left 30,000 wounded civilians and 7,000 of their soldiers behind, the Nazis executed all of them.

In mid-September, American planes attempted supply drops, but due to German antiaircraft fire they could not come in low enough to assure accuracy. As a result, the Germans recovered 80 percent of the American aid. The following week, a new German offensive in the city brought another hospital under Nazi control; patients and doctors were all executed.

The situation for the AK was clearly impossible, and negotiations ended the uprising with a promise that prisoners would be treated according to the Geneva Conventions. The two-month insurrection was over; on October 4, the Polish newspaper and radio station shut down. The toll was very high: 15,000 AK soldiers surrendered, 50,000 civilians were sent to concentration camps, and 150,000 additional civilians became forced laborers in Germany.

The Nazis fulfilled the wish of Hitler and Himmler. They first scavenged the city for anything of value and sent 30,000 railway cars stuffed with valuables toward Germany, and they then began the systematic destruction of neighborhoods block by block. This was, however, temporary revenge, as the Soviet army resumed its offensive and entered what used to be the city of Warsaw in January 1945.

Courage: Jozef and Wiktoria Ulma

This Polish Catholic family risked and sacrificed everything to help others in trouble. They lived in the south of Poland where he worked as the town librarian and she raised their six children. During the war they hid six Polish Jews in their attic, but in 1944 someone turned them in to the Gestapo. The massacre that ensued was brutal. Each one of the Jews was lined up and shot in the back of the head, followed by both Jozef and Wiktoria; she was not spared despite being eight months' pregnant. The Gestapo finished the job by shooting each of the Ulma children as well. In 1995, the Ulma family was recognized as "Righteous Among the Nations."

SOVIET UNION

Two factors helped create the resistance movement in the Soviet Union. The first was German atrocities, which quickly convinced people that Nazi occupation was as bad as the Soviet government claimed it would be. The second was the size and geography of the country, which made it impossible for the Wehrmacht to patrol everyplace, leaving forests and swamps as perfect shelters for partisan units.

Where the Wehrmacht controlled Soviet territory, the occupation was intentionally brutal. The Germans were not trying to win a war as much as they wanted to destroy a civilization. They made a point of carrying out public hangings in almost every town and village in order to intimidate the population. Resistors or partisans could be seen hanging from light posts with signs around their necks: "we are bandits who killed and plundered German soldiers and Russian citizens" or "partisans and their helpers end like this." In ancient times, rulers would sometimes decapitate opponents and leave their heads on stakes as a warning to others, and the Germans emulated this practice by leaving the bodies hanging for days to rot as well.

The partisan movement was weak for about a year after the invasion. There were civilians and soldiers who fled to the forests looking for places to hide, but they were unorganized and without effective weapons. The situation changed when the Soviet government realized that these fighters could be useful in disrupting German communications and transportation, and toward the end of 1942 the regular Soviet army was encouraged to coordinate with partisans and provide them with weapons. The increased fire power made the partisans more effective, and since they were often people on the run whom the Nazis wanted to kill, they had little to lose when operating behind enemy lines. After the Battle of Stalingrad, the partisan movement grew larger and eventually included several hundred thousand guerrillas who sabotaged German supplies and especially railways, helping to drive the Wehrmacht out of the country.

CONCLUSION

The story of the resistance can be divided into several parts. In 1939, with only Poland under attack, the rest of Europe watched and waited. In 1940 most of Western Europe was occupied, and the true nature of German rule slowly revealed itself. Nevertheless, resistance movements were hindered by the Nazi-Soviet Nonaggression Pact, which prevented local communists from opposing the Germans. The situation changed dramatically twice: first when Germany invaded the Soviet Union and Stalin ordered communists throughout Europe to oppose the occupation, and second after the Battle of Stalingrad demonstrated that the Wehrmacht was not invincible. The ever-growing German demand for forced labor, one of the most unpopular actions taken by the occupiers, added to local discontent.

The Nazis carried out mass atrocities wherever they went, stoking local anger and ultimately hatred of the German military. In countries like Poland, the Soviet Union, France, Greece, and Serbia, resistance grew and caused serious trouble for the occupiers. In addition, unexpected resistance came from ghettos, where the fight for human dignity created problems for the German army.

Resistance was extremely useful when combined with larger military actions such as the Soviet army offensive during 1943–1944 or the D-Day landing in 1944, but all acts of resistance were important, including those of conscience. At a time when Nazi occupation tried to deny what makes us human, thousands of Europeans insisted on hiding and feeding a neighbor in need, on offering a ration coupon to a starving family, or on sharing a last crust of bread with a bunk mate in a concentration camp. The Nazis could not kill that form of resistance.

FURTHER READING

Ashdown, Paddy. *The Cruel Victory: The French Resistance, D-Day and the Battle for Vercors 1944*. London: HarperCollins, 2014.

Golsan, Richard J. *The Papon Affair*. New York: Routledge, 2000.

Karski, Jan. *Courier from Poland: The Story of a Secret State*. Boston: Houghton Mifflin, 1944.
Kirkup, James. "Anna Marly: Troubadour of the Resistance." *Independent*, February 21, 2006.
Paxton, Robert O. *Vichy France*. New York: Columbia University Press, 1972.
United States Holocaust Museum, Washington.
Wieviorka, Oliver. Translated by Jane Marie Todd. *The French Resistance*. Cambridge, MA: Belknap Press of Harvard University Press, 2016.

9

THE HOLOCAUST

> Monsters exist, but they are too few in number to be truly dangerous. More dangerous are the common men, the functionaries ready to believe and to act without asking questions.
> Primo Levi, *Survival in Auschwitz*

INTRODUCTION

Is it possible to understand why Ukrainians killed Poles in vicious ways; why Romanians slaughtered Jews and Ukrainians in Odessa; why Croatians butchered Serbs as well as Jews; why members of the Gestapo engaged in torture and sadistic acts; why the Einsatzgruppen* shot so many children; or why millions of people listened with complete joy as Hitler and Goebbels spouted lies and abhorrence? Why did so many Germans and other Europeans accept this message of hatred?

Recent historical debates about anti-Semitism and other hate crimes during the war focuses on both long- and short-term causes. Some historians assert that anti-Semitism had its origins in early Christianity while others concentrate on modern causes such as the development of nationalism and ethnic romanticism after the French Revolution. Is it possible to combine these two positions to try to understand what happened in the twentieth century not only in Germany but in many other European countries as well, where enthusiastic supporters of the Nazis participated in the killing of millions of people that included Jews, Roma, homosexuals, and others?

Some Europeans heard anti-Semitic messages in church, making them susceptible to the program of an extremist political party. In addition, by the mid and late nineteenth century, Jews throughout Europe aspired to full rights as citizens, and some became successful in a variety of fields, including education, the arts, business, politics, science, and the military. While most Jews remained poor like most Christians, the success of some members of this minority group led to resentment by their neighbors who felt left out of modern society and looked for someone to blame for their own failures.

Beyond that underlying factor, was there an immediate reason why Germans responded enthusiastically to the Nazis? From the beginning, the Nazis did not attempt to hide their program or pretend to be moderates until they attained power; both *Mein Kampf** and Nazi propaganda made their objectives clear. Hitler and Goebbels did not kill eleven million people themselves; they were assisted by enthusiastic supporters and volunteers from many nations, as well as millions of people who stood by and pretended that the spread of evil was not their concern. While the economic instability of the 1920s and 1930s contributed to the appeal of the Nazis, so did a variety of other factors already mentioned: a history of anti-Semitism, ethnic romanticism, resentment and fear of minorities, and politicians who played on these sentiments. Despite these factors, most western countries that also suffered through the Great Depression did not succumb to the Nazi message.

GERMANY

The Nazis established the first prison camp for their political enemies in Dachau* near Munich. Nazi military success, conquests in Eastern Europe, and racist ideology all contributed to the transformation of prison camps to death camps. As a result of the invasions of Poland and the Soviet Union, the Nazis controlled millions of people who they had targeted for elimination. Nazis did not wonder whether it was right to kill these people; the only question was how to do it quickly. They experimented with two possibilities: the first was shooting each person individually, but this was slow and used up a lot of bullets; the second involved running carbon monoxide into the back of a van, but this did not kill large numbers quickly enough.

By January 1942, the numbers of Jews and other ethnic targets under German control had grown too numerous for existing killing methods, and Nazi officials called a meeting in the Wannsee* suburb of Berlin to consider how to make genocide more efficient. Reinhard Heydrich (1904–1942), a high-ranking SS official, organized the meeting. The Nazis discussed what they called the "final solution of the Jewish question."* The Nazi goal was the murder of all Jews in Europe, to be accomplished by expanding the concentration camp system and adopting twentieth-century industrial innovation, the assembly line, to the mass-production of death. Like industrialists building a factory near the source of raw materials, the Nazis planned to place the concentration camps in Eastern Europe, where the largest number of Jews lived.

Officially the camps fell under the administration of the SS, which was led by Heinrich Himmler (1900–1945), but he delegated the actual running of the system to Adolf Eichmann (1906–1962), who took seriously his job of keeping the assembly line moving efficiently. Twenty years later on trial in Israel, Eichmann expressed pride in his careful and successful management of the system. He never expressed remorse for his actions.

While several thousand prisoners survived the Nazi plan, many millions died in the camps. Most were killed in the gas chambers, and some died of disease. A smaller number committed suicide by running toward the barbed wire knowing they would be shot by guards. Guards had unlimited power to kill, torture, and mistreat prisoners, with no need to explain the abuse of a prisoner. The ever-expanding concentration camp system was independent of all legal restraints—it was basically a state within the state carrying out the racist policies that were essential to Nazi ideology.

Nazi Racism

Nazi racial policy led inevitably to the camp system. Nazi beliefs were not complicated; rather they were both simplistic and false. They claimed that the world was divided into opposing and antagonistic races, and these races were always in conflict for domination of the globe. As discussed previously, Nazis believed in the "survival of the fittest" in terms of race and nationality (see Chapters 1 and 7). Supposedly, the superior race in world history was the

Germanic people that Hitler called the "Aryan" race.* The Aryans were destined to rule the world, but first they had to defeat their enemies. According to this theory, the Jewish people were the primary obstacle, and the "Aryan race" had to destroy them, Roma,* homosexuals, people with disabilities, Jehovah's Witnesses, and Slavs in order to fulfill their destiny. These "inferior" groups lived all around Germany, especially to the east, and after victory the German people would expand into their territory. As Slavs would not move off their land voluntarily, they had to be conquered in war. The Nazis actually looked forward to this massive war, since according to their views the superior race was preordained to win.

T4

One aspect of Nazi racial policy, a plan to kill children with physical or mental disabilities, started before the war. While all Jewish children would be targeted for death eventually, the T4 plan (see also Chapter 7) included the murder of Christian children who did not live up to the Nazi concept of the perfect "Aryan" specimen. The killing program began in 1939 and was named T4 after the address in Berlin where its offices were located. The program asked doctors and nurses to identify children or babies with physical or mental disabilities. The children were taken from church asylums or psychiatric hospitals and placed in centers that were disguised as treatment clinics. These were actually killing facilities. Parents who enquired about their children were told they had already died or been transferred for better treatment, but of course there was no real medical facility or therapy. The program also killed adults who were already in homes for the disabled or mentally ill. This euthanasia program, targeting those the Germans called "incurably sick," lasted for two years and killed about 70,000 people.

The T4 program revealed one of the distressing aspects of Nazi racial policies—the involvement of medical staff in the killing process. Doctors take an oath to protect and heal the ill, but German doctors who participated in the T4 euthanasia program as well as other cruel experiments and murders in the concentration camps violated their promise to treat and help the sick.

The objection of Catholic bishops and others played a role in the suspension of the T4 program, but there is debate about whether the church acted quickly enough. Critics argue that the Vatican was slow to criticize even the persecution of Catholics in the T4 program. Despite a Vatican statement in 1940, the most direct protest came not from the pope but from Bishop August von Galen who delivered three strongly worded sermons in 1941. Shortly thereafter, Hitler suspended the program, but in practical terms it did not matter since the concentration camps were then in operation and carrying out the Nazi mission. Some historians consider Pope Pius XII's more forceful statement against T4 in 1943 too late, since by then T4 was out of date. In his statement, the pope did not criticize the continuing genocide against Europe's Jews, Roma, or other groups designated as inferior by the Nazis.

Einsatzgruppen

These German "mobile killing squads" followed the Wehrmacht* eastward; their task was rounding up and shooting Jews, Slavs, Roma, and other racial enemies of the Third Reich. Jews were the primary target, and Poland and the Soviet Union had the largest populations of Jews in Europe. Soon the Einsatzgruppen developed a killing routine: arrest all the Jews in a town or city, march them to a rural setting nearby, order them to dig deep trenches (sometimes the trenches had been prepared in advance), and make everyone turn over their valuables and undress. The victims were surrounded by machine guns, so there was little chance of escape. The next step was horrifying: they had to climb into the trench face down and receive a bullet in the back of the head or sometimes stand in front of the trench and allow the bullet to knock them over backward. They might be asked to hold a baby or young child in front of them so that one bullet could kill both.

The Einsatzgruppen shot over one million victims before Himmler decided that killing each person individually was time consuming and a waste of ammunition. To make the system more efficient, the Nazis tried a van that pumped carbon monoxide from the exhaust system into the back of the vehicle where prisoners were tightly packed together. Despite this new technique, the Nazis continued to search for an effective killing method that would employ twentieth-century techniques in the cause of mass execution.

Auschwitz I*

Auschwitz I opened in 1940 in the town of Oświęcim (in Polish) or Auschwitz (in German), incorporating about twenty buildings that had served as barracks for the Polish army. Prison labor was used to expand the camp and add various details, such as a sign over the entrance that proclaimed: "Arbeit Macht Frei"* or "Work

Makes You Free." Eventually it became the largest concentration camp and killed over one million victims.

At first Auschwitz served as a prison camp to handle the large number of Poles who had been arrested, but eventually it grew to include three main parts and several small parts, including Auschwitz I, Auschwitz II-Birkenau, and Auschwitz III-Monowitz. The subcamps were labor camps where prisoners were forced to work in industries or on farms for the German military.

Men and women were usually separated in the camp, at first by a high wall and shortly thereafter by the building of a new prison for women in Auschwitz II-Birkenau. Being female did not protect them in any way from the horrors of the camp, including SS beating and torture, rape, separation from their children, and death in the gas chamber. Pregnant women or nursing mothers were sent to immediate death. Survivors often mentioned being persecuted for both their religion and their gender. Mistreated as Jews, they were also victims of sexual abuse.

Auschwitz operated for about four and a half years until January 1945. More than one million Jews were sent to Auschwitz, and most of them died there. The camp also held or processed about 140,000 Poles, 23,000 Roma, 15,000 Soviet POWs, and a variety of other groups. In 1944, the Germans occupied Hungary and shipped over 400,000 more Jews from Budapest to Auschwitz.

The Selection

As the largest killing camp in the German system, Auschwitz used methods that became infamous and symbolic of all the camps. Prisoners arrived in railway cars, stuffed with people, some of whom had traveled for days without food, water, or sanitation. Typically, many of the old and the weak died in their railway car, packed together so tightly that no one could sit during the entire journey. When the train arrived at Auschwitz and the doors opened, the SS with their attack dogs were waiting to choose who would die immediately. This was called the "selection."

The sick and disabled, the old and the weak, and pregnant women and children were usually sent directly to the gas chamber. Like the iron gate with its slogan about work, the Germans tried to trick those selected for death so they would not panic or cause trouble. They were told they had to take a shower to be disinfected and were then led to a special building where they removed their clothes. Each person was even given a number to maintain the deception that they would reclaim their clothes after the shower. The four largest gas chambers at Auschwitz held 2,000 people at a time. The gas chamber itself had fake shower fixtures in the ceiling, but instead of water, poison gas was released into the room. Putting industrial ingenuity into this project led to the discovery of a pesticide called Zyklon B, a form of deadly hydrogen cyanide pellets easily transported in canisters. Once deployed, the pellets turned to gas and killed everyone in the chambers in no more than twenty minutes. It is impossible to imagine the terror that took place in the gas chamber during that time, as parents realized what was happening and tried to shield their screaming children. Of course, it was too late and there was no hope.

After the prisoners were killed in the gas chamber but before the crematorium (oven), guards were ordered to open the mouth of each dead person and examine their teeth for gold fillings. If gold was found, the tooth was then extracted, the filling drilled out, and eventually all the gold was melted into bars and stockpiled. The pulling of teeth out of dead bodies was too gruesome for volunteers, so prisoners were forced to perform this action and then take the body to the crematorium. After the crematorium, the ashes were dumped in mass graves. The guards who performed these tasks knew that they would eventually be killed by this same technique.

Other prisoners were killed using a variety of methods: shot, hanged, or given a fatal dose of phenol in the heart muscle. These punishments were usually for prisoners who broke the rules or civilians who were arrested for trying to help a prisoner. Between 1941 and 1943 in Auschwitz, the SS shot several thousand people along a wall in a courtyard between Blocks 10 and 11. Most of those executed were Polish political prisoners or leaders of resistance organizations, but even children were killed in front of the wall. In addition to shooting or hanging, the SS sometimes whipped and hung prisoners by their wrists with their arms straight up in the air.

Collection of Personal Items

With millions of prisoners in the camp system, the German authorities took the opportunity to collect the personal belongings of the victims and use those items for the army or German civilians. Before being sent to the gas chamber, women had their hair shaved off, supposedly for sanitary reasons. In reality, the hair was saved and used for a variety of purposes: to make wigs, to stuff mattresses, to make certain textiles or felt, and other items. In addition, many other personal belongings were confiscated, including shoes, clothing in good condition, toiletries, utensils, bowls, pots, glasses, and more. Clothing that was not wearable was sent to textile factories to be rewoven. On a visit to Auschwitz today, a tourist can see piles of these personal effects taken from inmates, including mounds of shoes from little children.

Dehumanization

Nazi policy was to make a prisoner feel like an animal rather than a human being—in other words to dehumanize the prisoner. There

Buchenwald* was a concentration camp located about 6 miles from the city of Weimar in Germany. Used primarily as forced labor in German armaments factories, prisoners in Buchenwald died at high rates (about 25%). The camp housed several well known inmates, including German theologian Dietrich Bonhoeffer (later moved and executed at Flossenburg concentration camp) and author Elie Wiesel, who was liberated and can be seen in this photo (second bunk from the bottom, seventh from the left). (National Archives)

were various ways to accomplish this goal. One was to separate families. As soon as the prisoners arrived, men were sent to one barrack and women to another, and in most cases, they never saw each other again. Another method was to deny the prisoners their own names by tattooing a number on the inside of their left arm. The prisoners were fed horrible food that was not enough to live on, forcing them to fight over the smallest crumbs. The SS enjoyed turning fathers against sons or brothers against each other, making them steal or fight over a drop of thin soup to try to stay alive. Due to the lack of medical treatment, disease was prevalent as well, with dysentery an especially difficult ailment. Each morning and evening the prisoners stood at attention for "roll-call," where the guards made sure that everyone was accounted for. A prisoner with dysentery remained in place with the others, sometimes for hours in the rain, snow, or heat. The result was predictable, but no exceptions were allowed. One had to stand or go to work in one's own filth, enduring an additional humiliation along with the pervasive brutality of camp life.

Guards

The guards were sadistic. Most of the camp personnel were in the SS, the most fanatical of all Nazi units. The SS followed the goals of Heydrich as established at the Wannsee Conference—their plan was to eliminate all of these "inferior" people. Sometimes the guards were from countries such as Ukraine or Croatia, where anti-Semitism was widespread. Some guards believed that they might save their own lives by being obedient to the Nazis, but eventually most of them died in the gas chambers as well.

Medical Experiments

Among the worst aspects of the concentration camps were the medical experiments performed on prisoners. These experiments were sometimes requested by German drug companies to test medicines—but to examine the effect of a new medicine, the prisoner first had to have the disease. Healthy prisoners would be injected with typhus or other deadly bacteria, and then the medical staff would watch and take notes on the advance of the illness. Sometimes the prisoner would die from this action, and sometimes an experimental drug would be administered as if the person were a lab rat. Either way the prisoner usually ended up in the gas chamber. Surgery without anesthesia was performed so doctors could observe organs still in operation. Some prisoners were lowered into a vat of boiling water or freezing water to see how their organs reacted to extreme temperatures. Women were subjected to cruel operations and forced sterilization experiments. Many died or were killed in the process; survivors suffered from lifelong physical as well as psychological injuries. To the Nazis and the medical teams who carried out this torture, the prisoners were subhuman.

The most infamous doctor at Auschwitz was Dr. Josef Mengele (1911–1979), who specialized in experiments on twins. He claimed that he wanted to build an "Aryan"* by transplanting parts from one twin to another, but his operations were simply cruel and sadistic and included injecting blue colored dye into eyeballs or infecting victims with deadly diseases. Along with other SS officers and doctors, Mengele waited for the arrival of train cars packed with prisoners and then participated in the "selection" of those who would be sent to the gas chambers. He enjoyed his position of power and control over the weak and helpless so much that Jewish inmates called Mengele the "Angel of Death." Mengele survived the war and escaped to South America. He lived there quite freely until his death about thirty years after the war ended. (See also Chapter 7).

Topography of Terror

Topography of Terror is a Berlin museum today housed in the former headquarters of the Gestapo. This incredible photo exhibit documents and exposes Nazi crimes clearly and explicitly. There is a photo of the smiling medical staff at Auschwitz with this caption: "Dr. Fritz Klein was involved in selecting Jews and Gypsies for death in the gas chambers at Auschwitz-Birkenau; Dr. E. Wirths, highest-ranking SS camp doctor, was responsible for selecting old, sick, and feeble prisoners for death as well as choosing inmates for medical experiments."

In addition to the photo of smiling doctors mentioned earlier, there are two other photos that show groups of guards at a picnic, smiling, laughing, and having fun, and the label says: "SS female auxiliary maids and SS men from Auschwitz at the SS retreat south of the camp in an idyllic mountain landscape taking a break and having a good time." In an exhibit that shows brutal arrests and piles of dead bodies, the maids and men laughing and enjoying their leisure time after a day at Auschwitz may be the most frightening photo in the entire collection.

Soviet Prisoners

The story of Soviet prisoners is one of the most horrific of the war. The Germans captured nearly six million Soviet POWs, and they quickly set up a special camp within Auschwitz for these prisoners. Considered devoid of human dignity, Soviet captives were kept in a fenced area, given little food, and literally worked to death. Some were shot, especially members of the Communist Party, while others were sent to the gas chambers. Many were brutalized by the SS. Those who refused to work or cooperate were taken outside naked and made to stand in freezing temperatures. The SS would spray them with cold water that would ice up on their skin, and a large number froze to death as a result.

As the war dragged on, German authorities realized that they were wasting the labor potential of these prisoners; one million Soviet POWs were then put to work for the German war machine. Due to poor treatment, these workers also died in large numbers. Germany violated all treaty agreements dealing with POWs in what was later recognized as a war crime on a massive scale. Over half of these prisoners died in German captivity.

Liberation

In early 1945, Soviet forces were on the offensive against the retreating Wehrmacht. The Germans were anxious to hide the evidence of their crimes so they started the evacuation of Auschwitz. The Nazis tried to destroy records, burning files and lists that they had carefully maintained for years. German guards destroyed part of the camp itself, including the gas chambers and other buildings. More than 50,000 prisoners were forced onto a "death march" in the direction of Germany. These prisoners were already in terrible shape—starving, weak, sick—and the forced march led to almost 10,000 of them dying on the way. The Soviet army arrived in the camp on January 27, 1945.

The first Nazi commandant of Auschwitz was Rudolf Höss. He was captured at the end of the war and testified at the Nuremberg Trials.* He talked about running a concentration camp as if it were a normal job, and he admitted that his goal was to murder millions of people as efficiently as possible. He was sentenced to death by a Polish court and hanged in April 1947 on the spot in Auschwitz where the Gestapo building used to be.

POLAND

Before 1939, three million Jews lived in Poland, making up about 10 percent of the Polish population, and in some towns the Jewish population comprised 30–40 percent of the inhabitants. While in the larger cities such as Warsaw or Kraków many Jews were successful and assimilated into Polish society, in smaller towns and villages the Catholic and Jewish populations lived side by side but had basically separate lives.

Over 90 percent of the three million Jews in Poland were killed during World War II. In addition, some Poles hid Jews and others turned them in to the Nazis. This is the basis of the controversy about Polish anti-Semitism. The problem is that defenders and critics of the Poles are both correct. In most cases, it was clearly the German military, SS, and Gestapo that carried out the murders of millions of Polish Jews, but in others, Polish Catholics themselves were responsible for assisting or carrying out these acts. While many Poles have been recognized for helping to save Jews, there were massacres of Jews such as the famous one in Jedwabne that raise questions to this day.

Jedwabne Pogrom

Jedwabne is infamous as a town where 340 Polish Jews were massacred by Polish Catholics who were their neighbors. In 1939 when the war started, this town in eastern Poland fell into the Soviet zone of occupation, but two years later, when Germany invaded the Soviet Union, the Wehrmacht established control over Jedwabne. At that time there were about 800 Jews living in this area, and Nazi propaganda encouraged the Catholics to turn against Jews, accusing the Jews of having supported the Red Army and the communists when the Soviets governed the region. According to this allegation, the Jews were traitors to Poland. The charges successfully convinced many Poles to hunt for Jews; when caught they were marched to the town square where they were mistreated and beaten. Beards of religious Jews were cut off as a form of humiliation. Finally, Polish Catholics forced the Jews into a barn, the barn was set on fire, and the Jews were killed.

The Nazis surrounded the barn with machine guns in the unlikely event that someone might escape. No one did.

While Nazis encouraged this massacre, it was neighbors who lived in the same town who carried out the killing, and then looted the apartments of people they had known for years.

Ponary Massacre in Poland/Lithuania

Wilno was a city of over one million people in northeast Poland in 1939. It was a contested area, claimed by both Poland and Lithuania, and today it is known as Vilnius and is the capital of Lithuania. Ponary is a suburb of the city, and on July 8, 1941, it was the scene of a massacre of thousands—perhaps as many as 100,000 people—who were shot and buried in mass graves. Prisoners were rounded up and marched to the killing ground, where they surrendered any valuables they carried, undressed, and marched in single file to the pit. The Germans opened fire, and each body fell into the trench. The next group of prisoners was brought forward to be killed; the second line fell onto the first victims, and then the process was repeated many more times. Estimates suggest that about 70,000 Jews or about 90 percent of the Jewish population of the area was killed using this form of execution. In addition, the Germans shot 20,000 Poles and 10,000 Russians (mostly POWs) in the same place. The total murdered was about 100,000, and it remains one of the most brutal massacres in a very brutal war.

The killings were carried out by both German and Lithuanian squads. An eyewitness account reported on the horror of the massacres, as hundreds of people were driven to the deserted area every day never to return. According to these reports, the executioners eventually tired of their work so they pushed wounded victims into the pits and let them writhe in pain as dead bodies were tossed on top of them.

Diary of Dr. Klukowski

Lublin, Poland, also had a large Jewish population that came under the jurisdiction of the General Government* of Hans Frank based in Kraków. The German occupiers quickly moved the Jewish population into the Lublin Ghetto,* but in 1942 the Nazis shipped all 26,000 Jewish inhabitants from the ghetto to Belzec* concentration camp.

Dr. Zygmunt Klukowski was a doctor in a hospital in a small town near Lublin. He kept a diary that expressed his increasing outrage as time went on. First he noted that Germans took over the nice houses in the town, which did not surprise him. Then he saw more extreme measures, such as forcing Jews to carry out manual labor that included sweeping the streets and cleaning the public outhouses. Every day the Germans changed various rules so that the Jewish population was unsure what was permitted. For example, one day they might be allowed to open their shops but the next day they could not do so. The Nazi plan was to keep the Jewish residents uninformed of the laws so they could be punished based on ever-changing regulations.

As a physician, Dr. Klukowski was shocked when he found out that Germans were killing mental patients in a nearby hospital. He wrote about SS soldiers who searched for Jews in hiding. If they discovered a family in a basement, the SS would throw grenades into the cellar. Anyone caught trying to escape would be beaten before being killed. He wrote about Jews being taken to the edge of town where the Jewish cemetery was located, ordered to dig trenches, and then forced inside before being shot. The doctor also commented on German troops who robbed and raped as they wished without anyone stopping them. "The Germans even killed small Jewish children.... It is so terrible that it is almost impossible to comprehend." Dr. Klukowski witnessed the Wehrmacht publicly executing the entire family of a partisan fighter and wiping out a village of 800 people, mostly women and children, also due to partisan activity (Klukowski, 1993).

Ghettos in Poland

The Germans distrusted Polish Catholics, but they hated Polish Jews. The first ghetto was established in the city of Lodz, which is about seventy-five miles southwest of Warsaw. A large Jewish population of almost 160,000 Jews was pressed into one square mile. Over the next year, another 40,000 Jews were forced into the ghetto, and soon 5,000 Roma were interned there as well. All of the Roma were quickly sent to Chelmno concentration camp where they were killed. In 1942, 70,000 Jews joined the Roma in the death camp. The Jews who stayed in the ghetto worked in factories for the Nazis but suffered horrible conditions, living without water, sanitation, or health care. Thousands more died of disease or starvation. In 1944 the ghetto was liquidated, with the victims sent either to Chelmno or to Auschwitz.

The Lodz Ghetto was the first one established in Poland, but those in Kraków and Warsaw were built immediately thereafter. They are best known due to their large size, the uprising in the Warsaw Ghetto, and the stories of a few survivors. In some cases, recent films have made these accounts familiar to many people: *Schindler's List* described a Nazi who developed a conscience and saved his Jewish workers, while *The Pianist* focused on the lucky survival of a classical musician in Warsaw. Jan Karski is not as well known as either Schindler or Szpilman the pianist, but he took great risks to warn the west about the genocide taking place in Poland.

Schindler

Oskar Schindler (1908–1974) was born in Moravia (part of Austria-Hungary and later part of Czechoslovakia) to German parents. In 1939 he joined the Nazi Party and moved to Kraków. The Germans were in the process of taking over Jewish-owned businesses, and the factory that Schindler leased at 4 Lipowa Street was in this category. It made enamelware, but since all factories were expected to contribute to the war effort, it made artillery shell fuses also.

As a member of the Nazi Party with good connections in the German military, Schindler signed contracts to provide enamel cooking pots and pans for the army. He employed Jewish workers, and his Nazi contacts allowed him to bribe officials whenever a roundup of Jews was taking place. On several occasions he was able to claim that his workers were essential to the war effort and had to remain in his factory in order to maintain productivity. Although Schindler's workers were forced to live inside the Kraków Ghetto, they had special papers that gave them permission to leave the ghetto each day to go to work. Nevertheless, the situation could be risky. The workers were searched entering and leaving the factory, and a military officer took roll-call to make sure that no one disappeared or escaped. Nevertheless, work in Schindler's factory, even with its twelve-hour shift, was better than life in the ghetto.

Schindler tried to provide decent food and even medicine for the workers. Using the black market, he traded pots and pans that the army did not need for vodka and cigarettes, and his workers could then trade the vodka for extra food and ration coupons.

In 1944, as the Red Army moved closer to Polish territory, the German military ordered factories closed and Jewish workers to be sent to death camps. Schindler bribed and convinced Nazi officials that his factory should move to the Sudetenland where he could continue to produce war material for the German military. It was at this time that "Schindler's List," the names of Jews who needed to be transferred with the factory, was drawn up. Schindler's secretary compiled a list of about 1,200 names. The next several months were full of intrigue, as Schindler struggled to keep his workforce together by handing out bribes. In the end Schindler saved over one thousand workers, as well as others he helped to liberate from the camps and certain death.

By the end of the war, Schindler had spent all his money on bribes and supplies for the workers. His business dealings did not go well, but Jewish groups remembered his role, and they helped him with donations. He died in 1974 and is buried in Jerusalem. He is recognized as "Righteous Among the Nations"* for this work.

In 1993, Steven Spielberg produced and directed the film *Schindler's List*, winner of seven Academy Awards.

The Pianist

Wladyslaw Szpilman (1911–2000) was a well-known classical pianist in Poland before the war. He played frequently on Polish radio in the 1930s, but he was trapped in Warsaw by the German invasion in 1939. Ordered to move with his family into the Warsaw Ghetto in 1940, Szpilman supported himself at first by playing music in the few cafes that opened inside the ghetto. When members of the ghetto, including Szpilman's family, were sent to Treblinka for extermination, Szpilman was saved by a Jewish policeman who recognized him from his concert posters and pulled him out of line just before he boarded the train to the camp. For most of 1942–1943, the former classical musician survived doing odd jobs, but when the ghetto was completely liquidated in May 1943, Szpilman went into hiding. For a while he had the assistance of other Polish musicians, but when those contacts disappeared, he was on his own and lived in an abandoned hospital and then a bombed-out building. He survived on rainwater and small pieces of food that he found or scavenged for.

In 1944, Szpilman was living secretly in a mostly destroyed building with an old piano in it. Suddenly, he was confronted by a German officer, and Szpilman expected to be arrested or shot. Instead the officer asked him a few questions, including what he did before the war. When Szpilman explained, the officer told him to demonstrate his skill on the abandoned piano. Szpilman played Chopin—the same Nocturne that he had played on the radio when the war started. Rather than turning Szpilman in to the authorities, the officer brought him some food and warm clothing.

Shortly thereafter, Szpilman was liberated by the Red Army, but the German officer was arrested. While the officer died in a Russian POW camp, Szpilman again became a featured performer on Polish radio after the war. Although Szpilman died in 2000, his story was told in the film *The Pianist* in 2002. Roman Polanski, who survived the German occupation of Poland by hiding and pretending to be Catholic, produced and directed the film. The movie, using Szpilman's memoir of his life story, won several Oscars.

Eyewitness: Jan Karski

Jan Karski (1914–2000) remains an unsung hero of the Holocaust. Before the war, he served as a diplomat and joined the army in 1939 to fight the German invasion. Subsequently, he joined the Polish underground, and in an act of bravery and significant risk, he was smuggled twice in and out of the Warsaw Ghetto to learn firsthand what was happening behind the high walls. The Polish underground then helped him travel to London where he told his story to the Polish government-in-exile and representatives of the British government, including the foreign secretary. The next summer he was in Washington and told President Roosevelt and the American secretary of state what he had witnessed. Many of those he told refused to believe the accuracy of his description. Karski was disappointed when western policy did not change. Roosevelt and Churchill feared that highlighting the plight of the Jews as a reason for the war might lose them support at home. Their military policy was to win but not specifically to target the concentration camps or even the train tracks leading to the camps. After the war, Karski taught at Georgetown University and became an American citizen. In 1982 he was recognized as "Righteous Among the Nations;" he had previously written about his mission in *Courier from Poland: The Story of a Secret State* (1944).

In recent years, historians have raised questions about the weak western reaction to Karski's information. Allied bombers hit targets in Poland in 1944 not far from Auschwitz, but never tried to bomb the railroad tracks or the crematoria in the concentration camp. While doing so might not have ended the genocide, destruction of the tracks and parts of the camp could have slowed down Nazi efforts.

THE NETHERLANDS

In May 1940, Seyss-Inquart became the administrator of the Netherlands with the title of Reich Commissioner (*Reichskommissar*). He ordered all government employees and civil servants to fill out a registration form, a "Declaration of Aryanism," that asked about ancestry and religion. With very few exceptions, everyone completed the paperwork. Dutch Jews who survived the war later stated that the form itself did not seem unreasonable. Since they did not know about the concentration camps, they did not have a good reason for disobeying the order.

The Nazis quickly used the forms to identify and fire Jewish civil servants as well as university professors. When students in some university cities went on strike, the Germans arrested more than 400 Jewish men and beat them as a warning. In response the strike spread, and soon public transportation in Amsterdam was at a standstill. German troops did not hesitate and opened fire on the strikers, killing nine and wounding hundreds more. A few days later the German authorities made their view of opposition clear: they took three strike leaders and fifteen other resistance members and shot all of them. The strike was over.

In April 1942, SS headquarters in Berlin ordered all Dutch Jews to sew a yellow star on their clothes with the word "JOOD" (Jew) in the middle. Each Jewish person received four stars to display on different items of clothing, and any protest or refusal to wear the star was harshly punished. The largely successful and rapid success of this program started the process of separating the Jewish population from Dutch Christians. Previously, everyone in the country was Dutch, and religion was a private matter; suddenly anyone walking down the street could be identified as Christian or Jew.

Slow but Steady

In their policy toward Dutch Jews, the Nazis tried not to move too quickly to avoid stirring up resistance. German authorities liked to use local Jewish representatives to help with the process of getting everyone registered; it was less trouble to have a so-called Jewish Council do this work for them.

How can we explain the behavior of members of the Jewish Council who checked the identity papers of Jews who were scheduled to be deported? In a few cases, members of the Council were able to change identity cards to save lives. For example, Walter Süskind was a member of the Council who manipulated the system of registration and may have saved 2,000 people, including many children, before he was sent to Auschwitz where he died on a death march in 1945. Another member of the council, David Cohen, hoped to slow down the process of registering and transporting Dutch Jews. Somewhat like Schindler in Poland, he drew up lists of indispensable workers and tried to protect them. Of course, the Nazis were not to be stopped by such actions. After a strike in May 1943, Nazi authorities sent all of Amsterdam's Jewish population, including David Cohen and his family, to concentration camps.

Before being shipped to Poland, Dutch Jews and Roma were kept in holding or transfer camps in the Netherlands; conditions were horrible with polluted drinking water and barely enough food for survival. Westerbork was the most notorious of these camps because every Tuesday a train left for Auschwitz, Sobibór,* Bergen-Belsen,*or Theresienstadt.* The total number of people shipped out of Westerbork was 100,000.

Why Did So Many Die in the Netherlands?

From a Nazi point of view, the destruction of the Dutch Jewish population was successful. The Netherlands lost 100,000 people or 70–80 percent of its Jewish population, one of the highest percentages in Europe. In comparison, 75 percent of French Jews survived the war, 60 percent of Belgian Jews survived, but only about 25 percent of Dutch Jews survived, despite the fact that the Netherlands was not known for anti-Jewish sentiment.

New studies emphasize the role of the government of Seyss-Inquart, a committed Nazi from Austria. Seyss-Inquart and other top leaders of the Netherlands were intense anti-Semites, and they were dedicated to their objective of finding and killing all Dutch Jews. Seyss-Inquart's enthusiasm for his work was proven by the high death toll among Dutch Jews. At the end of the war he was arrested, put on trial at Nuremberg, and hanged with other high-ranking Nazis convicted of war crimes.

ANNE FRANK

> Writing in a diary is a really strange experience for someone like me . . . it seems to me that later on neither I nor anyone else will be interested in the musings of a thirteen-year-old school girl. (June 1942)

Throughout Europe, approximately a million children died during World War II from disease, mistreatment, and murder. The vast majority of these young people disappeared and died anonymously. Anne Frank has become the war's best-known symbol of the suffering and heroism exemplified by so many of these victims. Anne's story was preserved in her diary, a manuscript turned into a book by her father after the war ended. Her diary does more than tell her story; it intrigues the reader due to her authentic testimony about the life of a teenager in her situation.

Originally published in Dutch in 1947, the diary was translated into English five years later and since then has appeared in more than fifty-five languages and sold twenty-five million copies. Today her house in Amsterdam is a museum, and there are foundations named for her that perform humanitarian work around the world.

Although Anne is often thought of as being Dutch, her family was from Germany. She was born in Frankfurt in 1929, about three and a half years after her sister Margot. Due to increasing anti-Semitism in Germany, the Frank family decided to relocate to the Netherlands. They settled in Amsterdam where Anne's father Otto ran a business that supplied spices and pectin for making jam. Like so many other refugee families, Anne's family was trapped after the German army moved west and occupied the Netherlands in the spring of 1940.

While restrictions against Dutch Jews started soon after the Nazis arrived, the constraints became significantly worse in October 1941. Jewish teachers were fired, government workers who were Jewish were removed, and Jewish-owned businesses had to be surrendered to "Aryans." Otto Frank formally signed his business over to one of his Christian friends. The company moved to a new address—Prinsengracht 263—the famous location where the family would soon go into hiding.

Jewish children such as Anne and her sister were no longer allowed to attend regular Dutch schools, and they had to transfer to a Jewish-only institution, where Anne quickly developed a reputation for being funny and also talkative. Nevertheless, the situation for the Frank family and other Jews became worse almost every day. The Nazis provided a long list of activities that were closed to Jews: they were not allowed to ride in cars, on trams, on bicycles, or other forms of public transportation; they could only shop between certain hours and only in stores owned by Jews; they were not allowed on the street at night and could not attend any public entertainment venues such as movies, theaters, or clubs; they could not participate in any athletic events, including swimming, tennis, or rowing; and finally they were not permitted to socialize with Christians in any way. With their mandatory yellow star on their clothes, they were totally segregated from normal society.

Hiding

The threat posed by tightening anti-Semitic policies led the family to prepare a hiding place. When Anne's sister received an order to report for work in Germany, the family decided to take fast action. Wearing several layers of clothes, family members proceeded a few at a time toward Prinsengracht. They settled into rooms behind a bookcase in Otto's place of business and called their new home the Secret Annex. Soon they were joined in hiding by another family—the Van Pels—and then the dentist Fritz Pfeffer. In this space, the Frank family lived on the second floor and the Van Pels lived on the third floor. Food was hidden in the attic. Soon a moveable bookcase that opened like a real door was added to conceal the entrance to the Secret Annex.

It seems remarkable that these families were able to survive for the next two years under these conditions, with food being smuggled into their hiding space by friends who also faced shortages. Friends sacrificed some of their own rations to feed all those who shared that Secret Annex—two years of nothing but potatoes, porridge, thin soup, sauerkraut, and some bread. For those in hiding, these friends were their only contact with the outside world, who, in addition to food, brought clothes and news whenever possible. The pressure on all of them was intense, but nevertheless Anne continued to chronicle her life in the diary she nicknamed "kitty."

She wrote about her daily life, including what she missed most— her education: "Most of all I long to have a home of our own, to be able to move around freely and have someone help me with my homework again, at last. In other words, to go back to school!" (July 1943). The family had stockpiled books to help everyone pass the time, and many of those in hiding studied English and read books on different topics; ultimately for Anne, Margot, and the others, there was nothing else to do day after day.

Anne's diary provided a glimpse of a life in hiding. First up in the morning was Mr. Van Pels at about 6:45, and everyone else got up soon thereafter. The time between 8:30 and 9:00 meant absolute silence since workers were in the business part of the building. Breakfast was at 9:00, followed by a visit by one of their friends to see what they needed. Early in the afternoon, at 1:00, they all listened to the BBC news on the radio, ate lunch, and then took a nap. Anne preferred to write in her diary rather than sleep at that time. Later in the day, around 5:30 or so, the workers in the business, who of course did not know about the Secret Annex, went home, and the family relaxed and talked a bit. Dinner and the evening news occupied most of the rest of the day, with bedtime around 9:00 or 10:00.

For a teenager like Anne, this daily routine was not easy. It was filled with concerns over food but also the fear of discovery. Any loud noise might reveal their situation to an informant and lead to arrest and death. "One day we're laughing at the comical side of life in hiding, and the next day (and there are many such days), we're frightened, and the fear, tension and despair can be read on our faces" (May 1944). Anne wrote faithfully until the dreaded day finally arrived early in August 1944—discovery, deportation, and a concentration camp.

Discovery and Deportation

Imagine the terror in the Secret Annex when they heard the Nazi agents searching the building around 11:00 AM on August 4, 1944. The secret bookcase door was discovered, and by 1:00 PM everyone had been arrested. They were searched for any valuables and then taken away at gunpoint. We still do not know if they were discovered by chance or by betrayal, but the Frank family was sent to Westerbork transit camp by train. One month later they were on the list of those to be sent to Poland. The family with about seventy other Jewish prisoners was loaded into a freight car on a long train carrying hundreds of prisoners; there was barely enough room to stand in each wagon. For three days there was no privacy; everyone shared a bucket in the corner as a toilet.

On arrival at Auschwitz in the middle of the night, guards with attack dogs screamed at everyone in German. Men and women were separated, some designated for immediate death and some sent to the barracks to work for the Nazis. Anne's mother remained at Auschwitz and died there, probably in January 1945. By then Anne and Margot had been sent to Bergen-Belsen in northern Germany, where they both died of typhus. After the war, Otto Frank, the lone survivor of the eight people hiding with Anne for two years, returned to Amsterdam and recovered the diary that had been saved by family friends.

Otto Frank devoted his life to preserving Anne's legacy through her diary. He remarried with Elfriede (Fritzi) Geiringer, another Auschwitz survivor. Eva, Fritzi's daughter from her first marriage, also survived the concentration camps. Eva learned that her father and brother, neither of whom survived the war, had placed paintings in the house where they were hiding before they were captured and deported. Just as Otto Frank, who died in 1980, had returned to the Netherlands to find Anne Frank's diary, so too Eva returned to the Netherlands and discovered the paintings of her father and brother. Like Anne's diary, the paintings express the desire for freedom and other emotions experienced while spending one's life in hiding and fear.

Legacy

While the diary seems to be all that remains of Anne Frank, her story continues to inspire millions of people around the world. The diary itself is fascinating due to Anne's honesty, as she explored her feelings toward family and friends without pretending that everything was perfect. She is believable because she never knew that her diary would be read by others; her description of the stress and fear is simple, unpretentious, and convincing.

Anne's diary and tragic death helped to put a personal touch on the larger catastrophe of the Holocaust. While she was only one of millions who died, her individual account and portrayal of life in the shadows brought her struggle to life for the many readers of her story. In 1960 the house where the Frank family hid from the Nazis opened as the Anne Frank Museum. *The Diary of a Young Girl* remains a classic tale of human persistence in the face of evil.

FRANCE

Restrictions on Jews in France started three months after the armistice. The Jewish population was ordered to register with the local police and also barred from various professions, including government, medicine, law, teaching, and entertainment. In July 1942, on German orders, the French police started the roundup of 13,000 Jews and confined them under very harsh conditions in the Vélodrome d'Hiver (Vél d'hiv),* an old bicycle stadium. From there the prisoners were moved to the internment camp at Drancy* in a northeastern suburb of Paris. At Drancy, the inmates were subjected to harsh treatment, including torture and execution, sometimes by members of the French police. While such brutal behavior was expected of Nazi guards, many people remain shocked that French police acted in this manner as well. From Drancy the condemned were transported by train to the concentration camp of Auschwitz. Few prisoners survived Drancy and Auschwitz.

The Vichy government in the south joined with the occupation forces in the north in arresting and sending Jews to Drancy and Auschwitz. As part of this collaboration, Gestapo head Klaus Barbie led a raid on an orphanage for Jewish children in Izieu about fifty-five miles east of Lyon. The "Butcher of Lyon" participated personally in throwing the crying and screaming children into the back of the vans, with a total of forty-four children and their seven adult caretakers arrested. All of the children were sent immediately to Drancy and then on the next train to Auschwitz, and all were killed.

By the end of the occupation, more than 75,000 prisoners had been held at Drancy, and almost all of them were killed in concentration camps. In addition to Jews, the Nazis and the French police targeted Roma, homosexuals, communists, and many immigrants who had come to France to escape the Nazis.

A Survivor's Story

Simon Igel was one of those immigrants who had come to France for a better life. Born in 1927 in Poland, his family moved to Vienna when he was one. He grew up with his two older brothers and recalled picnics and hiking on Sunday afternoons. When Simon was ten years old, the family moved to France seeking improved economic opportunities. He found school in France difficult, as he spoke German at home, and it took a while for him to learn a new language. Nevertheless, his German language skills would soon save him.

When the war broke out, his father tried to enlist but was rejected as a foreigner. The armistice found the Igel family living under German occupation, and the anti-Jewish statutes meant that his father could not even look for work. Soon Simon found himself humiliated with a yellow star on his clothes; he felt publicly ashamed just walking down the street. He remembered the day in July 1942 when the police came to the family apartment, and his father and brothers were frozen with anxiety; his mother started packing all of their belongings. All five members of the family were transported in silence to prison, but since Simon was only fifteen, he was taken separately to an orphanage. Three days later his family was gone—on their way to Auschwitz. "I never imagined for an instant that I would never see them again" (Igel, 20).

A month later, Simon was in hiding when three Gestapo agents knocked on his door and arrested him. He was sure that he had been betrayed, but he never learned who turned him in. Transported to prison in Lyon, he was held in the "barracks for Jews." His cell did not have a toilet, and it did not have a window so he never knew whether it was day or night; he was allowed one hour per day in the courtyard. After three weeks in prison, Simon was taken to the train station and sent to Drancy. While he recalled the ride to Drancy as horrible, it was nothing compared to what lay ahead of him.

In October 1943 Simon was included in a convoy of one thousand prisoners put on a train for Poland. With only the clothes he was wearing, he entered a train car that had a small grill for air, one bucket to serve as a toilet for everyone, no room to move or sit, and babies and children crying all the time. After three days and nights of this hell, as he called it, he was happy to arrive someplace even though he did not know where he was.

When the wagon doors opened, there were SS members yelling at everyone to line up and follow orders. "The scene was terrifying." Immediately men and women were separated, and Simon realized where one line was going: "Here you enter by the door and you leave by the chimney. I still did not understand and tried to look around for my parents. Eventually my line of men arrived at an SS officer who asked my age. I answered in perfect German, and the officer, surprised by my response, hesitated for a fraction of a second before sending me to another line where I was put on a truck to a work camp. That is where I got my tattoo on my left arm: 157085" (Igel, 47). Along with this new identity, Simon received a uniform with vertical stripes. Every day he was awake at 5:00 A.M. and on his way to work in the mines, and every day was the same except execution day, when all the inmates had to watch prisoners being shot.

Simon considered himself lucky when the SS officer sent him to work, but he was injured while performing heavy labor. In the infirmary, Simon's doctor turned out to be from Vienna and recognized Simon's Austrian accent. The doctor gave him small jobs in the clinic, including the stacking of dead bodies, but Simon discovered a positive side to this otherwise-gruesome detail. As he collected the bodies, he often found bits and pieces of food in the clothes of the dead; he was glad to have the extra nourishment.

Early in 1945, the rumor went around that the Soviet army was on its way. The inmates were moved out of the camp on a forced march that finally took him to Bergen-Belsen in Germany. Once again Simon was lucky, as that camp was liberated by the British. Since no one had any identification papers, the British asked everyone their nationality and then lined them up for transfer accordingly. Simon saw that the Jewish prisoners were held separately, and he was determined to avoid punishment due to his religion again. Hoping to avoid being sent to Poland, he told the officers he was French, and he was added to the train going in that direction. A short time later, he was dropped in Brussels, eighteen-years-old, alone in the world, with nowhere to go.

Simon Igel went on to spend much of his life talking to high school and college students about his experiences, determined that the Holocaust would not be forgotten and equally certain that young people had to be reminded always about the consequences of apathy (Igel, 110).

DENMARK

> The situation is very serious. We must take action immediately. You must leave the synagogue now and contact all relatives, friends and neighbors you know who are Jewish and tell them what I told you. You must also speak to your Christian friends and ask them to warn any Jews they know. You must do this immediately, within the next few minutes, so that two or three hours from now everyone will know what is happening. By nightfall we must all be in hiding.
> Dr. Marcus Melchior, Chief Rabbi, Krystalgade Synagogue, Copenhagen, September 29, 1943 (www.auschwitz.dk)

Denmark was occupied in April 1940. Without a large army, the country could not put up resistance to the Nazi invasion, and the battle for Denmark lasted little more than one day. A token force of approximately one hundred Germans occupied this nation of almost four million people that included about 7,500 Jews.

Hitler viewed the Danes as close relatives of Germans, and Denmark was allowed to retain a lot of autonomy. Based on his view of so-called racial affinity, Hitler's postwar goal was a merger between Germany and Denmark. Danish King Christian X and his government did not go into exile in London; the proud king refused to collaborate but remained in the country and continued to serve as the official head of state. Denmark became a protectorate of Germany.

In 1942, Werner Best was Germany's highest-ranking official in Denmark. Trade relations between Denmark and Germany were good, with Denmark providing up to 15 percent of Germany's agricultural needs at this time. Best was concerned that an aggressive assault on Danish Jews would upset the relationship between the two countries, and as a result he did not order the Jewish population to wear a yellow star or move into a ghetto. Despite some restrictions, the occupation of Denmark was mild compared to other nations under Nazi control.

Nevertheless, opposition to German occupation increased as the war dragged on. The Russian victory at Stalingrad* played a major role in Danish awareness that the Allies might win the war. In the summer of 1943 strikes and other protests against the Nazis took place and the situation quickly enflamed views on both sides. Relations between the two countries deteriorated. As the occupiers used more force, the Danish resistance grew stronger and bolder.

In retaliation, the Nazis decided to send Danish Jews to concentration camps. The German official (naval attaché) Georg Duckwitz, who had friendly relations with influential Danes, told several politicians what was going to happen. Duckwitz also informed the government in Stockholm about the plan to deport the Jewish population, and various Swedish officials began to work on obtaining passports for Danish Jews. The government of Sweden agreed to provide refuge.

The Gestapo began its search for Jews in hiding and about 200 Danish Jews were arrested; clearly, the opportunity to rescue the rest of the population was closing. With little time to spare, close to 7,000 Danish Jews were moved to the coast at night and taken across the Baltic Sea to Sweden. Although some fishermen charged for their service, the Danish resistance and the government provided funds to make the crossing possible. Fishing boats totaled 900 crossings to transport 7,000 people, while in Denmark the rest of the population refused to assist in the capture of Jews in hiding. In addition, the Torah (holy scroll) from the main synagogue was hidden in a Lutheran Church where the Nazis did not find it. It was a brave national effort that brought the king, the churches, and the Danish population together and prevented a repetition of the genocide taking place in the rest of Europe.

After the war, newspapers claimed that King Christian X wore an armband with a Star of David in solidarity with Danish Jews. This report is not true, but that does not detract from the brave act of the entire population in Denmark. While the absolute number of Danish Jews was not large, Denmark saved the highest percentage of its Jewish population of any occupied country in Europe. It was one heroic moment in a war filled with terrible moments.

Duckwitz stayed in Denmark for a while after the war, then returned to Germany and became a diplomat there. He died in 1973, but before his death Duckwitz received recognition as "Righteous Among the Nations."

The history of Denmark has become more nuanced since the end of the war. It is now clear that there were Danish collaborators,* but it is also apparent that when faced with a challenge to their sense of justice, most Danes rallied together to affirm that Christian and Jew could be members of the same nation.

BULGARIA

Bulgaria is often overlooked in the discussion of heroic responses to Nazi oppression. Neutral when war broke out in 1939, Bulgaria entered into an alliance with Germany in 1941 just before the invasion of the Soviet Union took place. By 1944, with the Soviet army approaching eastern Europe, Bulgaria changed sides and joined the Allies.

In 1943 while still allied with Germany, Bulgaria prepared to ship 20,000 of its 50,000 Jewish inhabitants to concentration camps. Popular opposition that included ordinary citizens, politicians, and clergy convinced the government to cancel the deportations. When the war ended, almost all of Bulgaria's 50,000 Jews had been saved.

SOVIET UNION

Berdichev and Babi Yar*

Wherever the Wehrmacht went in the Soviet Union, the Einsatzgruppen killing squads were with them, especially along the border areas near Poland, Belarus, and into Ukraine. About one hundred miles southwest of Kiev is Berdichev, a town with a long Jewish history. In September 1941, as soon as the German army occupied the town, the Einsatzgruppen arrived. They enlisted the help of the local Ukrainian police to find all of the Jewish homes and residents, and then marched 30,000 Jews to fields nearby where they were all executed.

As the German army occupied Kiev, the capital of Ukraine, about 100,000 Jews fled east, leaving 60,000 Jews still in the city. Only two weeks after the Berdichev massacre, the Einsatzgruppen executed another 33,000 Jews at a ravine called Babi Yar. Over the next few months, thousands more Jews, Roma, and others were shot there; eventually 100,000 victims were in those trenches. In all parts of Eastern Europe where the Einsatzgruppen operated, estimates suggest that they killed between one and two million people.

Odessa

This important port city on the Black Sea was abandoned by the retreating Soviet army in late summer and occupied in October 1941 by the Romanian army, one of Germany's allies. Much of the city's population had fled east, but 300,000 people, including 50,000 Jews, remained in Odessa. The Romanian army started the slaughter immediately, with Jews being arrested, shot, burned alive inside buildings, or hanged from electric lines running above trolley cars. Thousands of people were killed in a short time. Once the initial carnage was over, the remaining Jewish population was ordered to move into one part of the city only—a ghetto—and then in early 1942 sent out of the city entirely to camps in the countryside where lack of food and disease took a toll on the remaining 30,000.

CROATIA AND SERBIA

Croatia and Serbia had been unified before the war in the Kingdom of Yugoslavia, but they split into two separate countries during World War II. Croatia established a right-wing pro-Nazi government that carried out sadistic atrocities, killing 30,000 Jews, 25,000 Roma, and 350,000 Serbs in their own concentration camp. In Serbia, it was the German occupation forces that rounded up and killed about 16,000 Serbian Jews through shooting and carbon monoxide vans.

GREECE

The German army arrived in Greece to save Mussolini from defeat. The Nazis were able to kill 80 percent of the Jewish population, or about 70,000 people. Unlike churches in Croatia and Slovakia, the Greek Orthodox Church did not support the murders. The archbishop of Athens, Damaskinos, wrote a letter of protest to the Nazi authorities and promised protective documents for Jews in the country, but there was little he could do against the German military. The Jews of Greece were shipped to Auschwitz.

Kurt Waldheim

Kurt Waldheim (1918–2007) was born in Austria, and he served in the Wehrmacht in Greece and Serbia during the war. In subsequent years, he lied about his war record and claimed that he had been a student. With his supposedly clean record, he had a wonderful career—he served as secretary-general of the United Nations for ten years (1972–1982). In 1986 he was a candidate for president of Austria, but during the campaign his Nazi war record was revealed. Despite the evidence of his false testimony and role in the deportation of Greeks, Serbs, and Jews, he was elected president of Austria and served one term from 1986 to 1992.

HUNGARY

Raoul Wallenberg

In 1944, the situation in Hungary was chaotic; a pro-German Hungarian government that had protected the Jewish population was replaced by a Nazi puppet government that immediately started shipping Jews to Auschwitz. In less than two months, the new Nazi regime, advised by Adolf Eichmann, sent 150 freight trains carrying 400,000 Hungarian Jews to death. The Swedish government was alarmed by the situation, and it posted one of its diplomats, Raoul Wallenberg (1912–1947?), to its legation in Budapest with the specific mission of saving Jews. There were 200,000 Jews left in the country, and Wallenberg's plan was to issue documents called "protective passports" that identified the person as a Swedish subject. When he heard that Eichmann was planning to massacre the remaining Jews in the Hungarian capital, Wallenberg warned the German general who was to carry out the plan that he would be charged as a war criminal. The killing was cancelled shortly before

Table 9.1 Holocaust Deaths by Country (see United States Holocaust Memorial Museum)

Country	Killed	Percentage of Jewish Population Killed
Belgium	25,000 (out of 90,000)	27
Croatia	30,000 (out of 39,000)	90 (plus 350,000 Serbs and 25,000 Roma)
Denmark	60 (out of 7,500)	1
France	75,000 (out of 315,000)	22
Germany	165,000 (out of 214,000)	75
Greece	65,000 (out of 72,000)	90
Hungary	575,000 (out of 825,000)	70
Netherlands	100,000 (out of 140,000)	70
Poland	3,000,000 (out of 3,350,000)	90
Romania	250,000 (out of 350,000)	80
Serbia	15,000 (out of 17,000)	90
Slovakia	75,000 (out of 90,000)	80
Soviet Union	1,000,000 (out of 3,000,000)	33

the Red Army arrived in January 1945. There were 100,000 Jews remaining in Budapest after the war, and while Wallenberg had not handed each one a "protective passport," his efforts saved most of them. Shortly thereafter, however, the Soviet army arrested Wallenberg on suspicion of espionage. He was supposedly taken to Moscow and interrogated; recent evidence suggests he died in 1947 in Soviet custody.

CONCLUSION

As the war approached its end, Soviet and Allied troops entered and liberated the concentration camps. The extent and horror of the extermination program shocked the soldiers, who were confronted by piles of unburied bodies, remnants of gas chambers and crematoria, and walking-skeleton survivors. Allied photographers took photos and newsreels of the grisly sights, presented to the world for the first time at the Nuremberg Trials at the end of 1945. Ever since, historians, philosophers, theologians, and psychologists have tried to understand and make sense of these events, but most of their efforts fail in some way. The enormity of the crime, the level of hatred, and the exercise of sadistic acts all remain beyond comprehension.

It is not difficult to build a framework for what took place between the wars, starting with Germany's defeat in World War I, the discontent with both the Treaty of Versailles* and the Weimar Republic,* and the rise of an extremist political party with a charismatic leader. It is subsequent events that defy our understanding: a message of racial hatred and bigotry and the absence of voices in defense of democracy and freedom. Anyone who supported Hitler could not deny knowing what he stood for because his program was clearly spelled out in *Mein Kampf* and in continuous speeches, posters, and radio campaigns. Many observers have commented on the infatuation and devotion of average Germans listening to his speeches, followed by chants of "Sieg Heil" and Nazi salutes.

Testimony at the trial of high-ranking Nazi war criminals in Nuremberg revealed how the process of mass killing worked. Several witnesses talked easily about their role in the machinery of death—the concentration camps—without remorse or reflection. For them, assembly line techniques that killed people was a job similar to the mass production of automobiles. Rather than regretting their role in murder, they spoke proudly of the efficiency of their operation.

While it is important to remember the role of Germany in these events, it is also necessary to recall the Romanian treatment of Odessa, the Polish priests who supported the eradication of Jewish life in Warsaw or Kraków, the French Milice* under the Vichy regime, the "Butcher of Lyon" who tortured Jean Moulin and then raided the orphanage at Izieu and sent all the children to death, regular German soldiers who made it possible for the Einsatzgruppen killing squads to lead thousands of people to open ditches to be shot and dumped without remorse, the Croatian Ustashe* who murdered Serbs, Jews, and Roma with abandon, Bishop Hudal who ran the "ratline" to help war criminals escape to South America, the gangs in the Netherlands and France who hunted Jews for a fee, and Ukrainians who worked in the camps and rivaled the SS in cruelty.

In considering those events and the despair pervading them, one also does well to remember the individuals who restored faith in humanity; Jan Karski, who went into the ghetto and camps and took his report to Allied governments; Raoul Wallenberg, who turned his assignment to help some Hungarian Jews into a personal mission to save them all; the friends who fed Anne Frank and her family; the priests, nuns, ministers, pastors, and average folks who hid children; Father Pierre-Marie Benoît; the village of Le Chambon-sur-Lignon; Oskar Schindler; Sophie Scholl; Jozef and Wiktoria Ulma; Jan and Antonina Zabinski, who directed the zoo in Warsaw; the Jews of the Warsaw Ghetto who fought the German army for three weeks; Janusz Korczak who held the hands of the orphans under his care and walked them with dignity to the train; and more than 27,000 individuals designated as "Righteous Among the Nations."

FURTHER READING

Auschwitz.dk: one of several websites dedicated to remembering the Holocaust (established 1966).
Frank, Anne. *Anne Frank: The Diary of a Young Girl*. New York: Doubleday, 1952.
holocaustresearchproject.org. website established in 2006 as H.E.A.R.T. or Holocaust Education and Archive Research Team.
Igel, Simon. *Matricule 157085: Témoignage d'un adolescent rescapé d'Auschwitz*. Conde-sur-Noireau: Charles Corlet, 2011.
Jewishvirtuallibrary.org. established in 1993 to preserve information on the Holocaust.
Karski, Jan. *The Story of a Secret State*. Boston: Houghton Mifflin, 1944.
Klarsfeld, Serge. *The Children of Izieu: A Human Tragedy*. New York: Harry N. Abrams, 1984.
Klukowski, Zygmunt. *Diary from the Years of Occupation 1939–1944*. Champaign, IL: University of Illinois Press, 1993.
Seibel, Wolfgang. Translated by Ciaran Cronin. *Persecution and Rescue: The Politics of the "Final Solution" in France, 1940–1944*. Ann Arbor: University of Michigan Press, 2016.
Sporl, Gerhard. "How Denmark Saved Its Jews from the Nazis." *Spiegel Online*, October 17, 2013. https://www.spiegel.de/international/zeitgeist/book-examines-how-jews-of-denmark-were-saved-from-the-holocaust-a-928116.html
United States Holocaust Memorial Museum, Washington.
Anne Frank House. *The World of Anne Frank*. London: Macmillan, 2001.

Appendix A
FILMS ABOUT WORLD WAR II

This brief list is intended to provide the reader with another resource in addition to books and websites. The films included are primarily from or about the countries featured in this book. The list is highly selective and not intended to be complete. Each film's title is followed by the year of production and a brief description.

FRANCE
1. *Night and Fog* (1955): Vivid newsreel of concentration camps.
2. *Army of Shadows* (1969): A realistic look at the French resistance.
3. *The Sorrow and the Pity* (1969) (released in the United States in 1972): A four-hour documentary by Marcel Ophuls based on interviews with residents of Clermont-Ferrand in France. The film explores the occupation, collaboration, resistance, and the Holocaust.
4. *Au revoir les enfants* (1987): Based on a true story, the film deals with children in a Catholic boarding school and the Gestapo's search for Jewish children hiding there.
5. *Sarah's Key* (2010): This film focuses on the roundup of French Jews in 1942 and the conditions in Vel' d'Hiv.

GERMANY
1. *Das Boot* (1981): Focuses on life in a German U-Boat in 1942 in the Atlantic Ocean.

2. *Stalingrad* (1993): Made in Germany, this film depicts the battle from the perspective of the losers. The movie is realistic and considered an excellent view of war.
3. *Downfall* (2004): Using historical records, this drama re-creates Hitler's last days in his bunker in Berlin before the Soviet army arrived. It is considered one of the better historical depictions of this subject.
4. *Sophie Scholl—The Final Days* (2005): It tells the true story of the White Rose resistance movement based at the University of Munich and organized by Sophie and her brother. Unlike the officers in Operation Valkyrie who tried to assassinate Hitler only after Germany was losing, these students risked everything based on their moral objections to the Nazis.

NETHERLANDS

1. *Black Book* (2006): Set in the Netherlands, this film follows a Dutch Jewish woman who becomes a spy for the resistance. Her assignment involves infiltrating Nazi headquarters, where she meets both brutal and decent German officers.

POLAND

1. *Forbidden Songs* (1946–1947): The story of daily life for several residents in an apartment building during the occupation of Warsaw. Resistance and patriotic songs used by the underground are woven into the plot. The film's theme is the common suffering of Poles and Jews and their resistance to the Nazis. The film was popular and demonstrated the important role that music played for all Poles at that time. Nevertheless, it was pulled from theaters by the postwar government and reworked to add more Nazi cruelty and more Soviet liberation.
2. *Border Street* (1948): One of the first postwar films to deal with the Warsaw Ghetto and its destruction as shown through the eyes of several families.
3. *Kanal* (1956): Set during the Warsaw Uprising of 1944, the story follows resistance fighters traveling through the sewers of Warsaw to escape the Nazis.
4. *Ashes and Diamonds* (1958): Just as the war ends and Germans leave Poland, Russian and Polish fighters who were on the same side during the war confront the new reality of opposing each other.
5. *Eroica* (1958): A story in two parts set in Poland during the war: the Warsaw Uprising and a POW camp.

6. *Story of 700 Polish Children* (1966): A true story of the journey of Polish children orphaned during the war and sent to New Zealand. At the battle for Monte Cassino in Italy, Polish and New Zealand troops fought together, but the Polish soldiers paid a high price in lives lost. The children of those soldiers needed a home, and the New Zealand troops and government arranged for them to be sent there. The film shows the children arriving in Wellington, New Zealand, as well as their adaptation to their new lives.
7. *Europa Europa* (1990): Based on the autobiography of a Polish Jew named Solomon Perel, this film tells the story of how the author (then a teenager) survived by convincing the Nazis that he was of Aryan origin.
8. *Korczak* (1990): The true story of a Jewish orphanage in the Warsaw Ghetto and the idealistic pediatrician who hoped that the Nazis would spare the children. He died with them in Treblinka in 1942.
9. *Schindler's List* (1993): Based on the true story of Oskar Schindler and his attempt to save Jewish workers in his factory in Kraków.
10. *The Pianist* (2002): Based on the autobiography of Wladyslaw Szpilman who went into hiding after the Warsaw Ghetto was liquidated. He was helped by a German officer at the end of the war.
11. *Katyn* (2007): The massacre of 20,000 Polish officers and intellectuals in 1940 by the Soviet secret police. The mass grave was discovered by the Nazis in 1943, but the Soviet government denied any involvement.
12. *In Darkness* (2012): Based on a true story, a sewer worker in Lvov finds Jews hiding below ground and agrees to help them in exchange for money.

SOVIET UNION

1. *Two Soldiers* (1943): Two machine-gunners on the Leningrad front share a trench and an emotional bond. The song "Dark Night" is still popular in Russia.
2. *Rainbow* (1943): It is difficult to find the rainbow in the midst of German atrocities.
3. *The Cranes Are Flying* (1957): The film depicts two young lovers, Boris and Veronika. Boris goes to war and is killed. Veronika makes sacrifices that symbolize what Soviet women endured during the war.
4. *Ballad of a Soldier* (1959): The film tells the story of Alyosha and his experiences as he travels home from the front.

5. *Ivan's Childhood* (1962): This Soviet film follows young Ivan, who is captured by the Germans, escapes back to Russia, and returns to Germany to spy on the Nazis.
6. *Come and See* (1985): A story of a teenager in Belarus who joins the resistance and witnesses Nazi crimes.

OTHER COUNTRIES

1. *Casablanca* (1942): Made during the war, this film presents moral issues about resistance.
2. *On Their Own Territory* (1948): In Yugoslavia, partisans fight against Germans and Italians.
3. *The Man Who Never Was* (1956): Based on a 1943 attempt by the British called Operation Mincemeat to trick the Germans into thinking that the planned invasion of Sicily would take place in Greece and Sardinia. A British cadaver is planted to wash ashore in Spain with papers designed to fool German intelligence.
4. *The Longest Day* (1962): Historically based film about D-Day in Normandy in 1944. Despite the presence of well-known actors, the landing itself is the star of the movie.
5. *The Great Escape* (1963): Based on a true story of POWs digging a tunnel to escape from Stalag Luft III in Germany (now in Poland). The film changed several details to appeal to American viewers. In reality, the successful escapees were two Norwegians and a Dutch prisoner.
6. *Is Paris Burning?* (1966): A film version of the book about the liberation of Paris in 1944.
7. *A Bridge Too Far* (1977): This film deals with the failed Allied attempt to seize the bridges across the Rhine River in Operation Market Garden in 1944.
8. *Saving Private Ryan* (1998): The opening scene is recognized as a realistic depiction of the Allied landing in Normandy in 1944.
9. *U-571* (2000): This movie shows an American ship capturing a German submarine and with it an Enigma machine that helps the Allies break the German code. In reality, the United States was not in the war at that time, and it was the British destroyer HMS *Bulldog* that captured the machine.
10. *Enemy at the Gates* (2001): This is a film about two snipers during the Battle of Stalingrad. It is not a true story.
11. *Valkyrie* (2008): It is a re-creation of the failed July 20, 1944, plot to kill Hitler.
12. *Flame and Citron* (2008): Based on true events in Denmark, the film follows two resistance fighters who hunt for collaborators and are hunted in turn by the Gestapo.
13. *Defiance* (2008–2009): This movie deals with partisan warfare and is based on the Jewish Bielski brothers in the forests of Belarus.

14. *The Monuments Men* (2014): The attempt to recover stolen art hidden by the Nazis during the war.
15. *The Zookeeper's Wife* (2017): The film is based on the true story of Jan and Antonina Zabinski, who saved 300 Jews during the war.
16. *Dunkirk* (2017): The film tells the story of Dunkirk from the perspective of a couple of British soldiers.
17. *Darkest Hour* (2017): A film about Churchill coming to power as prime minister in 1940.

Appendix B
MUSEUMS VISITED

This brief list includes many of the war-related museums visited by the author. The purpose of this list is to indicate the variety of museums, mostly in Europe but increasingly in the United States as well, where objects of war, weapons, photo exhibits, and documentary films about the war can be visited and consulted. There are also many preserved battle fields, artillery and gun emplacements, and cemeteries that are available for the motivated traveler.

Amsterdam:
Verzetsmuseum Resistance Museum

Arromanches, France:
Musée du Débarquement

Bayeux, France:
Museum of the Battle of Normandy

Berlin:
German Historical Museum
German-Russian Museum Berlin-Karlshorst

Caen:
Caen Mémorial Museum

Kraków:
Auschwitz concentration camp
Oskar Schindler's Enamel Factory

Leningrad (St. Petersburg), Russia:
Museum of the Defense and the Siege of Leningrad

London:
Churchill War Rooms
Imperial War Museum
Royal Air Force Museum London

Moscow:
Museum of the Great Patriotic War

Munich:
Dachau concentration camp
Munich Documentation Centre for the History of National Socialism

New Orleans:
National World War II Museum

Nuremberg:
Documentation Center Nazi Party Rally Grounds
Nuremberg Court House

Paris:
Les Invalides
Musée du Général Leclerc de Hauteclocque
et de la Libération de Paris-Musée Jean Moulin

Portsmouth, U.K.:
D-Day Museum

Reims, France:
Museum of the Surrender (Musée de la Reddition)

Sainte-Mère-Église:
Airborne Museum

Warsaw:
POLIN Museum of the History of Polish Jews
Warsaw Uprising Museum

Washington, D.C.:
U.S. Holocaust Memorial Museum

BIBLIOGRAPHY

Ament, Suzanne. *Sing to Victory: The Role of Popular Song in the Soviet Union During World War II*. Ann Arbor: University of Michigan Press, 1996.
Andrews, Evan. "8 Things You Should Know About WWII's Eastern Front." History.com, May 27, 2014. https://www.history.com/news/8-things-you-should-know-about-wwiis-eastern-front. Accessed October 2, 2017.
Aragon, Louis. *Le crève-coeur*. London: Horizon/La France Libre, 1942.
Armstrong, John A. *Ukrainian Nationalism 1939–1945*. New York: Columbia University Press, 1955.
Ashdown, Paddy. *The Cruel Victory: The French Resistance, D-Day and the Battle for Vercors 1944*. London: HarperCollins, 2014.
Bank, Jan with Lieve Gevers. *Churches and Religion in the Second World War*. Translated by Brian Doyle. London: Bloomsbury, 2016.
Barber, John and Mark Harrison. *The Soviet Home Front, 1941–1945: A Social and Economic History of the USSR in World War II*. London: Longman, 1991.
Barrett, Thomas M. "No, a Soldier Doesn't Forget the Memory of the Great Fatherland War and Popular Music in the Late Stalin Period." *Canadian-American Slavic Studies*. Vol. 48, no. 3, 2014, 308–328.
Beevor, Anthony. *The Second World War*. New York: Little, Brown and Co., 2012.
Benioff, David. *City of Thieves*. New York: Plume, 2009.
British War Blue Book: Documents Concerning German-Polish Relations. New York: Farrar & Rinehart, 1939.

Children of War: Diaries 1941–1945. Translated by Andrew Bromfield, Rose France, and Anthony Hippisley. Moscow: Argumenty i Fakty, AIF Kind Heart Charitable Foundation, 2016.

Collingham, Lizzie. *The Taste of War: World War Two and the Battle for Food*. New York: Penguin Books, 2011.

Cottam, Kazimiera J., ed. *Women in War and Resistance: Selected Biographies of Soviet Women Soldiers*. Nepean, Canada: New Military Publishing, 1998.

Crowther, Bosley. "Terror Reign by Nazis." *New York Times*, October 23, 1944. https://www.nytimes.com/1944/10/23/archives/terror-reign-by-nazis.html. Accessed September 6, 2017.

Cunard, Nancy. *Poems for France*. London: La France Libre, 1944.

Dublin, Louis. "War and the Birth Rate—A Brief Historical Summary." *American Journal of Public Health*. Vol. 35, April 1945, 315–320.

Eye Witness to History. "The Nazi Occupation of Poland." 1997. https://www.eyewitnesstohistory.com/poland.htm

Frank, Anne. *Anne Frank: The Diary of a Young Girl*. New York: Doubleday, 1952.

French Yellow Book: Diplomatic Documents. London: Hutchinson & Co., 1939.

Gardner, Brian. *The Terrible Rain: The War Poets 1939–1945*. London: Methuen, 1966.

Gildea, Robert, Olivier Wieviorka, and Anette Warring, eds. *Surviving Hitler and Mussolini: Daily Life in Occupied Europe*. Oxford: Berg, 2006.

Glantz, David M. *The Battle of Leningrad 1941–1944*. Lawrence: University Press of Kansas, 2002.

Golsan, Richard J. *The Papon Affair*. New York: Routledge, 2000.

Hamblett, Charles. *I Burn for England: An Anthology of the Poetry of World War II*. London: Frewin, 1966.

Hamilton, Ian. *The Poetry of War, 1939–1945*. London: Ross, 1965.

Hassing, Arne. *Church Resistance to Nazism in Norway, 1940–1945*. Seattle: University of Washington Press, 2014.

Higgins, Ian. *An Anthology of Second World War French Poetry*. London: Methuen, 1982.

Igel, Simon. *Matricule 157085: Témoignage d'un adolescent rescapé d'Auschwitz*. Conde-sur-Noireau: Charles Corlet, 2011.

Karski, Jan. *The Story of a Secret State*. Boston: Houghton Mifflin, 1944.

Kedward, H. R. *Occupied France: Collaboration and Resistance 1940–1944*. Oxford: Blackwell, 1985.

Klarsfeld, Serge. *The Children of Izieu: A Human Tragedy*. New York: Harry N. Abrams, 1984.

Klemann, Hein and Sergei Kudryashov. *Occupied Economies: An Economic History of Nazi-Occupied Europe, 1939–1945*. Oxford: Berg, 2012.

Klukowski, Zygmunt. *Diary from the Years of Occupation 1939–1944*. Champaign: University of Illinois Press, 1993.

Kosmala, Beate and Georgi Verbeeck. *Facing the Catastrophe: Jews and Non-Jews in Europe During World War II.* Oxford: Berg, 2011.

Lehnstaedt, Stephan. *Occupation in the East: The Daily Lives of German Occupiers in Warsaw and Minsk, 1939–1944.* Translated by Martin Dean. New York: Berghahn, 2016.

Liebreich, Karen. "The Nazi Marilyn Monroe: Goebbels Had Very Nice Eyes—But He Was a Devil." *The Guardian*, April 3, 2017. https://www.theguardian.com/the-nazi-marilyn-monroe-goebbels-had-very-nice-eyes

Longman, Jeré and Andrew W. Lehren. "World War II Soccer Match Echoes Through Time." *New York Times*, June 23, 2012. https://www.nytimes.com/a-soccer-match-in-ukraine-during-world-war-ii-echoes-through-time

Madigan, Kevin J. "How the Catholic Church Sheltered Nazi War Criminals." *Commentary*, December 1, 2011. https://www.commentarymagazine.com/how-the-catholic-church-sheltered-nazi-war-criminals

Marquand, Robert. "A Protestant Town's 'Conspiracy of Good' in Vichy France." *Christian Science Monitor*, May 15, 2008. https://www.csmonitor.com/World/Europe/2008/0515/p01s01-woeu.html

Mazower, Mark. *Hitler's Empire: How the Nazis Ruled Europe.* New York: The Penguin Press, 2008.

Merridale, Catherine. *Ivan's War: Life and Death in the Red Army, 1939–1945.* New York: Picador, 2006.

Milward, Alan S. *War, Economy and Society, 1939–1945.* Berkeley: University of California, 1979.

Murdoch, Brian. *Fighting Songs and Warring Word: Popular Lyrics of Two World Wars.* London: Routledge, 1990.

Myles, Bruce. *Night Witches: The Untold Story of Soviet Women in Combat.* Chicago: Academy Chicago Publishers, 1990.

Naliwajek-Mazurek, Katarzyna. "The Use of Polish Musical Tradition in the Nazi Propaganda." *Musicology Today*, 2010, 243–259. Files.musicologytoday.hist.pl/files/Musicology_Today-r2010-t7-s243-259.pdf

Nazi-Soviet Relations: Documents from the Archives of the German Foreign Office. Washington, DC: U.S. Department of State, 1948.

The New York Review of Books, September 28, 1989, Vol. 36, No. 14; March 29, 1990, vol. 37, No. 5; September 27, 1990, Vol. 37, No. 14 for an exchange on Denmark in the war.

Nicholas, Lynn H. *The Rape of Europa: The Fate of Europe's Treasures in the Third Reich and Second World War.* New York: Vintage Books, 1994.

O'Neill, William L. *World War II: A Student Companion.* New York: Oxford University Press, 1999.

Overy, Richard. *Russia's War: A History of the Soviet War Effort 1941–1945.* New York: Penguin Books, 1997.

Overy, Richard. *Why the Allies Won.* New York: W.W. Norton, 1997.

Paxton, Robert O. *Vichy France*. New York: Columbia University Press, 1972.
Pennington, Reina. *Wings, Women, and War: Soviet Airwomen in World War II Combat*. Lawrence: University Press of Kansas, 2002.
Plevy, Harry. *Norway 1940: Chronicle of a Chaotic Campaign*. Havertown, PA: Casemate, 2017.
Polyudova, Elena. *Soviet War Songs in the Context of Russian Culture*. Cambridge, UK: Cambridge Scholars, 2016.
Prusin, Alexander. *Serbia Under the Swastika: A World War II Occupation*. Urbana: University of Illinois Press, 2017.
Rhodes, Richard. *The Making of the Atomic Bomb*. New York: Simon and Schuster, 1987.
Riding, Alan. *And the Show Went On: Cultural Life in Nazi-Occupied Paris*. New York: Vintage, 2010.
Roberts, Andrew. *The Storm of War: A New History of the Second World War*. New York: HarperCollins, 2011.
Rozin, Igor. "Russia's Forgotten WWII Heroes Gain Recognition Thanks to Online Project." *Russia Beyond*, April 14, 2015.
Russia Beyond (official name *Russia Beyond the Headlines* or RBTH) provides news about Russia. RBTH is part of the newspaper *Rossiyskaya Gazeta*, which is a newspaper owned by the Russian government. https://www.rbth.com
Schnitker, Harry. "Catholic Church in WWII." *Catholic News Agency*, June 27, 2011. https://www.catholicnewsagency.com/the-catholic-church-in-the-second-world-war
Seghers, Pierre. *Poésie 39–45*. London: Editions Poetry, 1947.
Seibel, Wolfgang. *Persecution and Rescue: The Politics of the "Final Solution" in France, 1940–1944*. Translated by Ciaran Cronin. Ann Arbor: University of Michigan Press, 2016.
Shrayer, Maxim D., ed. *An Anthology of Jewish-Russian Literature: 1801–1953: Two Centuries of Dual Identity in Prose and Poetry*. Armonk, NY: M.E. Sharpe, 2007.
Snyder, Timothy. *Bloodlands*. New York: Basic Books, 2010.
Sontheimer, Michael. "Germany's WWII Occupation of Poland: When We Finish, Nobody Is Left Alive." *Spiegel Online*, May 27, 2011. Accessed November 7, 2017. https://www.spiegel.de/germany-s-wwii-occupation-of-poland-when-we-finish-nobody-is-left-alive
Sporl, Gerhard. "How Denmark Saved Its Jews from the Nazis." *Spiegel Online*, October 17, 2013. https://www.spiegel.xe/book-examines-how-jews-of-denmark-were-saved-from-the-nazis
Stites, Richard, ed. *Culture and Entertainment in Wartime Russia*. Bloomington: Indiana University Press, 1995.
Stites, Richard. *Soviet Popular Culture: Entertainment and Society Since 1900*. Cambridge, UK: Cambridge University Press, 1992.
Suleiman, Susan Rubin. *Crises of Memory and the Second World War*. Cambridge, MA: Harvard University Press, 2006.
Taylor, Richard. *Film Propaganda: Soviet Russia and Nazi Germany*. London: Croom Helm, 1979.

Tooze, Adam. *The Wages of Destruction: The Making and Breaking of the Soviet Economy*. New York: Penguin Books, 2008.
Watt, George. *The Comet Connection: Escape from Hitler's Europe*. Lexington: University of Kentucky, 1990.
Weinberg, Gerhard L. *A World at Arms: A Global History of World War II*. Cambridge, UK: Cambridge University, 1994.
Werth, Alexander. *Russia at War 1941–1945*. New York: Carroll & Graf Publishers, 1964.
Wieviorka, Oliver. *The French Resistance*. Translated by Jane Marie Todd. Cambridge, MA: Belknap Press of Harvard University Press, 2016.
The World of Anne Frank. London: Macmillan, 2001.
Wright, Gordon. *The Ordeal of Total War, 1939–1945*. Prospect Heights, IL: Waveland, 1997.
Yosomono, Eric. "Top 10 Surprising Facts About Poland During WWII." History.com, January 26, 2014. https://www.toptenz.net/top-10-surprising-facts-about-poland-during-wwii.php Accessed October 5, 2017.

WEBSITES

Airsports.fai.org
Allpoetry.com
Auschwitz.dk
Avalon.law.yale.edu
Eyewitnesstohistory.com
Gherkinstomatoes.com
History.com
Holocaustmusic.ort.org
Holocaustresearchproject.org
Ibiblio.org
Jewishvirtuallibrary.org
Kinoglaz.fr
Marxists.org
Nizkor.org
Ordredelaliberation.fr
Prokonsul.blogspot.com
Sovietlit.net
Spiegel.de
Todiscoverrussia.com
Toptenz.net
Ushmm.org
Warsaw.com
Wiesenthal.com
Zchor.org

INDEX

Note: Page references for photographs are *italicized*.

Agriculture/food production: Denmark and, 93–94, 241; farm worker shortages, 57, 63–64, 83, 85; France and, 84–85; Nazi racial policy and, 129; Poland and, 79–80, 82–83; Soviet Union collectivization, 20, 61; Soviet Union food production, 60–62; Ukraine and, 55–56, 61, 73; war-time impacts throughout Europe, 90
Airborne forces (paratroopers), 40, 43
Aircraft/air warfare: Allied air superiority, 39; British, 43; German, 43, 48; Soviet Union, 43, 47, 48. *See also* Luftwaffe
Albania, 21
Alexander Nevsky (Soviet film, 1938), 157–58, 159–60
Alexei/Alexy I (Russian Orthodox Patriarch), 177

Aliger, Margarita, 159
All Quiet on the Western Front (Remarque), 110
American Battle Monuments Commission, 92
American Civil War, 72
American War for Independence, 72
Anderson, Lale, 142
André, Joseph (priest), 179
Anglo-German Naval Treaty of 1935, 8
Anne Frank Museum, 237
Anschluss, xxiv, xxix, 9–10, 26, 168
Antelme, Robert, 123
Anti-Semitism: Catholic clergy and, 174, 181, 182; about cause and acceptance, 215–16; collaborationists and, 122; depiction in films, 141; individual expressions of, 145,

170; Pétain and Vichy France, 30, 126, 195; Poland, 226; as program in occupied territories, 21, 178, 179, 233

Appeasement, xxix, 9–13, 26, 27. *See also* Munich Pact (1938)

Aragon, Louis, 123

Arbeit Macht Frei ("Work makes you free"), xxix, 219–20

Ardennes Counteroffensive. *See* Battle of the Bulge (Ardennes Counteroffensive 1944–45)

Arletty, 145

Aryan race: creating/maintaining "purity," 97, 165, 200, 224; about the definition, xxix; Hitler and the mythology of, 4–5, 22, 53, 108, 110, 206, 217–18; implementation in Denmark, 93, 232–34; incorporation into art and daily life, 110–11, 144; incorporation into Poland, 78–79, 129–30, 147; Olympic athletes, superiority of German, 136–41; purging non-Aryan opposition, 117, 122, 170–71

Atlantic Wall, 86, 93

Atomic bomb, xxxi, 42, 48, 117–21

Aubrac, Lucie, 198

Auschwitz (concentration camp), xxix; arrival and selection process, 220–21, 236; construction, 219–20; dehumanization of prisoners, 221–23; Mengele and medical experimentation, 169, 223–24; photo exhibit, 224–25; Red Army liberation, xxviii, 225–26; sending Jews to, xxvi, 195, 199, 228–29, 233, 236–37, 239; transport of Catholics to, 173, 180; transport of French Jews, 237–38; transport of Greek Jews, 244; transport of Hungarian Jews, 244–45; transport of Roma, 199, 228; treatment of Soviet POWs, 225; Western reaction/response, 231–32. *See also* Holocaust

Austria: Anschluss, xxiv, xxix, 9–10, 26; Hitler art collection, 111, 115; Third Partition of Poland, 14, 28; value to German war effort, 72–73; Waldheim as president, 244

Avengers (United Partisan Organization), 208

Babi Yar, massacre, xxv, xxix, 39, 242–43

Baez, Joan, 198

Baker, Josephine, 194

Balkans, 31, 164. *See also* Albania; Bulgaria; Croatia; Romania; Serbia

Baltic Sea, 241

Baltic States: Ponary massacre, 227; religions, 164; resistance efforts, 208; Soviet occupation, xxiv, 20

Barbie, Klaus ("The Butcher of Lyon"), 170, 190–91, 195, 238

Barth, Karl, 179

Battle of Britain (1940), 30–31, 43

Battle of Kiev (1941, 1943), xxv, 32, 39

Battle of Kursk (1943), xxvii, xxxi, 38–39, 46

Battle of Moscow (1941–42), 32, 36–37, 55, 72, 152

Battle of Normandy (1944). *See* Normandy/D-Day landings

Battle of Smolensk (1941), xxv, 45, 64–65, 152, 155–56

Battle of Stalingrad (1942–43), xxxii, 37, 76, 158–59, 189, 212

Battle of Stalingrad (film *Enemy at the Gates*), 252

Battle of the Bulge (Ardennes Counteroffensive 1944–45), xxviii, xxx, 40–41
Baudrillart, Alfred-Henri-Marie (Cardinal), 174
Beckett, Samuel, 125
Being and Nothingness [L'Être et le néant] (Sartre), 125
Belarus (Belorussia), 32, 44–45, 58, 242, 252
Belgium: food shortages and rationing, 96, 101; Holocaust deaths, 245; invasion and occupation, 19, 21, 29, 76; life during the occupation, xviii–xxi, 179; looting and theft of art, 113; post-war recovery, 42; resistance movement, 198–99; value to German war effort, 72–73
Belzec (concentration camp), xxix, 227
Benioff, David, 66
Benoît, Pierre-Marie (Father), 175, 247
Berdichev massacre, 242–43
Bergen-Belsen (concentration camp), xxviii, xxix, 233, 237, 240
Berggrav, Eivind (Bishop), 176
Bernes, Mark, 153
Best, Werner, 241
Bethe, Hans, 118
Bialystok Ghetto, 207
Bielski brothers (partisans), 45, 252
Birkenau (Auschwitz subcamp), 220, 224
Bismarck, Otto von, 166
Blitz, xxv, xxix
Blitzkrieg (lightning war), xxx, 14, 15, 28, 43, 54–55
Bohr, Niels, 118–20
Bolsheviks/Bolshevik Party, 19, 197

Bonhoeffer, Dietrich, xxviii, 171, 222
Bonny, Pierre, 196
Borkowska (Borokowska), Anna (Sister), 173
Born, Max, 118–20
Braddock, Jim, 137
Brasillach, Robert, 122
Brecht, Berthold, 110
Breker, Arno, 124
Bridge Too Far, A (film, 1977), 40, 252
Briedé, William, 204
Britain: American Lend-Lease support, 62–63; Chamberlain appeasement policy, xxiv, xxix, 1, 9–13, 29; declaration of war on Germany, 14–15; evacuation at Dunkirk, xxv, xxx, 30
Britain, weapons of war: aircraft, 43, 48; encryption/code breaking, 47–48; radar, 47
Broz, Josip ("Tito"), 31
Bruder, Jean, 123
Bubnova, Mayya, 69–70
Buchenwald, xxviii, xxx, 222
Bulgaria, xviii–xxi, 41–42, 242

Camus, Albert, 123
Cannes Film Festival, 160
Carpet bombing, xxx, 116
Casablanca Conference (1943), xxvi, xxx, 38
Casablanca (film, 1942), 252
Casualties. *See* War-time deaths and casualties
Catholic Church: Belgium, 179; Bishop Hudal and the "ratline," 168–70; Croatia and Slovakia, 180–81; France, 124, 127, 174–77; German hatred toward, 55, 76, 166; Hitler born and raised as, 165; Hitler destruction of, 172; Jewish conversion, 119–20, 180;

Netherlands, 179–80; Pius XII relationship with the Nazis, 166–68, 218–19; Poland, 16, 79–81, 83–84, 171–74; prevalence in Western Europe, 164; relationship with Jews, 172–76; role in German politics, 3, 7, 166; signing of the Concordat, 166–67; Vichy, France, 17
Céline, Louis-Ferdinand, 122
Censorship, 19, 38, 125, 129, 131, 143–44, 147, 150, 152, 160
Chagall, Marc, 116
Chamberlain, Neville, xxiv, xxix, 1, 9, 11–13, 29
Champs-Élysées (Paris), xxvii, xxx, 192–93
Chanel, Gabrielle ("Coco"), 145–46
Chelmno, Poland, 172
Chelmno concentration camp, 28, 228–29
Cherkasov, Nikolai, 158
Chevalier, Maurice, 146
Children: caring for war-time orphans, 100–101, 206; fitting the Aryan racial stereotype, 82–83, 200; indoctrination by Hitler Youth, 128, 166, 176; psychological impact of war, 103; resistance activities, 190; smuggled to safety, 202; surviving the "Hunger Winter," 95; surviving the Leningrad siege, 66–71; T4 euthanasia program, 168, 169, 218–19; WWII films, 249, 251
Children of War: Diaries 1941–1945, 66–71
Chopin, Frédéric, 115, 147, 149, 231
Christianity, 163–65.
See also individual religious denominations

Christian X (king of Denmark), 241, 242
Churchill, Winston: becoming prime minister, xxiv, 29, 253; Casablanca Conference, xxvi, xxx, 37–38; confidence in defeating Germany, 72; Dunkirk evacuation, xxv, 30; policy toward Nazi Final Solution, 231–32; Tehran Conference, xxvii; Yalta Conference, xxviii, xxxiii, 41
Ciano, Galeazzo (Count), *10*
City of Thieves (Benioff), 66
Claudel, Paul, 124
Clausewitz, Carl von, 48
Clermont-Ferrand, France, 249
Cocteau, Jean, 124
Cohen, Leonard, 198
Colette, Sidonie-Gabrielle, 124
Collaborator/collaboration, xxx; awareness of Nazi agenda in Germany, 186; France, 121–23, 194–96; about the occupation and, 185; sleeping with the enemy as, 98–99; Soviet Union dealing with, 100, 98–99
Collateral damage, xxx, 26, 116
Colleville-sur-Mer (American cemetery), 92
Combat (resistance magazine), 123
"Comet Line," 198–99
Communism/communists: blamed for burning the Reichstag, 7, 166; Catholic Church and, 167, 173, 174; civil war in Greece, 21; about Hitler attacks on/hatred of, 5, 8, 22; influence in France, 188, 192; post-war takeover in Eastern Europe, 41–42; role in Weimar government, 6; Russian revolutions, 19

Concentration camps.
See individual camps by name
Courier from Poland: Story of a Secret State (Karski), 231
Croatia: alliance with Germany, xviii–xxi; formation of Ustashe, 31; Holocaust deaths, 245; invasion and occupation, 22; life during the occupation, 180–81
Cromwell, Dean, 136
Czechoslovakia: alliance with France and Soviet Union, 9, 12; assassination of Heydrich, xxvi, 200; destruction of Lidice, xxxi, 200; 1938 Germany given the Sudetenland, xxiv, xxxi, xxxii, 10–12; 1939 occupation by Germany, 181; post-WWII Soviet takeover, 41–42; religious life, 164; Theresienstadt concentration camp, xxxii, 233; value to German war effort, 72–73; war-time deaths, 26, 200
Czerniaków, Adam, 206

Dachau (concentration camp), xxiii, xxviii, xxx, 7, 166, 172, 196, 216
Daladier, Edouard, xxiv, 111
Damaskinos (archbishop of Athens), 244
Danzig (Gdansk), Hitler demands for, xxiv, 12, 14, 27
Darwinism/Charles Darwin, xxxii, 4, 165
Da Vinci, Leonardo, 114
D-Day and the Battle of Normandy. *See* Normandy/D-Day landings; Operation Overlord (Normandy invasion)
Deaths. *See* War-time deaths and casualties
Defense of Tsaritsyn (Soviet film, 1942), 158–59

Defiance (film, 2008), 45, 252
De Gaulle, Charles: birth of, 175; leadership in the resistance, 121, 188–89, 192–93, 198; leadership of France in exile, 145; liberation of France, 146, 174; liberation of Paris, xxvii, xxx, 191–93; postwar return to power, 124
De Gaulle-Anthonioz, Geneviève, 193–94
Degenerate art, xxx, 111–13, 116
De Hevesy, George, 118–19
De Jong, Johannes (Archbishop), 180
Dekker, Hilde, 179–80
Denmark: construction of Atlantic Wall, 93; Holocaust deaths, 245; invasion and occupation, 76, 240–41; life during the occupation, xiv, xviii–xxi; postwar recovery, 42; shipping Jews to concentration camps, 241–42; trade relations with Germany, 93–94, 241; value to German war effort, 72–73
De Visser, Hendrica, 180
Diary of a Young Girl, The (Frank), 237
Dietrich, Marlene, 141–42
Domestic and Material Life: burial of the dead, 91–92; creation of ghettos, 80–82; destruction of history and culture, 77–79; drop in birth rate, 85; effects of occupation on, xv, 75–77; exploitation of agriculture, 84–85, 90; exploitation of labor and industry, 82–83, 88–89, 92–95, 100, 104; food shortages and rationing, 79–80, 87–88, 95–96, 96, 101; innovation and coping mechanisms, 101–4; lack of goods and housing, 83–84, 86; medicine, hygiene, health care, 91, 102; paying the cost

of occupation, 86–87; sexual relations with the enemy, 96–99, 101; women as replacement workers, 89–90, 99
Donskoi, Dmitri, 177, 178
Drancy, France (internment camp), xxx, 169, 195, 238–39
Drôle de guerre (French strange war or Phony War), 28–29
Dumon (Dumont), Aline Micheline ("Michou"/"Lily"), 198–99
Dunkirk (British Army evacuation), xxv, xxx, 30, 253
Duras, Marguerite, 123

Economics/economic planning: blitzkrieg tactics and, 54–55; effects of occupation on, xiv–xv; German racism and war planning, 53–54; invasion of the Soviet Union, 51–52, 55–56; Soviet Union industrial production, 20, 59–60; about principles and model of, 53; worker shortages and productivity, 63–64. *See also* Agriculture/food production; Forced labor
Eden, Anthony, 185
Ehrenburg, Ilya, 154
Eichmann, Adolf, 169–70, 217, 244
Einsatzgruppen (killing squads), xx, xxx, 186, 215, 219, 242–43, 246. *See also* SS (*Schutzstaffel*)
Einstein, Albert, 48, 117–20
Eisenhower, Dwight D., xiii, xxvii, 40, 51, 191–92
Eisenstein, Sergei, 158
Éluard, Paul, 123
Enigma (coding machine), xxx, 47, 252
Estonia. *See* Baltic States

Eternal Jew, The (film, 1940), 141
Exodus (French civilians fleeing from Nazis), xxx, 30, 187–88

Fadeev, Aleksandr, 154–55
Faý, Bernard, 126
Fermi, Enrico, 118–20
Filipovic, Miroslav (priest), 180–81
Final Solution, xxvi, xxx. *See also* Holocaust; Wannsee Conference of 1942
Finland, xxiv, 28–29, 137
Flies, The [Les Mouches] (Sartre), 125
Flossenbürg concentration camp, 222
Follett, Ken, xiii
Food, shortages/rationing: Belgium, 96, 101; France, 87–88, 96; Germany, 96; about the need/problems of, 95–96; Netherlands, 96; Poland, 79–80; replacement innovations, 102
Forced labor: building the V-1/V-2 rockets, 44; concentration camps as source of, 58–59, 222; about the German use of, xix, 51; occupied territories as source of, 56–58, 82–83, 92–95, 104, 200, 210; post-war arrest for collaboration, 104; resistance to/criticism of, 148, 212; Vichy STO system, 88–89. *See also* Slave labor
Four-Year Plan, xxx, 54
France, resistance movement: beginnings of, 18, 187–88; collaboration and German retaliation, 194–97; daily life in, 121–25, 189–90; about de Gaulle and, 188–89, 192–93; individual stories, 190–91; invasion support on D-Day, 191;

invoking the memory of Joan of Arc, 175; liberation of Paris, 191–92; music in the expression of, 197–98; Oradour-sur-Glane massacre, 196; Tulle massacre, 196; Vercors massacre, 197; women in, 193–94

France/Vichy France: Appendix A (WWII Films, 249); collaborators/Vichy collaboration, 121–23, 194–95; creating a Pétain cult of personality, 126–28; declaration of war on Germany, 14–15; establishment of the Vichy government, xxv, xxxiii, 17–18, 30, 121–22, 124; food shortages and rationing, 87–88, 96; German invasion and surrender, 16–17, 29–30, 76; Gestapo activities, 196–97; Holocaust deaths, 245; innovation and coping mechanisms, 102–3; life during the occupation, xiv, xviii–xxi, 121–28; post-war cemeteries, 92; post-war recovery, 42; protection of art collections, 111–13; relationship of Catholic Church to Vichy, 174–76, 193–94; role of women, 89–90; shipments to concentration camps, 237–40; STO forced labor system, 88–89; value to German war effort, 72–73; wartime agricultural production, 84–85, 88–89; WWII films, 249, 252; youth camps, 128

Franck, James, 118, 120

Franco-Prussian War, 22

Frank, Anne, xvi, xxix, 52, 247

Frank, Elfriede Geiringer ("Fritzi"), 237

Frank, Hans, 15–16, 78, 80–84, 115, 129, 147, 169, 172, 227, 234–37

Frank, Otto, 237

Führerprinzip (principle of Hitler's leadership), xxiv, 7–8, 171

Führer, Hitler as, xvii, xxiii, 11, 82, 135

Galen, August von (Bishop), 218–19

General Government (Nazi government of Poland), xxx, 15, 81–82, 129, 172, 227

Genocide, 18, 34, 39, 73, 183, 186, 242. *See also* Holocaust

George II (king of Greece), 21

Germany, about the build-up to war: 1918 creation of Weimar Republic, 2–3; 1919 Treaty of Versailles, xiv, xxiii, xxix, xxxii, 3; 1923 Munich beer hall putsch, xxiii, 4; 1932 Reichstag elections, 5–6; 1933 collapse of Weimar Republic, 6–7; 1933 Hitler appointed chancellor, xxiii, 6, 17, 22, 165; 1933 Nazi book burnings and Enabling Act, 7, 109; 1933 Reichstag burns, 7, 166; 1934 Hitler named Führer, xxiii, 7–8; 1935 rearmament and occupying the Rhineland, xxiv, 7, 9, 26, 42–44; 1936 start of the Four Year Plan, xxx, 54; 1938 Anschluss with Austria, 9–10; 1938 Western appeasement/Munich Pact, xxiv, 9–12; 1939 demand for return of Danzig, 12, 26–27; 1939 Nazi-Soviet Nonaggression Pact, 13–14, 27; 1939 occupation of Czechoslovakia, 26, 181; as the lead-up to WWII, 1–2, 26

Germany, actions of WWII, 202; 1939 attack on Poland, 14–16, 27–28; 1939–40 the Phony War, 28–29; 1940 battle for France, 29–30; 1940 Battle of

Britain, 30–31; 1940 Spring Offensive, 29; 1941 invasion of the Balkans, 31; 1941 invasion of the Soviet Union, 31–35, 51, 55–56, 76–77, 177; 1941–42 Battle of Moscow, 36–37; 1941–44 Siege of Leningrad, 32, 35–36, 39, 55, 64–71; 1942–43 Battle of Stalingrad, xxxii, 37, 76, 158–59, 189; 1943 Battle of Kiev, 39; 1943 Battle of Kursk, 38–39; 1944 Operation Valkyrie, xxvii, 187, 252; 1944–45 Ardennes Counteroffensive, xxviii, xxx, 40–41; fighting a two-front war, 13, 27, 56–57, 73; WWII films, 249–50. *See also* France/Vichy France, Appendix A (WWII Films)

Germany, Allied actions: 1941–43 North Africa campaign, 37–38; 1942 invasion of North Africa (Operation Torch), 188; 1943 invasion of Italy, xxvii; 1944 D-Day and the Battle of Normandy, xxvii, 39–40; 1944 liberation of Rome, xxvii, 38; 1944 Operation Market Garden, 40; 1944–45 Battle of the Bulge, 40–41; 1945 victory in Europe, xxviii

Germany, weapons of war: aircraft, 43, 48; tanks, 43, 48; U-Boats, 44; V-1/V-2 rockets, 43–44

Gestapo (*Geheime Staatspolizei*): actions of, 26, 53, 122, 203–4, 211; arrest and torture of Jean Moulin, 170, 190–91, 246; about the creation of, xxiii, 199; film depictions, 249, 252; Heydrich role in, 199; infiltration of the churches, 181; Klaus Barbie role in, 170, 195, 238; Müller as leader, 170; presence in Belgium, 179; presence in Denmark, 204, 241; presence in France, 123–24; presence in Poland, 78, 226; pursuit of the resistance, 189, 198, 203, 239; rape and abuse of women, 97; use of torture, 131, 187, 215. *See also* Milice (French Gestapo)

Getter, Matylda (Sister), 173

Ghetto, xxx. *See also individual ghettos by name*

Glickman, Marty, 136–37

Glossary of terms, xvi

Goebbels, Joseph, xxviii, 41, 77, 109–10, 115, 130–31, 134–35, 141, 186, 215–16

Göring, Hermann, 10, 43, 57, 111–12, 116

Great Depression, xxiii, 2, 5, 22–23, 216

Great Patriotic War, 64, 152

Great Patriotic War Museum (Moscow), 64, 177–78

Great Turningpoint, The (Soviet film, 1945), 160

Greece: invasion and occupation, 21–22, 31, 114; life during the occupation, xviii–xxi; Orthodox Church, 164, 244; protection of art and culture, 113–14; shipping Jews to concentration camps, 244; value to German war effort, 72–73; war-time deaths, 26

Grossman, Vasili, 155

Guernica (Picasso), 126

Haakon VII (king of Norway), 176

Hemingway, Ernest, 110

Henneicke, Wim, 204

Hess, Rudolph, 4

Heydrich, Reinhard, xxvi, 77, 199–200, 217

Hindenburg, Paul von, xxiii, 5–7, 17, 22
Hiroshima, Japan, 48
Hitler, Adolf: appeasement by the West, 9–13, 26; appointed chancellor, xxi, 6–7, 17, 22, 165; assassination attempt, xxvii, 187; belief in the message of, 31; destruction of democracy, xxi, 7, 22–23; as *Führer*, xvii, xxiii, 7–8, 11, 82, 135, 171; ideology of *Mein Kampf*, xxiii, 4–5, 31, 108, 110, 186, 216, 246; as megalomaniac racist, 71; 1923 beer hall putsch, xxiii, 4; 1932 Reichstag elections, 5–6; quotations, xvii, 1, 25; suicide/death, xxvii, 41, 250; WWI military service, 3–4
Hitler youth, 128, 166, 176
Hlond, August (Cardinal), 172–73
HMS *Bulldog*, 252
Holocaust: Allied liberation, 225–26; Auschwitz I, establishment of, 219–20; creating the camp system, 216–17; deaths, 220, 225; denial, 123; Eichmann and, 170, 217, 244; Einsatzgruppen and, 219; Heinrich Himmler and, 217; humiliation and dehumanization, 222–23; legacy of Anne Frank, 234–37; about the meaning and underlying factors, xvi, xxx, 215–16; medical experimentation, 223–24; Nazi justification, 141; Nazi racial policy and, 4–5, 217–18; Pius XII and the Catholic Church, 168, 218–19; program in occupied territories, 233; selection and collecting personal belongs, 220–22, 236; survivor story, 238–40;

T4 euthanasia program, 168, 218–19; Topography of Terror (museum), 224–25. *See also* Auschwitz (concentration camp); Genocide; Wannsee Conference of 1942
Holocaust in the occupied territories: Croatia and Serbia, 243; Denmark, 240–42; France, 237–40; Greece, 244; Hungary, 244–45; Netherlands, 232–37; Poland, 226–32; Soviet Union, 225, 242–43
Homosexuality, 5, 124, 216, 218, 238
Honor of Poets, The [L'Honneur des Poêtes] (Éluard), 123
Hoover, Herbert, 23
Hudel, Alois (Bishop), 168–70, 246
Huguenots (French Protestants), 175–76
Humboldt University (Berlin), 7
Hungary: alliance with Germany, xviii–xxi; Holocaust deaths, 245; post-WWII Soviet takeover, 41–42; shipping Jews to concentration camps, 244–45

I Am Everywhere [Je suis partout] (Brasillach), 122
If War Comes Tomorrow (Soviet film, 1938), 158
Igel, Simon, xvi, 238–40
Igosheva, Lera, 68
Intellectual life: attack on education, 107–8, 117–21, 128–30; book burnings, 108–10; censorship and restrictions on news, 130–31; control of artistic production, 110–11; destruction of "degenerate" art, 111, 113, 116; about the impact of occupation on, xv; looting and theft of art, 111–13;

preservation of art and culture, 113–15; recovery of stolen art and treasures, 115–16; war-time scientific advances, 117–21
Invincible (Soviet film, 1942), 159
Israel, xxxii, 134, 170, 217
Italy: alliance with Germany, xviii–xxi; Balkan invasion, rescued by Hitler, 31; defeat in North Africa, 37–38; destruction of Monte Cassino, 38, 116, 149; liberation of Rome, xxvii, 38; World Cup victories, 138

Jagiellonian University, 129–30, 147
Japan: attack on Pearl Harbor, xxv, 72; attack on Russia, 37; bombing to end the war, 48, 71; fighting ability, 49; treatment of women, 98; Yalta Conference plans for, xxxiii, 41
Jaujard, Jacques, 112
Jedwabne Pogrom, 226–27
Jehovah's Witnesses, 5, 218
Jew Named Süss [Jud Süss] (film, 1940), 141
Jews: conversion to Catholicism, 119–20, 180; creation of the "Final Solution," xxvi, xxx; enactment of Nuremberg Laws, xxiv, 77; about the Hitler hatred of, 5; Kristallnacht, xxiv, xxxi, 138; Nazi racial policy and, 16, 34, 53, 217–18; numbers killed, xxv, xxix, 21–22, 58, 84, 137, 169, 173, 179–80, 200, 204–8, 220, 226–28, 233, 242–45
Joan of Arc (Saint), 175
John Paul II (Karol Józef Wojtyla), 173–74
Journey to the End of the Night [Voyage au bout de la nuit] (Céline), 122
Joyce, James, 125

Karlshorst Museum, 70
Karski, Jan, 229, 231–32, 246–47
Katyusha rockets ("Stalin's Organ"), 45–46
Keller, Helen, 110
Kellogg-Briand Pact (1928), 2
Kiev, Ukraine: German capture and occupation, xxv, 32, 45, 55, 64–65; German defeat, 39; survival of occupation, 70–71. *See also* Ukraine
Kirchner, Ernst Ludwig, 111
Klein, Fritz, 224
Klukowski, Zygmunt, 227–28
Kolbe, Maximillian (Father), 173
Kolkhoz (Soviet collective farms), xxxi, 20, 56, 61
Komorowski, Tadeusz ("Bor"), 209
Komsomolskaya Pravda (newspaper), 156
Korczak, Janusz, 206, 247
Korczak (film, 1990), 206, 251
Kosmodenyanskaya, Zoya, 159
Kovner, Abba, 208
Krahelska, Krystyna ("Danuta"), 149
Kraków, Poland: Aryanization of the city, 78–79, 83–84; closing Jagiellonian University, 129–30; creation of the ghetto, 80–83; eliminating the ghetto, xxvi; looting and theft of art, 114; restrictions on daily life, 83–84
Kristallnacht (Night of Broken Glass), xxiv, xxxi, 138
Kursk, battle of (1943), xxvii, xxxi, 38–39, 46
Kutuzov, Mikhail, 178
Kutuzov (Soviet film), 159

Lafont, Henri, 196
Lake Ladoga, xxxi. *See also* Leningrad, siege of (1941–44)

Latvia. *See* Baltic States
Laval, Pierre, 194–95
League of Nations, 8, 11, 41
Lebensraum (living space), xxxi, 4, 77
Le Chambon-sur-Lignon (village), 175–76, 247
Lend-Lease Act of 1941, xxv, xxxi, 62–63
Lenin, Vladimir I., 19–20, 65
Leningrad, siege of (1941–44), 32, 35–36, 39, 52, 55, 64–66, 91–92, 251
Leningrad diaries, accounts from survivors of the siege, 52, 66–71
Leopold III (king of Belgium), 21
"Les Éditions de Minuit" (resistance publisher), 123
Levi, Primo, 215
"Liberty" (poem, Éluard), 123
Lidice, Czechoslovakia, xxvi, xxxi, 200
"Lili Marlene" (song), 141–42
Lindbergh, Charles, 124
Lithuania. *See* Baltic States
Litvinov, Maxim, 9, 12–13, 27
Lódz, Poland, 129, 172
Lódz ghetto, 28, 228–29
London, Jack, 110
Los Alamos National Laboratory, 120
Louis, Joe, 137–38
Loutrel, Pierre, 196
Lublin, Poland/Lublin Ghetto, xxvii, xxxi, 227–28
Luftwaffe, xxxi: attack on London ("The Blitz"), xxv, xxviii; attack on Poland, 15; Battle of Britain, 30–31; destruction of air supremacy by Allies, 39; development/production of aircraft, 43
Lukov, Leonid, 153
Luther, Martin, 164, 176

Lutheran Church, 76, 164–65, 170–71, 176
Luxembourg, xviii, xxiv, 55
Lynn, Vera, 142

Maginot, André, 29
Maginot Line, xxxi, 29–30, 43
Majdanek (concentration camp), xxvii, xxxi
Malraux, André, 123, 124
Manhattan Project (development of atomic bomb), xxxi, 42, 48, 117–21
Mann, Thomas, 110
Man's Fate [La Condition Humaine] (Malraux), 124
Marly, Anna (aka Anna Betulinskaia), 197–98
Marseille, France, 138, 175, 193
Marshall Plan, 42
Marx, Karl, 110
Matejko, Jan, 114
Matisse, Henri, 116
Medical care: battlefield innovations, 91; concentration camps, 223; ghettos, 205; murder of doctors and nurses, 209–10; Nazi experimentation, 169, 172, 223–24; soap/making soap, 102; Soviet Union, 34; T4 euthanasia program, 218–19
Mein Kampf [My Struggle], xxiii, xxxi, 4–5, 31, 108, 110, 186, 216, 246
Melchior, Marcus (Rabbi), 240
Mengele, Josef, 169, 224
Metcalfe, Ralph, 136
Milice (French Gestapo), xxxi, 195, 197, 246
Military Life: effectiveness of women, 46–47; medicine and health care, 91; number of WWII casualties, 25–26; partisan (resistance) warfare,

44–45; post-WWII aftermath, 41–42; about war and, xiv, 49; weapons, British and U.S., 47–48; weapons, German, 42–44; weapons, Soviet, 45–46; weapons as the tools of war, 48–49. *See also* Germany, actions of WWII; Germany, Allied actions
Minin, Kuzma, 178
Minsk, Belarus, *58*
Mitterrand, François, 123
Mizoch (Mizocz) Ghetto, 207
Moldagulova, Aliya, 46
Molotov, Vyacheslav, 12–13, 27, 33, 65
Molotov cocktail, xxxi, 29, 207
Monet, Claude, 116
Monowitz (Auschwitz subcamp), 220
Monuments Men, xxxi, 113, 115–17, 253
Moscow, battle for/defense of, 32, 36–37, 55, 72, 152
Moulin, Jean, 170, 190–91, 195, 246
Mukhina, Lena, 69
Müller, Bruno, 129–30
Müller, Heinrich, 170
Munich beer hall putsch (1923), xxiii, 4
Munich Pact (1938), xxxi, 10–12. *See also* Appeasement
Museum of Fine Arts (Switzerland), 116
Mussert, Anton, 19
Mussolini, Benito: execution/death, xxviii, 41; invasion of Albania and Greece, 21–22, 244; invasion of the Balkans, 31; named premier of Italy, xxiii, 17; negotiating the Munich Pact, 10–11; removal as premier of Italy, xxvii, 38; World Cup celebrations, 138

Nagasaki, Japan, 48
National Socialist Movement (Dutch), 19
Nazis (National Socialist German Workers Party), 4–6
Nazi-Soviet Nonaggression Pact (1939), xxiv, xxxi, 13–16, 20, 27, 112, 212
Netherlands: collaborators, 204; escaping to England, 202–3; food shortages and rationing, 96; German retaliation for resistance, 203–4; Holocaust deaths, 233, 245; "Hunger Winter," 95; invasion and occupation, 18–19, 29, 76, 232–33; legacy of Anne Frank, 234–37; life during the occupation, xviii, 104, 179–80; "Milk Strike," 94; neutrality policy, 18; Operation Market Garden, failure of, 95; postwar recovery, 42; protection of art and culture, 113; Putten Raid, 203–4; resistance efforts, 200–204; shipping Jews to concentration camps, 232–33; value to German war effort, 72–73; WWII films, 250. *See also* France/Vichy France, Appendix A (WWII Films)
Nevsky, Alexander, 157–58, 177, 178–79
New Mexico, 48, 120
New York Times, 6, 160
New Zealand, 251
Nicholas II (Russian tsar), 19
Niemöller, Martin, 163, 170–71
Nietzsche, Friedrich, 164–65
Nieuwlande (village), 176
Night (Wiesel), 182
Nobel Prize for Literature, 123
Nobel Prize for Physics, 117–20
Normandy/D-Day landings: Allied plans for, xxvii;

assaulting the beaches, 39–41; film depiction of, 252; French resistance efforts, 18, 181, 193; German defenses, 93–95, 191; post-war cemeteries, 92. *See also* Operation Overlord (Normandy invasion)
North Atlantic Treaty Organization (NATO), 42
Norway: invasion and occupation, 29, 76; life during the occupation, xviii–xxi, 176; post-war recovery, 42; value to German war effort, 72–73
Nowogródek, Belarus, 173
Nuremberg Laws, xxiv, 77
Nuremberg Trials, xxviii, xxxi, 23, 58–59, 225–26, 233, 245–46

Odessa, Ukraine, 39, 46, 65, 70–71, 215, 246. *See also* Ukraine
Olympic Charter, quotation from, 133
Olympic Games, 134–37, 141
Operation Barbarossa (German invasion of USSR), xxv, xxxi, 31–35
Operation Citadel (Battle of Kursk), xxvii, xxxi, 38–39, 46
Operation Dragoon (Operation Anvil), *193*
Operation Market Garden, 40, 252
Operation Overlord (Normandy invasion), xxvii, xxxi, 39–41. *See also* Normandy/D-Day landings
Operation Reinhard (retaliation for Heydrich assassination), xxxii, 200
Operation Sea Lion (plans for invasion of England), 30–31
Operation Tempest (Warsaw Uprising), xxvii, xxxii, 208–10

Operation Torch (Allied invasion of North Africa), xxxii, 37–38, 188
Operation Typhoon (German campaign against Moscow), xxxii, 36
Operation Valkyrie (assassination attempt on Hitler), 187, 252
Ophuls, Marcel, 249
Oppenheimer, J. Robert, 120
Oradour-sur-Glane, France, xxxii, 196
Orthodox Church, 76, 164, 177–78, 182, 244
Overy, Richard, 71
Owens, Jesse, 136–37

Pabiance ghetto (Poland), *28*
Pankiewicz, Tadeusz, 81–82
Papon, Maurice, 195
"Paris Under Occupation" (Sartre), 125
Partisan warfare: Belarus, 45, 252; executions/killings, 228; Italy, xxviii, 41; Poland, 207–8; Soviet Union, 44–45, 56, 100, 159, 197–98, 211–12; Ukraine, 44–45, 242–43; WWII films, 45, 252. *See individual camps by name*
Pavlichenko, Lyudmila ("Lady Death"), 46–47
Peierls, Rudolf, 118, 120
Perel, Solomon, 251
Pétain, Philippe, xxv, 17–18, 30, 89, 121–22, 124, 126, 146, 174, 188, 194, 194–95
Petrova, Nina, 47
Phony (Phoney) War (1939–1940), 28–29
Piaf, Edith, 146
Pianist, The (film, 2002), 229, 230–31, 251
Picasso, Pablo, 111, 123, 126
Pius XI (Pope), 167–68

Pius XII (Pope), 166–68, 219
Poland: anti-Semitism and killing Jews, 226–28; attack on education and intellectual life, 128–31; concentration camps, 233, 236, 239–40; creation of occupation government, xxx, 15, 81–82, 129, 172; divided by Germany and Soviet Union, xxiv, 15–16, 20, 28, 104; eliminating culture and people, xxxi, 77–79, 171, 216, 219, 226–28; food shortages, 79–80; forced labor requirements, 82–83; about the German invasion, xxiv, 13–14, 27–28, 55, 76; ghettos, creation of, 80–84, 228–29; ghettos, eliminating, xxvi, 204–8; Holocaust deaths, 245; Jedwabne Pogrom, 226–27; life during the occupation, xiv, xvi, xviii–xxi, 16, 75, 77–84, 86, 128–31; Nazi book burnings, 115; post-WWI politics, 14–15; post-WWII Soviet takeover, 41–42; presence/power of the Catholic Church, 164, 166, 171–74, 180, 182; providing slave labor, 57, 82–83, 100; resistance, music as expression of, 147–49, 160; resistance movement, growth of, 212; restrictions on education and information, 128–31; restrictions on recreational activity, 138, 139–40; surviving the war years, 79–80; taking of children, 82–83; theft of art and culture, 114–15; value to German war effort, 72–73, 79; war-time deaths, 26, 205, 210, 226; work of Oskar Schindler, 229–30; WWII films, 250–51. *See also* Danzig (Gdansk), Hitler demands for; France/Vichy France, Appendix A (WWII Films); Kraków, Poland; Warsaw Ghetto

Polanski, Roman, 231
Polish Home Army (AK), xxvii, 149, 206, 208–10
Polish Underground Army, 148, 149
Political life: creation of the Weimar Republic, 2–3; entry of Adolf Hitler, 3–5; about Germany between the wars, xiv, 1–2; Hitler named chancellor, 5–8; invasion and occupation of Belgium, 21; invasion and occupation of France, 16–18; invasion and occupation of Greece, 21–22; invasion and occupation of Poland, 14–16; invasion and occupation of the Netherlands, 18–19; invasion and occupation of Yugoslavia, 22; Munich Pact/appeasement, 9–12; Nazi-Soviet Nonaggression Pact, 13–14, 21; opposition to Treaty of Versailles, 3; rearmament and occupation of Rhineland, 8–9; Soviet Union under Stalin, 19–21
Ponary massacre (1941), 227
Portugal, 202
Pozharsky, Dimitri, 178
Pravda (newspaper), 155
Prokoviev, Sergei, 158
Protestant Reformation, 164; creation of the Weimar Republic, 2–3; entry of Adolf Hitler, 3–5; about Germany between the wars, xiv, 1–2; Hitler named chancellor, 5–8; invasion and occupation of Belgium, 21; invasion and

Index

occupation of France, 16–18; invasion and occupation of Greece, 21–22; invasion and occupation of Poland, 14–16; invasion and occupation of the Netherlands, 18–19; invasion and occupation of Yugoslavia, 22; Munich Pact/appeasement, 9–12; Nazi-Soviet Nonaggression Pact, 13–14, 21; opposition to Treaty of Versailles, 3; rearmament and occupation of Rhineland, 8–9; Soviet Union under Stalin, 19–21

Quisling, Vidkun, 176

Racism, ideology/policy: American segregation/treatment of Blacks, 91, 121; Aryan purity and theory of evolution, 165; destroying a sense of right and wrong, 23; destroying education and intellectual life, xv, 108–10, 117, 121; development of the "final solution," 216–18; diversity of treatment based on culture, xviii, 57; Himmler and, 59; about the Hitler obsession, 5, 71; killing people as a focal point, 25–26; Olympic Games (1936), 134–37; opposition by churches, 180; overriding German economic policy, 53–54; Pétain and Vichy France, 30, 121–23; support by collaborators, 122–24, 145–46; Ustashe of Croatia, 31
Rainbow, The (Soviet film), 159–60
Raphael (artist, Raffaello Sanzio da Urbino), 114

Raskova, Marina ("Night Witch"), 47
"ratline" (aiding post-war escape of Nazis), 168–70, 181, 182, 246
Rauter, Hans, 204
Ravensbrück (concentration camp), xxxii, 194, 201
Recreation and entertainment: effects of occupation on, xv, 133–34; France, 142–46; German films and music, 140–42; German "Strength Through Joy" movement, 140; Poland, 146–49; Soviet Union, 149–60. *See also* Sports, during the occupation era
Reichstag, xxxii
Religious life: Belgium, 179; about the occupation and, xv, 163–64, 182–83; Croatia and Slovakia, 180–82; France, 174–76; Nazi beliefs and participation, 164–65; Netherlands, 179–80; Norway, 176; Poland, 171–74; Soviet Union, 177–79. *See also individual religious denominations*
Remarque, Erich Maria, 110
Rembrandt (Rembrandt Harmenszoon van Rijn), 113, 114
Renoir, Pierre-Auguste, 116
Resistance/resistance movement: Belgium, 198–99; Catholic Church and, 172; Czechoslovakia, 199–200; Germany, events within, 186–87; growth during occupation, 56; life during the occupation, 186–87; literary opposition, 123–25; music as expression of, 147–49, 197–98; Netherlands, 200–204; about

the occupation and, xv–xvi, 185, 212; Poland, 204; Polish ghettos, 205–10; Soviet Union, 211–12; WWII films, 249, 250. *See also* France, resistance movement; Partisan warfare
Ribbentrop, Joachim von, xxiv, 13, 27
Riefenstahl, Leni, 140–41
Righteous Among the Nations: about the designation of, xxxii, 246–47; Father Pierre-Marie Benoît, 175, 247; Georg Duckwitz, 241–42; Hanna van der Voort, 202; Jan Karski, 229, 231–32, 246–47; Joseph André, 179; Jozef and Wiktoria Ulma family, 210–11, 247; Le Chambon-sur-Lignon, village of, 175–76, 247; Mother Superior Matylda Getter, 173; Nieuwlande, village of, 176; Oskar Schindler, 229–30, 247; Sister Anna Borkowska, 173; Tadeusz Pankiewicz, 81–82
Robertson, Lawson, 136
Roman Catholic Church. *See* Catholic Church
Romania: alliance with Germany, xviii–xxi, 54; Holocaust deaths, 245; occupation of Odessa, 65, 243; post-WWII Soviet takeover, 41–42
Roma (Sinti), xxxii; church response to killings, 182, 219; German killing, 18, 34, 73, 76, 83, 199, 216, 218; about the Hitler hatred of, 5; killings at Babi Yar, 243; shipment to concentration camps, 228, 233, 238; Ustashe killing of, 22, 31, 180, 246; war-time deaths, 220, 243, 245
Roosevelt, Franklin: approval of the Manhattan project, 118, 120; Casablanca Conference, xxvi, xxx, 37–38; death of, xxviii, 41, 48; declaration of war on Japan, xxv; election as president, 23; internment of Japanese Americans, xxvi; policy toward Nazi Final Solution, 231–32; quotation, 107; Tehran Conference, xxvii; Yalta Conference, xxviii, 41
Rudykovskaya, Tanya, 67
Russian Revolution (1917): abdication of the Tsar, 19; Stalin, role in, 159
Ryabinkin, Yura, 67

Sabine, Jacques, 190–91
Saint-Exupéry, Antoine de, 124–25
Samogon, xxxii
Sandberg, Willem, 113, 116
Sapieha, Adam (Archbishop), 173
Sartre, Jean-Paul, 125
Sauckel, Fritz, 57–59
Savicheva, Tanya, 67
Schaft, Hannie, 201
Schindler, Oskar, 229–30, 247
Schindler Museum, 82, 129–31
Schindler's List (film, 1993), 229, 230, 251
Schmeling, Max, 137–38
Scholl, Sophie and Hans, xxvi, 186–87, 247, 250
Scorched earth, xxxii
Seelig, Erich, 135
Serbia: descent into civil war, 31; Holocaust deaths, 245; invasion and occupation, 22; life during the occupation, xviii–xxi, 104; Orthodox Church, 164, 244
Sergei (Russian Orthodox Patriarch), 177
Serova, Valentina, 155

Service du travail obligatoire (STO), xxvi, xxxii, 88
Seyss-Inquart, Arthur, 19, 179–80, 232–33
Shanina, Roza ("Invisible Horror of East Prussia"), 47
She Defends Her Motherland (Soviet film), 159
Shostakovich, Dmitri, 153, 159
Sieg Heil (Hail Victory), xxxii, 8, 136, 186, 246
Simonov, Konstantin, 155–56, 159
Sinti (Roma), xxxii
Sitzkrieg (German sitting war or Phony War), 28–29
Six O'clock in the Evening After the War (Soviet film), 160
Slave labor, 70, 73, 82, 154. *See also* Forced labor
Slovakia: alliance with Germany, xviii–xxi; Holocaust deaths, 245; life during the occupation, 180–81; Orthodox Church, 244
Sobibór (concentration camp), xxvii, xxxii, 207, 233
Social Darwinism, xxxii, 4, 166
Söderbaum, Kristina, 141
Sophie Scholl—The Final Days (film, 2005), 250
Sorrow and the Pity, The (documentary film), 185
Soviet Union: American Lend-Lease support, xxxi, 62–63; Babi Yar massacre, 243; Baltic States, occupation of, xxiv, 20; Berdichev massacre, 242–43; church-state relations, 177–78, 182; collectivization of agriculture and food shortages, xxxi, 20, 56, 60–62; crime and looting, 59–60; culture, art, music and film, 149–60, 197–98; deaths, Holocaust, 245; deaths/casualties, war-time, xx–xxi, xxx, 25–26, 34, 39, 52, 61–62, 65, 70; economic and industrial capacity, 43, 47, 59, 62–66, 71–73; elimination of the Jews, 216–17, 219, 242–43; about the German occupation, xiv–xvi, xviii–xxi; German theft of art and culture, 114–15; invasion of Finland ("Winter War"), xxiv, 20, 28–29; 1917 abdication of the Tsar, 19; 1917–23 Bolshevik Revolution results, 19–20; 1941 German invasion, 21–22, 31–35, 51–52, 55–56, 72, 76–77; orphans and homeless children, caring for, 100–101; partisan (resistance) warfare, 44–45, 211–12; Poland, division with Germany, xxiv, 15–16, 20, 28, 104; post-war occupation of Eastern Europe, 41–42; relationship with churches/religion, 177–79, 181–82; relationship with France, 8–9, 188–89; relationship with Romania, 54; resistance effort, 212; source of forced/slave labor, 100, 104; support of the Warsaw Uprising, 209; women, role in Soviet Army, 46–47; WWII films, 251–52. *See also* Battle of Kursk (1943); Leningrad, siege of (1941–44); Moscow, battle for/defense of; Stalingrad, battle of (1942–43)
Soviet Union, weapons of war: aircraft, 43, 47, 48; BM-13 Katyusha rockets, 45–46; partisans as, 44–45; T-34 tanks, 46, 48; women as, 46–47
Spain: influence of Catholic Church, 164; about Nazi support in, xviii; post-war

recovery, 42; protection of art collections, 113; role in escape of Allied pilots, 198–99; role in escape of refugees, 175, 202–3
Spanish Civil War, 126
Speer, Albert, 56
Spielberg, Steven, 230
Sports, during the occupation era: chess tournaments, 139–40; Italian World Cup soccer wins, 138; 1936 Berlin Olympic Games, 136–37, 141; 1936 Schmeling-Louis boxing match, 137–38; tennis tournaments, 139; Ukrainian-German soccer match, 138–39
SS (*Schutzstaffel*), xxxiii; about the actions by, 53; about the actions of, xx, 154, 232; destruction of education and intellectual life, 129–30; Eichmann as leader in, 217; execution of American soldiers, xxviii; Heydrich as leader in, 217; Himmler as chief of, 58–59, 77, 141, 217; joined by French volunteers, 174; killing civilians and partisans, 44; killing Polish Jews, 226–28; post-war escape of leaders, 169–70; punishment of resistance, 196, 204; running the concentration camps, 220–25, 239–40; Sobibór rebellion against, xxvii, 207; treatment of women, 97, 220. See also Einsatzgruppen (killing squads)
Stalin, Joseph: leadership during German invasion, 21, 32–35, 150, 177; left out of Munich Pact, xxiv, 11–13; 1918 Civil War, role in, 159; nonaggression pact with Hitler, xxxi, 13–14, 27; post-war division of Europe, xxviii; quotation, xvii, 25; reputation in Vichy France, 126; as successor to Lenin, 20–21; Tehran Conference, xxvii; Yalta Conference, xxviii, xxxiii, 41
Stalingrad, battle of (1942–43), xxxii, 37, 76, 158–59
Stalin Prize (for film), 159–60
Stalin Prize (for poetry), 156, 159
Stangl, Franz, 169
Stauffenberg, Claus von, 187
Stein, Edith, 180
Stein, Gertrude, 126
Stoller, Sam, 136
Stranger, The [L'Étranger] (Camus), 123
"Strength Through Joy" movement, 140
Stroop, Jürgen, 206–7
Stwosz, Wit (Veit Stoss), 114
Submarines (U-boats), 39, 44, 49, 63, 249, 252
Sudetenland, xxiv, xxxi, xxxii, 12, 26, 230
Suhard, Emmanuel (Archbishop), 174
Surkov, Alexei, 156
Survival in Auschwitz (Levi), 215
Suvorov, Alexander, 178
Swastika (symbol/flag), 8, 78, 98, 134, 143
Szilard, Leo, 118, 120
Szpilman, Wladyslaw, 229, 230–31, 251
Sztutowo concentration camp, 80

T4 euthanasia program, 168, 169, 218–19
T-34 tanks, 47
Tank Men, The (Soviet film), 158
Tehran Conference of 1943, xxxii
Teller, Edward, 118, 120
Theresienstadt concentration camp, xxxii, 233

Tillion, Germaine, 194
Tito (Josip Broz), 31
Todt, Fritz, 56, 89
Toklas, Alice B., 126
Topography of Terror (museum), 224–25
Touvier, Paul, 195
Treaty of Versailles, xxxii; banning of Anschluss, xxix; as blow to German national pride, 107–8; creating a new Polish state, 14, 28; Hitler campaign against, xiv, xxxii, 3, 26; leading to racial hatred and bigotry, 246; 1919 signing the treaty, xxiii
Treblinka concentration camp, 205, 206, 207
Triolet, Elsa, 123
Triumph of the Will (Nazi documentary film), 140–41
Trocmé, André (pastor), 175
Trotsky, Leon, 19–20
Truman, Harry S., xxviii, 48, 118
Tulle massacre, 196
Tvardovsky, Aleksandr, 156

U-boats (*Unterseeboot*). See Submarines (U-boats)
Ukraine: agricultural collectivization, 20, 61; film depiction of German atrocities, 159–60; killing civilians and partisans, 44–45, 242–43; liquidation of Mizoch ghetto, 207; rape and abuse of women, 97; resistance efforts, 154; source for German labor, 82; source German labor, 100; source of concentration camp guards, 223; value to German war effort, 55–56, 61, 73; win in soccer against Germans, 138–39. See also Kiev, Ukraine; Odessa, Ukraine

Ulma, Josef and Wiktoria, 210–11, 247
United Nations (UN), xxxiii, 41, 244
United States: bombing of Pearl Harbor, 72; development of the atomic bomb, 48, 117–21; election of Roosevelt, 23; Germany declares war on, xxv; Joe Louis as boxing champion, 137–38; Lend-Lease program, xxv, xxxi, 62–63; participation in 1936 Olympic Games, 136–37; post-war Marshall Plan and NATO alliance, 42; securing German rocket technology, 44; war-time industrial capacity, 43, 71
University of Göttingen, 117, 120
U.S. Central Intelligence Agency (CIA), 170
Ustashe (Croatian pro-Nazi party), xxxii, 22, 31, 180, 246

V-1 rocket ("buzz bomb"), 43–44
V-2 rocket ("Retribution weapon"), 44
Valland, Rose, 112, 116
Van der Voort, Hanna, 202
Van Gogh, Vincent, 111, 113
Van Roey, Jozef-Ernst (Cardinal), 179
Vélodrome d'Hiver (Vel d'hiv), xxxii, 238
Venereal disease, 98
Vercors massacre, 196
Vichy, xxxiii. See also France/Vichy France
Victory of Faith, The (Nazi documentary film), 140
Vilnius (Wilno) Ghetto, 208, 227
Von Neumann, John, 118, 120

"Wait for Me" (poem), 141, 155, 178
Wait for Me (Soviet film, 1943), 159
Waldheim, Kurt, 244
Wallenberg, Raoul, 244–45, 247
Wannsee Conference of 1942, xxvi, xxx, xxxiii, 170, 199–200, 217, 223. *See also* Holocaust
Warsaw Ghetto, xxx, xxxiii; establishment and life in, xiv, xxv, 205–7, 229, 229–31; film depiction of, 141, 250, 251; uprising (Operation Tempest), xxvi–xxvii, xxxii, 129, 204, 208–11; work of Jan Karski, 231–32; work of Wladyslaw Szpilman, 230–31. *See also* Poland
Warsaw Uprising, 208–10, 250
War-time deaths and casualties: American, 41; civilians and partisans, 44, 44–45; Czechoslovakia, 26; Greece, 26; Holocaust, 245; Nazi racism and, 25–26; Poland, 26, 226–28, 245; Soviet Union, xx–xxi, xxx, 25–26, 34, 39, 52; Ustashe killing of Roma, 31; Yugoslavia, 26
Wehrmacht, xxxiii; attack on the Soviet Union, 31–35; defeat at Normandy beaches, 39–40; defeat in Battle of the Bulge, 40–41; defeat in North Africa and Italy, 37–38; defeat in the Soviet Union, 35–37; destruction of Warsaw, 209–10; joined by French volunteers, 174; liquidation of Warsaw Ghetto, 205–6; rape and abuse of women, 97; retreat from Soviet Union, 38–39; saving Mussolini from defeat, 31; swearing obedience to Hitler, 7–8
Weimar, Germany, 2, 222
Weimar Republic, xxxiii, 2–3, 134, 246
White Rose (student resistance effort), 186–87, 250
Why the Allies Won (Overy), 71
Wiesel, Elie, 182, 222
Wigner, Eugene, 118, 120
Wilhelm II (Kaiser), 2
"Winter War" (Soviet-Finnish War), xxiv, 28–29
Wirths, E., 224
Women: prostitution, 90, 98, 146; as resistance fighters, 193–94; role in Soviet Army, 46–47; sexual abuse and rape, 96–98; sexual relations with the enemy, 98–99; taking over male roles, 99
Woortman, Semmy, 202
World Cup soccer tournaments, 138
World Holocaust Remembrance Center, xxxii
World War I (the Great War), the war to end all war, 2

Yalta Conference (1945), xxxiii
Young Guard, The (Fadeev), 154–55
Yugoslavia: division into Croatia and Serbia, 243; invasion and occupation, xxv, 22, 31; resistance movement, 104; value to German war effort, 72–73; war-time deaths, 26; WWII films, 252

Zabinski, Jan and Antonina, 247, 253
Zhukov, Georgy, 32, 37
Zimnitskaya, Gayla, 68–69
Zookeeper's Wife, The (film, 2017), 206, 253
Zoya (Soviet film), 159
Zweig, Stefan, 110

About the Author

Harold J. Goldberg, the David E. Underdown Distinguished Professor of History at the University of the South in Sewanee, Tennessee, is the author of *D-Day in the Pacific: The Battle of Saipan, Competing Voices from World War II in Europe,* published in paperback as *Europe in Flames,* and the four-volume series *Documents of Soviet-American Relations* (1917–1945). He teaches courses on World War II and Russian history as well as other topics, and has also been a visiting professor at Moscow State Humanities University and Rikkyo University in Tokyo. In addition to his own frequent travels in Europe and Asia, including a recent trip from Mongolia to Moscow on the Trans-Siberian Railroad, he leads a study-abroad summer trip for his students to war sites in Europe.